Transient Apostle

SYNKRISIS: Comparative Approaches to Early Christianity in Greco-Roman Culture

SERIES EDITORS: Dale B. Martin (Yale University) and L. L. Welborn (Fordham University)

Synkrisis is a project that invites scholars of Early Christianity and the Greco-Roman world to collaborate toward the goal of rigorous comparison. Each volume in the series provides immersion in an aspect of Greco-Roman culture, so as to make possible a comparison of the controlling logics that emerge from the discourses of Greco-Roman and early Christian writers. In contrast to older "history of religions" approaches, which looked for similarities between religions in order to posit relations of influence and dependence, Synkrisis embraces a fuller conception of the complexities of culture, viewing Greco-Roman religions and early Christianity as members of a comparative class. The differential comparisons promoted by Synkrisis may serve to refine and correct the theoretical and historical models employed by scholars who seek to understand and interpret the Greco-Roman world. With its allusion to the rhetorical exercises of the Greco-Roman world, the series title recognizes that the comparative enterprise is a construction of the scholar's mind and serves the scholar's theoretical interests.

TIMOTHY LUCKRITZ MARQUIS

Transient Apostle

PAUL, TRAVEL, AND THE
RHETORIC OF EMPIRE

Yale UNIVERSITY PRESS
New Haven &
London

Published with assistance from the Mary Cady Tew Memorial Fund.

Yale University Press books may be purchased in quantity for educational,
business, or promotional use. For information, please e-mail sales.press@yale.edu
(U.S. office) or sales@yaleup.co.uk (U.K. office).

Set in Sabon type by IDS Infotech Ltd., Chandigarh, India.
Printed in the United States of America.

Library of Congress Cataloging-in-Publication Data
Luckritz Marquis, Timothy.
Transient apostle : Paul, travel, and the rhetoric of empire / Timothy Luckritz
Marquis.
    p. cm. — (Synkrisis)
Includes bibliographical references and index.
ISBN 978-0-300-18714-4 (alk. paper)
1. Paul, the Apostle, Saint—Travel. 2. Apostles. 3. Travel—History—To
1500. 4. Rome—Description and travel. I. Title.
BS2506.3.L825 2013
225.9'2—dc23
                                                            2012031682

A catalogue record for this book is available from the British Library.

This paper meets the requirements of ANSI/NISO Z39.48–1992 (Permanence
of Paper).

10 9 8 7 6 5 4 3 2 1

For Christie

Contents

Preface

This study investigates Paul's use of travel motifs as a rhetoric of social change under imperial rule, focusing on the letter preserved in canonical 2 Cor 1–9 as a significant test case and providing context for Paul's language among various ancient literary traditions linking travel with death. I hope to engage New Testament scholars with my own reading of Paul's letters within their social contexts, but I have also intentionally framed this study for a broader academic audience interested in Roman imperial ideologies, the formation of hegemonic discourses, and recent post-Marxist approaches to new social movements. As much as possible, I have relegated to notes technical issues and references to the important work of other scholars. In addition, I have transliterated ancient Greek terms for nonspecialists. Through such efforts, I hope readers find this book to stand at the intersection of biblical studies, ancient history, and postcritical theory. Translations from ancient languages are my own unless otherwise noted.

Starting with my dissertation work at Yale University, I have undertaken much of this project in new homes, first in Durham and Greensboro, North Carolina, then in Bethlehem, Pennsylvania. Dale Martin deserves more credit than anyone if my interpretations in any way hit the mark; his ideas inspired me to study with him, and his attention to scholarly expression, rigor, and amiability continue to influence me whenever I write, present, or teach. Harold

Attridge, Adela Yarbro Collins, and Diana Swancutt offered much advice over and above their years of mentoring. In Elizabeth Clark I have found a guide and advocate for whom I will always be grateful. Derek Krueger and Eugene Rogers offered me much needed encouragement during my time at UNCG and beyond. I thank my current colleagues and students at Moravian Theological Seminary, especially Dean Frank Crouch, for their support and openness. At various points, I received helpful suggestions from Hans Arneson, Cavan Concannon, Emma Dench, Susanna Drake, Bart Ehrman, John Fitzgerald, Karen King, Sean Larsen, Colin Miller, Candida Moss, Laura Nasrallah, Brent Nongbri, Michael Peppard, Elizabeth Schüssler Fiorenza, and Matthew Thiessen. I am also grateful for the time and efforts of my anonymous reviewers, whose comments have greatly improved my argument. Throughout the review process, Jennifer Banks and Laurence Welborn have been unfailing sources of advice and support. Piyali Bhattacharya, Jessie Dolch, and Jeff Schier at Yale University Press have also provided invaluable help.

Portions of my research were presented at Society of Biblical Literature meetings in 2004, 2006, and 2010, at which I received constructive feedback. The Graduate School at Yale provided a Dissertation Fellowship in 2006–2007 without which my research would not have been possible.

My parents, Ann and Paul Marquis, have always been a foundation of love and support, as have Sarah, Gregg, Evan, Brendan, Michelle, Denzil, Lisa, Robin, and Christian. Maggie has long been an impetus for working and playing. Elias Blue, my new heart, inspired the project's completion. I dedicate this book to my true home, Christine Luckritz Marquis.

Abbreviations

Abbreviations follow *The SBL Handbook of Style*, supplemented by the *Oxford Classical Dictionary*.

Ancient Sources and Collections of Ancient Texts

Aeschylus	*Prom.*	*Prometheus vinctus* (*Prometheus bound*)
ANET		*Ancient Near Eastern Texts Relating to the Old Testament*. Ed. James B. Pritchard. 3rd ed. Princeton, NJ: Princeton University Press, 1969.
Aristophanes	*Ach.*	*Acharnenses* (*Acharnians*)
	Plut.	*Plutus* (*The Rich Man*)
Aristotle	*Eth. nic.*	*Ethica nichomachea* (*Nichomachean Ethics*)
	Rhet.	*Rhetorica* (*Rhetoric*)
Arrian	*Anab.*	*Anabasis*
BGU		*Aegyptische Urkunden aus den Königlichen Staatlichen Museen zu Berlin, Griechische Urkunden*. Berlin: 1895–.
Chariton	*Chaer.*	*De Chaerea et Callirhoe* (*Chareas and Callirhoe*)

Cicero	*Att.*	*Epistulae ad Atticum* (*Letters to Atticus*)
	Div.	*De divinatione* (*On Divination*)
	Fam.	*Epistulae ad familiares* (*Letters to his Friends*)
	Flacc.	*Pro Flacco*
	Off.	*De officiis* (*On Duties*)
	Red. Pop.	*Post reditum ad populum*
	Sen.	*De senectute* (*On Old Age*)
	Tusc.	*Tusculanae disputationes* (*Tusculan Disputations*)
CIL		*Corpus inscriptionum latinarum.*
Clement	*Protr.*	*Protrepticus* (*Exhortation to the Greeks*)
	Quis. div.	*Quis dives salvetur* (*Who Is the Rich Man Who Is Saved?*)
Corp. Herm.		*Corpus hermeticum*
Demetrius	*Eloc.*	*De elocutione/Peri hermēneias* (*On Style*)
DK		*Die Fragmente der Vorsokratiker* I. Ed. H. Diels and W. Kranz. 6th ed. Berlin: 1952.
DL		Diogenes Laertius, *Lives of Eminent Philosophers*
Epictetus	*Diatr.*	*Diatribai* (*Diatribes*)
Euripides	*Bacch.*	*Bacchae*
	Tro.	*Troades* (*Daughters of Troy*)
Eusebius	*Praep. Ev.*	*Praeparatio evangelica* (*Preparation for the Gospel*)
Galen	*Plac.*	*De placitis Hippocratis et Platonis* (*On the Doctrines of Hippocrates and Plato*)
Hesiod	*Op.*	*Opera et dies* (*Works and Days*)
Homer	*Il.*	*Iliad*
	Od.	*Odyssey*
Horace	*Ep.*	*Epistulae* (*Epistles*)
	Saec.	*Carmen saeculare*
IG		*Inscriptiones graecae.* Editio minor. Berlin: 1924–.
Ignatius	*Eph.*	*Epistle to the Ephesians*
ILS		*Inscriptiones Latinae selectae.* Ed. H. Dessau. 1892–1916.

Jerome	*Comm. Eph.*	*Commentary on Ephesians*
John Chrysostom	*Hom. 2 Cor.*	*Homilies on 2 Corinthians*
Josephus	*A.J.*	*Antiquitates judaicae (Jewish Antiquities)*
	B.J.	*Bellum judaicum (Jewish War)*
	Vita	*Vita (Life)*
LCL		Loeb Classical Library
Lucian	*Anach.*	*Anacharsis*
	Char.	*Charon*
	Dial. d.	*Dialogi deorum (Dialogues of the Gods)*
LXX		Septuagint (Greek translation of the Old Testament)
MT		Masoretic Text (Hebrew version of the Hebrew Bible/Old Testament)
OTP		*Old Testament Pseudepigrapha.* Ed. J. H. Charlesworth. New York: 1983.
Ovid	*Fast.*	*Fasti*
P.Cair.Zen.		*Zenon Papyri.* Ed. C. C. Edgar. Cairo: 1925–1940.
P.Col.		*Columbia Papyri* (1929–1998).
P.Eleph.		*Elephantine Papyri.* Ed. O. Rubensohn. Berlin: 1907.
P.Flor.		*Papiri Greco-egizii, papyri fiorentini.* Ed. D. Comparetti and G. Vitelli. Milan: 1906–1915; repr. 1962.
P.Giss.		*Griechische Papyri im Museum des oberhessischen Geschichtsvereins zu Giessen.* Ed. O. Eger, E. Kornemann, and P. M. Meyer. Leipzig-Berlin: 1910–1912.
P.Köln		*Kölner Papyri.* Opladen and Paderborn: 1976–2007.
P.Lips.		*Griechische Urkunden der Papyrussammlung zu Leipzig.* Ed. L. Mitteis. Leipzig and Munich: 1906–2002.
P.Lond.		*Greek Papyri in the British Museum.* London: 1893–1974.
P.Mich.		*Michigan Papyri* (1931–).
P.Oslo		*Papyri Osloenses (Oslo Papyri).* Ed. S. Eitrem and L. Amundsen. Oslo: 1925–1936.

P.Oxy.		*Oxyrhynchus Papyri* (1898–).
P.Zen.Pestm.		*Greek and Demotic Texts from the Zenon Archive.* Ed. P. W. Pestman. Leiden: 1980.
Philo	*Conf.*	*De confusione linguarum* (*On the Confusion of Tongues*)
	Congr.	*De congressu eruditionis gratia* (*On the Preliminary Studies*)
	Legat.	*Legatio ad Gaium* (*Embassy to Gaius*)
	Mos.	*De vita Mosis* (*On the Life of Moses*)
	Prob.	*Quod omnis probus liber sit* (*That Every Good Person Is Free*)
	QG	*Quaestiones et solutiones in Genesin* (*Questions and Answers on Genesis*)
	Spec.	*De specialibus legibus* (*On the Special Laws*)
Philostratus	*Vit. Apoll.*	*Vita Apollonii* (*Life of Apollonius*)
Plato	*Apol.*	*Apologia* (*Apology of Socrates*)
	Ep.	*Epistulae*
	Phaed.	*Phaedo*
	Pol.	*Politicus* (*Statesman*)
	Resp.	*Respublica* (*Republic*)
Pliny the Elder	*Nat.*	*Naturalis historia* (*Natural History*)
Pliny the Younger	*Ep.*	*Epistulae* (*Letters*)
Plutarch	*Aem.*	*Aemilius Paullus*
	Alex.	*Alexander*
	Cons. Ux.	*Consolatio ad uxorem* (*Consolation to His Wife*)
	Demetr.	*Demetrius*
	Exil.	*De exilio* (*On Exile*)
	Is. Os.	*De Iside et Osiride* (*On Isis and Osiris*)
	Pel.	*Pelopidas*
	Praec. ger. rei publ.	*Praecepta gerendae rei publicae*
	Quaest. Conviv.	*Quaestionum convivialum* (*Table Talk*)
	Sol.	*Solon*
Ps.-Plutarch	*Cons. Apoll.*	*Consolatio ad Apollonium* (*Consolation to Apollonius*)

Ps.-Philo	*L.A.B.*	*Liber antiquitatum biblicarum (Biblical Antiquities)*
Ps.-Plato	*Ax.*	*Axiochus*
PSI		*Papiri Greci e Latini (Pubblicazioni della Società italiana per la ricerca dei papyri greci e latini in Egitto).* Florence: 1912–.
SB		*Sammelbuch griechischen Urkunden aus Ägypten.* Marburg: 1915–.
Seneca	*Ben.*	*De beneficiis (On Benefits)*
	Brev. Vit.	*De brevitate vitae*
	Helv.	*Ad Helviam (To Helvia)*
	Marc.	*Ad Marciam de consolatione (To Marcia on Consolation)*
	Polyb.	*Ad Polybium de consolatione (To Polybius on Consolation)*
SVF		*Stoicorum Veterum Fragmenta.* Ed. Hans von Arnim. Stuttgart: 1903–1925.
T. Ab.		*Testament of Abraham*
Tactitus	*Hist.*	*Historiae*
Tertullian	*Res.*	*De resurrectione carnis (The Resurrection of the Flesh)*
Theodoret	*Affect.*	*Graecorum affectionum curatio (Remedy for the Diseases of the Greeks)*
Vergil	*Aen.*	*Aeneid*

Journals and Other Modern Sources

ABR	*Australian Biblical Review*
AJP	*American Journal of Philology*
BTB	*Biblical Theology Bulletin*
BZ	*Biblische Zeitschrift*
CBQ	*Catholic Biblical Quarterly*
CJ	*Classical Journal*
CP	*Classical Philology*
DHA	*Dialogues d'Histoire Ancien*
GR	*Greece & Rome*
HTR	*Harvard Theological Review*
Int	*Interpretation*
JBL	*Journal of Biblical Literature*

JHS	*Journal of Hellenic Studies*
JJS	*Journal of Jewish Studies*
JRH	*Journal of Religious History*
JRS	*Journal of Roman Studies*
JSJ	*Journal for the Study of Judaism in the Persian, Hellenistic, and Roman Period*
JSNT	*Journal for the Study of the New Testament*
JTS	*Journal of Theological Studies*
Neot	*Neotestamentica*
NovT	*Novum Testamentum*
NTS	*New Testament Studies*
OCD	*Oxford Classical Dictionary.* Ed. S. Hornblower and A. Spawforth. 3rd ed. Oxford: 2005.
RE	*Real-Encyclopädie d. klassischen Altertumswissenschaft.* Ed. A. Pauly, G. Wissowa, and W. Kroll. (1893–).
TDNT	*Theological Dictionary of the New Testament.* Ed. G. Kittel and G. Friedrich. Trans. G. W. Bromiley. 10 vols. Grand Rapids, MI: 1964–1976.

Transient Apostle

Introduction

In 17 B.C.E., heralds sent out by Augustus declared the advent of a new age. The emperor had revived the ancient rite of the *ludi saeculares* (the "Secular Games"), marking the passage of a new *saeculum*, or "age," a period of about 110 years, thought to be the limit of the human lifespan. The games capped off his achievements at an auspicious moment. Romans expected the return of a comet that had visited one of his early public appearances following the death of his adoptive father, Julius Caesar, an event that had led many to acclaim him as Caesar's rightful heir. Moreover, he had recently secured peace at the Empire's borders and passed a series of moralistic legal reforms. An innovative version of the ritual was planned, featuring, in addition to the traditional, nocturnal rites to fertility deities, daytime offerings to Jupiter, Juno, Diana, and Augustus's personal patron, Apollo. The event made a considerable impression in Rome and its immediate surroundings. A coin minted that year, depicting the head of Julius Caesar topped by the expected comet, commemorated the games. The reverse of the coin shows a herald, journeying with his traditional shield and staff in hand, proclaiming the good news of the coming era.[1]

Romans were not the only people at this time expecting a major break in history. In some cases, non-Roman imperial subjects predicted the arrival of a new age of their own, often in response to the Augustan image. Near the end of Augustus's *saeculum*—or around the end of the first century C.E.—the pseudepigraphic text 4 Ezra portrayed Ezra, the fifth-century B.C.E. scribal leader of the exilic Judean community, lamenting the delay of God's promised rescue of Israel. In a stubborn argument, Ezra repeatedly demands that the angel Uriel divulge the time of the destruction of the present unjust age (*saeculum*) and the advent of the new. Why, he asks, does iniquitous Babylon (here a transparent cipher for Rome) prosper over God's chosen people? "Has another nation known you besides Israel? Or what tribes have so believed the covenants as these tribes of Jacob? Yet their reward has not appeared and their labor has borne no fruit. For I have traveled widely [*pertransiens enim pertransivi*] among the nations and have seen that they abound in wealth, though they are unmindful of your commandments" (3:32–34). He mourns the fate of his countrymen: "We journey from this world [*pretransivimus de saeculo*] like locusts, our life is like the mist, and we are not worthy to obtain mercy" (4:24). The angel nevertheless promises, "If you are alive, you will see, and if you live long, you will often marvel, because the current age is departing" (*saeculum pertransire*; 4:26). For this anonymous, first-century author, eschatological fatigue was not only a pressing and contemporary concern, but a sentiment that could plausibly be retrojected into the sixth century B.C.E. A new age, it seems, was an old idea. At the conclusion of the text, Ezra is sent to instruct and warn his people before being taken up to heaven, to "travel away from these terrible times" (14:15).[2]

About halfway through this intervening era (in the 50s of the first century), another self-styled divine herald wandered the Mediterranean proclaiming the advent of a different new age, one to be inaugurated by the return of the Messiah of the God of Israel. In his final piece of correspondence, Paul the apostle writes to a group of Christ-believing communities in the Empire's capital concerning

> the favor that has been given to me by God so that I might be a minister to the Gentiles, performing a priestly duty for the gospel of God, so that the offering of the Gentiles might prove pleasing, sanctified by the Holy Spirit. So I have a reason to boast in Christ Jesus of the things I have accomplished before God. For I am not so bold as to speak of anything except what Christ has accomplished through me, in word and deed, for the obedience of the Gentiles, in the power of signs and miracles, in the power of the Spirit; so that from Jerusalem and all around until Illyricum I have fulfilled the Gospel of Christ, and so I have the ambition to proclaim the Gospel not where Christ has been mentioned by name, lest I build upon another's foundation; but, rather, as it is written: "Those to whom he has not been reported will see, and those who have not heard will understand." (Rom 15:15–21)

At the conclusion of the passage, Paul cites Isa 52:15, part of a prophecy foretelling the arrival of divine heralds who proclaim in advance the return of God to his royal throne on Zion. Like the messengers announcing Augustus's *imperium*, like Ezra proclaiming good news of redemption and return, Paul portrayed himself as a traveling herald of a new age.[3]

Travel was a central aspect of Paul's self-definition as "apostle," or "sent one"—a novel social role as leader of a new social movement. And in his emphasis on travel in both word and deed, message and lifestyle, Paul followed the rhetorical paths of centuries of Greco-Roman leaders and heroes both historical and mythical. Paul alternately drew upon the imagery of heralds proclaiming a new empire, of the prophet announcing the intentions of a god, of the ambassador proclaiming the will of a king. He styled himself as a cosmopolitan philosopher and as a despised foreigner. A wandering preacher of the Jesus movement, he resembled other traveling cultic practitioners and moralists of his day. The Apostle Paul has been known for centuries as a figure who transgressed and even straddled boundaries: a Diaspora Jew with facility in Greek language and idiom; a reputed Roman citizen sustaining himself as a common tentmaker; a fervent devotee of the Jewish god who insisted that non-Jews were being called to that god's worship; a leader who rejected open resistance to Rome while working to establish an alternative, international, divine "empire." His vision was not uncontroversial even among his own colleagues and communities; as a wandering practitioner of a foreign cult, Paul's itinerancy left him open to common ancient suspicions about travel. In order to succeed in his mission, Paul shaped his rhetoric to respond to and redefine such suspicions, attempting to portray himself as a new type of leader for a new age. For the modern scholar studying social change in the ancient world, then, Paul's use of travel motifs offers a unique window into the rhetorical construction of a new social movement at the advent of empire.

I recount the stories of Augustus and Ezra not to imply that Paul was directly influenced either by the Secular Games or by apocryphal tales of the ancient Jewish scribe. Nor do I wish to place Paul between the all-too-deeply entrenched scholarly constructs of "Greco-Roman culture" and "Judaism" that have framed more than a century of critical analysis of ancient Judaism and Christianity. (If anything, I wish to describe the apocalyptic strand of Judaism in which Paul shared as an integral part of the larger, Roman world.) Rather, I mean to create as broad a cultural background as possible against which to highlight and understand Paul's deployment of travel in his writings and form of life. Throughout my study, I illustrate the pervasiveness of travel as a motif of social change, suitable in its ambivalence, connoting both hope and fear, blessing and curse. In his attempts to institute a new age in the midst of Roman dominance and local anxieties, Paul harnessed the power of travel's semantic excess in order to forge an international community uniting various subject positions around the truth he proclaimed from city to city.[4]

We can clearly see travel's multiple meanings by returning briefly to Augustus's Secular Games. In a hymn composed for and performed at the event, the poet Horace evokes the divine providence that had prospered Rome from a legendary group of refugees to a city defending peace and virtue across the known world: "If Rome be your monument and if Ilian bands held the Etruscan shore, a remnant ordered to change their homes and city in a course that brings no harm [*sospite cursu*], for whom chaste Aeneas, survivor of his fatherland, without harm through Troy's conflagration paved a way for freedom [*liberum munivit iter*], about to bestow more good things than were left behind at Troy: gods, grant peace to those in the calm of old age, grant to the race of Romulus resources and offspring and every distinction" (*Saec.* 37–38).[5] Rooted in Aeneas's long journey from the ruins of Troy to the Italian coast, Rome has become a "monument" of the gods, deserving of peace, wealth, and stability. The new Empire is rooted in the epic wanderings of exiles. From such humble beginnings, Rome has come to wield a power crossing and expanding international boundaries.

For Horace, Augustus himself provides the strength requisite to ensure an abundant future through his conquest of the world's warring peoples: "Now the Parthian fears our troops, lords of sea and land, and the axes of Alba; now the Scythians and the Indi, haughty until recently, seek answers from us. Now Fidelity and Peace and Honor and ancient Modesty and neglected Courage dare to return, and blessed Plenty, with full horn, makes her appearance" (*Saec.* 53–60). Nations once inimical to Rome now seek its advice. The inhabited cosmos, previously a diverse set of races at odds with one another, now respects the power and wisdom of Rome. Peace, in turn, allows the return of the deified Virtues, themselves exiles until the advent of the Augustan age. In its expansion and acquisitions, the Empire had created a worldwide space for a new chapter in human history.

In the years preceding the Secular Games, texts supporting the Augustan reforms had already deployed as an image for the Empire the ancient notion of the "Golden Age," an era in which gold from abroad would flood the city and enrich it. So it is curious that Horace avoids altogether the mention of the trope. Rome's tranquility and wealth depended on its conquests abroad and the international commerce they allowed, but the gold that entered Rome also brought foreign customs and innovations, often perceived as threats to cherished traditions. The greater the expanse of Rome's dominion over the world, the more the world, in turn, infiltrated the Roman way of life, as its money and morals made their way to the metropolis. Thus, in the hymn, when Plenty brings a "full horn" from abroad, it is only in the company of foundational virtues and without the conspicuous lavishness often associated with triumphs over distant nations. Austerity and native fecundity—of crops and of population—characterized Augustus's new age. Horace explicitly praises Augustus's marital legislation, the *lex Iulia de maritandis ordinibus*, of the preceding year, which restricted upper-class Romans from marrying below their stations, thereby encouraging the propagation of the city's best elements. "Goddess," he prays to Ilithyia, deity of childbirth, "rear our youth and bless the decrees of the fathers concerned with women and the need for wedlock and on the marriage law, fruitful of new progeny" (*Saec.* 17–20). Although the voyages of refugees, soldiers, and merchants crisscrossed Rome's history, its future as expressed at the Secular Games lay in the promise of an autochthonous prosperity both material and spiritual. Horace's hymn asserts Rome's roots despite its wandering and motley past. Augustus's articulation of a new age encapsulated the peculiar mixture of stability and novelty that had long characterized Roman self-identity. Rome was, like the sun depicted in Horace's hymn, "reborn another and the same" (*Saec.* 10–11).[6]

Within the Augustan ideological program surrounding the performance of the Secular Games, travel periodically emerged as a troubling concept, its multiple meanings often expressed in dichotomous terms, alternately (or sometimes simultaneously) representing innovation and tradition, prosperity and poverty, status and shame, virtue and vice, life and death. Geographic factors often played into instances of social mobility during the turbulent days at the end of the Republic. For Roman writers at the outset of the Empire, the expanding boundaries of Roman influence were often best expressed through the ease of worldwide travel and the proliferation of geographic and ethnographic knowledge. Philo of Alexandria, a first-century writer now famous for negotiating the intersections among Jewish, Greek, and Roman worlds, attributed to the imperial office the mobility and peace inaugurated by the new world order:

> We owe to the art of government that . . . merchant ships safely navigate every sea to exchange the goods that countries offer to each other in their desire to associate . . . For the family of the Augusti has banished all the evils that used to flourish and be found in our midst over the frontiers to the ends of the earth and the depths of Tartarus, while it has brought back to the world that we inhabit all those benefits and blessing that had been, as it were, in exile from the limits of earth and sea. (*Legat.* 47, 49)

Philo and other Roman writers would credit the godlike powers of the emperor with the preservation of free movement across the inhabited world. The sheer military might that paved the way for ease of travel provided a necessary foundation for the *pax Romana*. At the same time, the entry into the city of foreign elements—whether led captive in triumphal procession or in honor as newly minted citizens—complicated traditional construals of Roman identity. Horace's hymn at the Secular Games is just one example of literary attempts to harness the anxiety of newness through the theme of the journey. In 17 B.C.E., Augustus's traveling heralds assured the inhabitants of Rome's immediate environs that, despite the novelty of empire, the prosperity brought by foreign conquest could remain distinctly Roman.[7]

As leaders attempting to forge new social movements, both Augustus and Paul operated within a new, international environment that both required mobility and harbored suspicions against wandering. For Romans in particular, travel encapsulated all the dangers and necessities of newness. Even though the most revered heroes of Rome's mythic history were regaled for braving stupendous adventures as they traversed the earth, audiences and authors alike understood these epic journeys as conveying both glory and curse. Those who took to road and sea for business or curiosity were alternately praised and scorned. The arrival of a stranger could be met with duty-bound hospitality or reflexive suspicion.

Within the Roman imperial context of freer yet still dangerous travel, ancient Christian literature portrays Paul as its heroic traveler par excellence. As a preacher and miracle-worker dedicated to bringing the message of the Jewish Messiah to non-Jews, Paul deployed travel as a central aspect of his lifestyle and self-presentation. The Acts of the Apostles, a late-first-century account of the spread of the early Jesus movement dedicated to glorifying its first leaders, has drawn the most attention of scholars highlighting the role of travel in Paul's public life. In particular, the climactic account of Paul's shipwreck en route to Rome in Acts 27 emphasizes his dedication to bringing his message to the political center of the Empire. In his own letters, however, Paul lays before his followers his afflictions on road and sea in long lists of sufferings on behalf of the gospel. The following passage from 2 Cor 11:25b–28 is a notable case in point: "Three times I have been shipwrecked. For a night and a day I was stranded in the open sea. Often on journeys, through dangers from rivers, dangers from bandits, dangers from my own people, dangers from Gentiles, dangers in the city, dangers in the country, dangers on the sea, dangers from false brothers, in hardship and labor, often through sleepless nights, in hunger and thirst, often starving, in cold and nakedness—and, apart from other things, I experience daily pressure because of my anxiety for all my communities."

An ancient audience would quickly recognize this list of travel hardships. At the end of it, however, Paul adds and emphasizes his concern for his followers while journeying to and from them. Over and above any physical hardship, Paul claims, he is beset by worry over his communities while absent from them.[8]

Death, of course, was a very real threat in any ancient journey. Travel by land or sea was risky. During classical and Hellenistic eras, sailing, though hardly safe (piracy being the most pressing danger, next to weather), offered far more speed and security than travel by land. Few Greek roads—usually only those leading to the most popular sanctuaries and games—were maintained. With the advent of the Roman Empire, voyages on land and sea became far easier and safer. The military built and maintained new roads, while piracy was all but stamped out. Nevertheless, imperial travel continued to present many dangers. Wild beasts and bandits were still troublesome on the road, and even the might of the Empire was no match for storms at sea. Yet in most cases, ancient literature pairs the fear over the physical dangers of travel with a more ideological anxiety about how the journey stretches, transgresses, or questions cultural borders and relationships. Paul may well be employing a clever rhetorical strategy in claiming that absence from his followers is a worse fate than shipwreck or starvation. As I discuss throughout my argument, Paul often felt the need to shame the Corinthians into honoring their original relationship with him. Yet the overall sentiment that the worst part of travel is separation from homeland and loved ones—and the prospect of never returning to them—was common among many types of ancient literature.[9]

So, in the *Odyssey*, Odysseus's mother dies not of sickness, but of longing for her son, as her spirit tells him from the edge of Hades (*Od.* 11.225–32). At the outset of the *Argonautica*, Jason's parents, Aeson and Alcimede, lament that the departure of their son to complete a near-impossible task is a fate worse than death. "Surely better had it been for him," cry the women of Iolcus about Aeson, "if he were lying beneath the earth, enveloped in his shroud, still unconscious of bitter toils (1.253–55, LCL trans.). Dying at home was considered preferable to oblivion at sea, both for voyagers and for those they left behind. In Greek and Roman lyric traditions, laments over travel also focus on death, as preserved in a central feature of the formal genre of farewell poems (*propemptika*, or "send-offs"). Horace writes an ode to Virgil as he leaves for Greece and curses the danger and insanity of travel:

> All to no avail did God deliberately separate countries by the divisive ocean if, in spite of that, impious boats go skipping over the seas that were meant to remain inviolate. The human species, audacious enough to endure anything, plunges into forbidden sacrilege. The audacious son of Iapetus by an act of criminal deception brought fire to the nations. After the theft of fire from its

heavenly home, a wasting disease and an unprecedented troop of fevers fell upon the earth, and the doom of a distant death, which up to then was slow in coming, quickened its step. Daedalus made trial of the empty air on wings that were never meant for men; Hercules (he of the labours) burst through to the region of Acheron; nothing is too steep for mortals. In our folly we aspire to the sky itself, and by our crimes we do not allow Jove to lay aside his bolts of wrath. (*Odes* 1.3.17–40, LCL trans.)

For the grieving Horace, travel is not only risky, it verges on impiety. The act of seafaring is as blasphemous and hubristic as Daedalus's foolhardy flight. In a send-off for his friend Maecius Celer, Statius similarly laments: "What bold creative thinker made the sea a novel, isolated kind of highway for us poor creatures, banished loyal sons of solid ground to the waves, made them go into the yawning ocean? . . . Into the void we go, and everywhere we flee our native lands, shut up inside skimpy timber and brass, exposed and bare" (LCL trans.). As do other authors, Statius curses the very invention of travel, since it pulls people from the safety and security of "solid earth" and their "native lands."[10]

The fear and shame of travel stemmed from its crossing, stretching, or breaking of cultural boundaries. Growing out of a concern for the preservation of the traditional structure of the homeland, depictions of travel as risky and suspicious also pervaded much political and economic discourse. So, though mercantile activity was a necessity that secured Hellenistic and Roman international interests, writers would denigrate trade in relation to agriculture, constructing a common topos. Much of the identity of the citizen of the polis as constructed by Greek law rested in land ownership. The attachment of Greek and Roman upper classes to gentleman farming can be construed more as a moral judgment of the best, most proper, and most natural lifestyle than as any assessment of the most financially profitable vocation. Although those who made their livings through trade and commerce were not the most contemptible on the social ladder, they fell below the landed aristocracy in prestige. The estimation is made clearly by Cicero:

Trade, if it is on a small scale, is to be considered vulgar; but if wholesale and on a large scale, importing large quantities from all parts of the world and distributing to many without misrepresentation [*sine vanitate*], it is not to be greatly disparaged [*non est admodum vituperanda*]. Nay, it even seems to deserve the highest respect, if those who are engaged in it, satiated [*si satiata*], or rather, should I say, satisfied [*contenta*] with the fortunes they have made, make their way from the port to a country estate, as they have often made it from the sea into a port. But of all the occupations by which gain is secured, none is better than agriculture, none more profitable, none more delightful, none more becoming to a freeman. (*Off.* 1.151, LCL trans.)

A few points from this passage deserve emphasis. First, Cicero claims that mercantile activity is respectable only if it is abandoned once sufficient resources have been acquired—once the trader is *satiata et contenta*. Trade connoted greed among ancient writers, as we will continue to see. In fact, Cicero implies that many traders are dishonest; another prerequisite of honorable trade is that the trader sell his imports *sine vanitate*. Finally, Cicero expresses ancient suspicions toward trade by depicting landowning as a refuge from mercantile activity. Just as a traveling merchant often finds the safety of the port, so a satiated and honest trader should flee to the security and honor of an estate.[11]

Ancient ethnographic accounts reinforce the suspicious and lowly nature of trade and the superiority of agriculture. At least twice in his *Geography*, Strabo uses the topos to characterize foreign peoples: in discussing the Scythians (once models of primitive, natural purity), he claims that they originally knew nothing of trade. Yet, as with most barbarian peoples, their contact with Greek culture, including seafaring and "trading" (*kapēleia*), led to their corruption (7.3.7). Strabo also describes the primitive essence of the Albanians as being devoid of interest in travel and trade (11.4.4). Dealers in religious teachings and practices—Paul included—would struggle against accusations that their vocations were mere endeavors at *kapēleia*, a petty trade in falsified divine knowledge and a fundamental degradation of natural human ends.

Jewish depictions of Judea also privilege agriculture over mercantilism. In *Contra Apionem*, Josephus adopts the notion that trade is an inferior ethnic quality when compared with agriculture; he claims that Judeans stay to themselves and thus avoid mercantilism, preferring to live off the land (1.60–61). An extensive section of the *Letter of Aristeas* describes the agricultural countryside surrounding Jerusalem. According to the narrator (as explained to him by the high priest), Judean agriculture thrived despite the hilly terrain. "Continuous attention to husbandry and the care of the land is necessary, to ensure good yield as a result for the inhabitants" (107). Just as the Ptolemaic king had prohibited Alexandrian citizens from leaving the city and their farming interests for too long in order to prevent lack of agricultural income (109–11), the Judean people constructed their cities so that the majority of the population could be devoted to cultivation of their bounteous environs (112–13), leaving the importation of goods to the neighboring Arabs (114–15). To describe a people as avoiding trade is to describe it as noble and devoid of guile, a stable society, self-sufficient within its own boundaries and culture. In ancient fashioning, travel and trade are linked to shame and death as practices that threaten the closure and cohesiveness of native ties and ideologies.[12]

As a minority population embedded in a larger, Greco-Roman culture, Jewish groups—including apocalyptic communities, such as those behind 4 Ezra and Paul's letters—also conveyed the ambivalent nature of travel. Throughout Ezra's lament in 4 Ezra, the twin notions of a new age (*saeculum*) and that of travel (expressed through the verb *pertranseo*) occur with remarkable frequency. Woven into Ezra's complaint about the present evil *saeculum* (alternately translated as "age" and "world") is the claim that, throughout the earth, one can roam extensively and find no goodness—or, as the angel Uriel predicts, a crisis is coming in which "one kingdom will inquire of its neighbor, 'Has any justice or person acting justly wandered [*pertransiit*] through you?' And the neighboring realm will reply in the negative" (5:11). At the same time, the new era is depicted as "arriving" using the same terminology. The angel encapsulates the metaphorical "journey" to the blessed age in a parable:

> There is a city built and set on a plain, and it is full of all good things; but the entrance to it is narrow and set in a precipitous place, so that there is fire on the right hand and deep water on the left. There is only one path lying between them, that is, between the fire and the water, so that only one person can walk on the path. If now the city is given to someone as an inheritance, how will the heir receive the inheritance unless by traveling [*pertransierit*] through the appointed danger? (7:6–9)

For the author of 4 Ezra, travel is an ambivalent marker of the state of world affairs, simultaneously a sign of all that is wrong and the means by which restoration will occur. As this study shows, Paul similarly deployed travel as an essential aspect of his apocalyptic rhetorical strategies.

In fashioning his identity as a wandering apostle, Paul had to take into account the ambivalence embedded in the socioeconomics of travel. An impoverished, peripatetic lifestyle could be read as either deceptive or insulting—but in both cases, it connoted social shame. The success of Paul's mission depended on his ability to acknowledge the many valences of his itinerancy and rhetorically refashion them. Nowhere is this refashioning more apparent than in the correspondence preserved in the biblical book 2 Corinthians, in which his controversies in Corinth come to a head. In my argument about itinerancy and social change in Paul, I direct most of my focus toward one, long letter fragment in 2 Cor 1–9 as a telling example of how the apostle created a new social movement through his self-portrayal as traveler. Through my analysis, I hope to show how a vague motif such as travel could provide rhetorical raw material for social change and to explore the ways in which a first-century leader brought newness into the world by journeying the discursive paths of a previous age.[13]

* * *

This study of Paul and travel within the context of the first century takes both a social-historical and rhetorical approach in order to investigate how Paul's rhetorical treatment of his itinerant form of life served to found, form, maintain, and expand both his local communities and their corporate role in the larger, international Jesus movement. I provide context for Paul's use of travel motifs within a broad understanding of the various meanings that travel communicated to an ancient audience. As theoretical supports, I also engage recent theories of social change and the construction of hegemony found among postcritical writers, as well as post-Marxist philosophers, some of whom have directed their attention to Paul's letters in the past two decades. Numerous recent works have found social history and postcritical theory to be congenial fellow travelers in the exploration of first-century Christianity. Sociohistorical approaches to Paul have helped clear the way for modern reassessments of the birth of Christianity and its relevance for contemporary concerns. The rise of feminist and postcolonial criticism in Pauline studies often takes thick, materialist description of Paul's social (and especially political) world as a launching point for examining the trajectories of his thought and practice and how these trajectories interface with the patriarchal and colonial legacies of the Western intellectual and political tradition—a tradition often bolstered by older interpretations of Paul. Contemporary approaches have adopted theoretical angles borrowed from a wide range of postcritical thought, engaging the theories of writers such as Jacques Derrida, Michel Foucault, Edward Said, Gayatri Spivak, and Judith Butler. The past decade, in fact, has seen a reversal of the trend of borrowing critical theory for the study of Paul, as continental philosophers have turned to Paul as a figure of political action and social intervention on an international scale, one who laid "the foundation of universalism."[14]

The postcritical Paul challenges reconstructions of the apostle that undergird the colonial tradition. Yet more recently, theoretical reimaginings of Paul also shy away from producing an egalitarian, liberal voice suitable for unproblematic application to the social injustices of our time. Rather, the postcritical Paul is revealed as embedded within first-century matrices of politics, rhetoric, and lines of power. As an imperial subject and member of a minority ethnic group, Paul lived in an environment of Roman imperial oppression. Yet as a subaltern voice recycling the language of empire to speak, he replicates strategies of domination in his own leadership tactics. The postcritical Paul, then, is a locus of reflection on how a leader of an alternative social movement might function within the context of various types of cultural hegemony.[15]

Attention to travel serves to flesh out the social-historical picture of Paul, insofar as he was one of a growing number of mercantile and spiritual wanderers taking advantage of the increased mobility that attended Roman dominance. This social-historical Paul is more a product of the material forces of his age than of his own theological imagination, an observation that may displace his central position within the early Christian story. After all, when read closely, Paul's letters (not to mention the book of Acts) testify to other traveling preachers of the gospel traversing the Mediterranean: Apollos, Priscilla and Aquila, anonymous "brothers" from other communities, numerous Greek-speaking preachers from Jerusalem bringing the word to Jew and Gentile alike, and various "opponents" of Paul, inimical to his mission on theological and/or personal grounds. Scholars have begun to suspect that the dominant picture of Paul as founding theologian has obscured other figures and communities that may have been as (or even more) foundational. Paul's letters, then, bear witness not so much to his actual, central role in Christianity's early expansion as to his attempt to creatively and consistently assert his own importance to his local communities and within the worldwide movement.[16]

Postcritical readings of the apostle call to mind another picture of Paul, an instance of self-presentation from his own writings: the Paul of many faces, who shifted his identity to fit his context. For centuries of his readers, Paul's genius was his ability to communicate his devotion to Christ and the coming messianic age in multiple, strategic ways depending on his audience. His rhetoric displayed a creativity and agility that allowed him to translate his message to individuals in various contexts, to address multiple subject positions—Jew and Gentile, rich and poor, male and female, slave and free— sometimes simultaneously. The passage in 1 Cor 9:23 where Paul claims that he "becomes all things to all people" stands as the best-known expression of the accommodating nature of his approach. The many faces of Paul throughout history may have roots in the apostle's strategy of shifting his self-image to fit different situations.[17]

First Corinthians 9 shows that Paul felt he needed to alter not just his message, but his very "form of life" to reach the various subject positions to which he appealed. For Paul, his self-image stood at the center of his message. Throughout his collected correspondence, he insists that his words and actions reflect the presence of Jesus's spirit. "Become imitators of me," he tells the Corinthians, "as I am of Christ" (1 Cor 11:1). Similar exhortations to imitation appear throughout Paul's extant letters to his communities, for example, 1 Cor 4:16 and 1 Thess 1:6 and 2:14. He presents himself as a model of sexual restraint (1 Cor 7:7), honest labor (1 Thess 2:9 and 5:14), and Christlike humility and suffering (Phil 1:29–30). While the crucifixion and resurrection of Jesus were at the heart of his proclamation, Paul tended to interject himself between Christ and his communities as an intermediary exemplar. If pressed to proffer a concise statement of what it meant to follow in Jesus's footsteps, Paul was likely to say, "Be like me." That centuries of Christian thought (and thought about Christianity) have turned to Paul as a foundational figure is in part a product of his rhetorical efforts. The image of Paul the apostle stood at the center of the alternative discursive universe he was constructing in the mid-first century C.E.

At one point in the letter preserved in 2 Cor 1–9, Paul reframes the travel motif he uses so often in the epistle, claiming that, in his traveling apostleship, he suffers afflictions similar to those that Jesus faced at the end of his life: "We are afflicted in every way but not crushed; distressed but not despaired; pursued but not left abandoned; attacked but not destroyed; always carrying around [*peripherontes*] the death of Jesus in our body so that even the life of Jesus might be made manifest in our mortal flesh" (4:8–10). Falling as it does in a letter largely composed of travel metaphors (as I argue), the image at the heart of the statement makes a bold claim: Paul and his co-workers, in their traveling ministry, bodily express the death of Jesus and the sufferings he endured. For Paul, his own travels were a sign of the presence of Christ in his mission.[18]

Yet Paul's wandering lifestyle proved a liability. As I discuss in Chapter 1, it seems likely that many of his followers in Corinth felt shame or offense at his preference for menial labor over accepting their financial support. From his earliest extant correspondence, Paul asserts that he tried never to demand material support from his communities but rather worked his own trade while proclaiming the message about Christ. In an ostensible paradox, however, it may well have been his refusal of material support from believers that led to one of his greatest controversies—that with his followers in Corinth. Other apostles of Christ who came to the city after him raised doubts about the authenticity of Paul's lifestyle, especially regarding his professed self-sufficiency. For even though Paul declined direct contributions to his own welfare, he actively promoted a financial contribution to the poor community of believers in Jerusalem, a gift to be collected and delivered by Paul and his co-workers. His Christian opponents smelled a scam, and they portrayed him as just another in a long line of itinerant con artists attempting to get rich off falsified cultic knowledge. On the other hand, Paul's Corinthian followers may have been offended at his refusal of support. Wealthier members of the community in particular may have felt deprived of the opportunity to keep Paul on retainer, as it were, as an intellectual client. Disputes over Paul's itinerancy centered over the question of leadership in the fledgling Jesus movement.

Within the context of ancient suspicions about travel as wandering, the exigencies of Paul's journeys reflected poorly on his character. Frequent allusions in the Corinthian correspondence indicate that his followers questioned his sincerity and authenticity because of the discrepancy between his words and deeds. In some cases, the Corinthians felt as if Paul did not follow the plans he made to come visit them, leading them to believe that he was too weak, fickle, or mendacious to keep a promise. In my reading, Paul's itinerant and poor form of life engendered suspicions against him. Yet Paul's writings (especially 2 Cor 1–9) concentrate on travel as a sign of his strength and authenticity. Paul's apocalyptic assertion—that the one God of the Jewish people was about to intervene decisively in history to bring about a new age—only amplified the dissonance between strength and weakness in his message. Why would he focus on the most ostensibly shameful aspect of his apostleship in order to strengthen it in the eyes of his followers? In trying to place himself at the center of the movement as the divine herald of imminent judgment, why concentrate on his marginality?

Modern scholars of Paul's letters, observing how frequently Paul mentions and even boasts about his misfortunes, emphasize the ubiquitous motif of "power in weakness" that characterizes his writings, thought, and life. Such observations more often, however, assert the idea as a Pauline theological principle without analyzing its internal consistency or its rhetorical function within the apostle's larger mission of building his communities. New resources for thinking through the rhetorical value of appeals to marginality in the formation of new social movements might be suggested by the analyses of Paul offered by post-Marxist philosophers, for whom the identity and values of a new community are best discerned in the way in which its identity and values are excluded or can be subtracted from current regimes of discourse— sometimes construed by philosophers as being that particular community's "universality." While all members of an established community share some aspect of what the group holds as universally true or good, no single member can stand as a paradigmatic example of that group's identity; that is, no member embodies all that characterizes the group in the abstract. Individuals excluded from the group, however, are a mirror image of the group's total values insofar as they bear no characteristics of the group. Universality is truly borne only by the marginalized, though as a photonegative of that universality. Additionally, the boundary between "inside" and "outside" created by every community simultaneously creates a boundary at the heart of every subject within the group, demarcating that which the group accepts (and which coincides with the group's universal values) and those aspects the group rejects (by virtue of which the individual may feel in part or at times excluded). In this way, the boundaries drawn by a group's values and truths form communal identity as well as individual subjectivities. The establishing of group identities—the boundaries that determine who is excluded from the laws and values of society—is a constitutive and foundational decision, so that the community's universal truths can be determined by examining the inhabitants of the margins. A corollary of this observation is that all communities leave a remnant, in terms of both the subject positions that are excluded and the fact that all members of the group, despite their membership, at times or in part are marginalized—again, insofar as no individual perfectly embodies abstract communal values.[19]

I explicate at length the preceding theme, common among post-Marxist readers of Paul, only because the relationship between Paul's rhetoric and the social composition of his communities resonates with contemporary analysis of the role of marginality with respect to communal truth. The beginning of 1 Corinthians offers a telling glimpse of Paul's communicative strategy toward a diverse population. Generally, his followers, like an overwhelming majority of the general population, appear to have been poor or of otherwise low status. He indicates that his communities in Macedonia (specifically, at Philippi and Thessaloniki) experience economic and social hardships (2 Cor 8:1–5). As has long been recognized, however, the situation in Corinth was somewhat mixed. As Paul explains at the outset of 1 Corinthians, both his message and his choice of audience displayed a focus on the marginalized:

> Christ did not send [*apesteilen*] me to baptize but to proclaim the gospel—and not through a wise-sounding speech, lest the cross of Christ be made empty. For the message of the cross is foolishness to those who are being destroyed, but to those being saved it is the power of God. For it is written: "I will destroy the wisdom of the wise, and the understanding of those with understanding I will thwart" [Isa 29:14]. Where is the wise man? Where is the scribe? Where is the debater from among this age? Has not God made foolish the wisdom of the world? For since, in God's wisdom, the world did not know God through wisdom, God was pleased to save those who believed through the foolishness of a proclamation [*kērugmatos*]. And since Jews ask for signs and Greeks seek wisdom, but we proclaim [*kērussomen*] Christ crucified—a stumbling block for Jews and foolishness for Gentiles, but to those who are called, both Jews and Greeks, Christ the power of God and the wisdom of God, because the foolishness of God is wiser than humans and the weakness of God is stronger than humans. Think of your own call, brothers: not many of you are wise according to the flesh, not many powerful, not many noble. Instead, it was the world's foolish things that God chose, in order to shame the wise; and it was the weak things of the world that God chose, in order to shame the strong things; and it was the low-born and despised that God chose—that which is not—in order to render invalid the things that are, lest any fleshly thing boast before God. (1 Cor 1:17–29)

This rather lengthy passage has been foundational both for social-historical reconstructions of Paul's Corinthian community and for recent, postcritical attention to his rhetoric of social change. First, the section is a traditional locus for investigating the role of suffering and marginality in Paul's "apostolic" and "heraldic" proclamation. (The passage contains verbal forms of the words for "apostle" and "herald" [*kērux*]: *apostellein* and *kērussein*.) Furthermore, social critics of Paul's letters place great emphasis on the repetitive "not many" of 1 Cor 1:26 and its implication that, although most of the group were uneducated, poor, and common, *some* were not. Additional evidence from the letter confirms the analysis: some Corinthians named in the letter seem to have status or power of one type or another. In 1:11, Paul speaks of having heard news from "Chloe's people," a circumlocution almost universally taken to refer to a woman and her household, including both immediate and extended family as well as clients and slaves—a woman of more than average material means. Paul also refers to "the household of Stephanas" in 1:16; in 16:15–18, he mentions Stephanas's household again as having "appointed themselves for the service of the saints." Paul mentions a certain Gaius at Rom 16:23 (written from Corinth) as the owner of a household at which "the entire congregation" of Corinth met and then signs off by claiming that "Erastus, the city treasurer [*oikonomos*], greet[s] you." At least some among the Corinthian community, then, had means beyond subsistence and the status such means might grant, at least among those at or below the poverty level.[20]

Paul's rhetorical goal in 1 Corinthians, however, seems geared toward bridging the gap between those above and those below subsistence in the community. Paul attempts to persuade the "strong," as he calls the more well-off members, to accommodate the needs and beliefs of the "weak" with regard to a range of issues, including sexual morality, behavior at their eucharistic meals, the need for orderly worship, and controversies over food purity. Paul deploys a common ancient trope for communal concord, seeing the group as a unified body with diverse members working toward a common goal (1 Cor 12 and 14). In Paul's use, though, the communal body is that of the crucified Christ, and the hierarchy of members is thus reversed. The "strong" must focus on the needs of the body as a whole and its "weak" members. All are members of Christ's body only insofar as they attend to the marginalized.[21]

Paul's rhetoric of communal formation in the Corinthian correspondence (as elsewhere) draws new boundaries based on new communal values targeting the despised among the Empire through the figure of Christ. And as we have seen, Paul viewed himself as imitating Christ's humiliation, becoming a more immediate paradigm for the group's formation. As a leader and exemplar, Paul emphasized marginality in his self-presentation; as an apocalyptic messenger, he proclaimed a new age in which God would invert existing communal values, a worldwide intervention that primarily conveyed a message of justice to the excluded—or, indeed, justice to all insofar as they were excluded. Likewise, according to Paul, he was a true apostle because he was marginalized. The role of marginality in Paul's mission, then, is more than just a matter of the social composition of his communities. The rhetoric of his address targeted excluded elements in every social location.

Both social-historical and philosophical-theological approaches to Paul should take into account the relationship between rhetoric and marginality in his letters. And while recent postcolonialist attention to Paul's background within the Roman Empire has succeeded in setting his discursive efforts within the social contexts of his various communities, post-Marxist analysis has raised the question of how he was successful at uniting these diverse communities into a more or less coherent, international movement. For many postcritical theorists, in particular, the construction of new social movements entails a series of rhetorical appeals to the despised, the remainder or excess left by the closure of a society's values, rights, and organization. The central dilemma in theorizing how new social movements coalesce entails explaining how diverse individuals and groups with diverse concerns and needs come together under one cause, under one figure or idea, to form a united and functional community—especially one that radically critiques, alters, or at least persists as an alternative to the status quo. As postcolonialist approaches argue, even though such discourses set out to critique or provide an alternative to existing power structures, the only discursive resources available to marginalized subjects are those provided by the hegemonic regime. The rupture with the regime that a new social movement creates, then, is a product of rhetoric, of creatively appropriating the language of empire in order to undermine empire.

The sheer diversity among and within Paul's local communities provided a fundamental obstacle to his rhetorical efforts at building or maintaining them. And as the letters preserved in 2 Corinthians show, Paul's efforts in 1 Corinthians at maintaining unity in the community proved ultimately unsuccessful. Many in Corinth expected a leader conforming to more stable, traditional, and patriarchal models of leadership—an apostle whose words more closely matched his deeds, who accepted financial support for his preaching, or (at the very least) whose message focused more on strength than suffering, on status and not servitude. Readers have long noted that 2 Corinthians as a whole stands as one of Paul's most emotional letters, as the apostle struggles to repair his ruptured relationship with his followers in Corinth. At the outset, he asserts that his feelings toward the community and the recent turmoil in his relationship with them are what dictated his changing travel plans: "it was to spare you that I did not come to Corinth . . . I decided this for myself—to not come again to you in pain" (1:23, 2:1). Paul attempts to reveal that his emotional outbursts and shifting itinerary are the products of clear planning and devotion to the community, of a consistent and directed "intention" or "desire." Ancient philosophers and moralists in general feared both physical and emotional wandering. The classic definition of a "passion" among the Stoics was an emotional impulse that "exceeded" (*pleonazein*) the control of reason. Thus, for the Stoic philosopher Chrysippus, passions are comparable to a man running so fast he cannot immediately stop himself. Emotions constitute uncontrolled motion. Indeed, as we will see, the act and idea of travel had such strong links to lack of control, social shame, and deception that travel was often linked to death.[22]

In 2 Cor 1–9, then, we see Paul trying a new rhetorical strategy, one in which he deploys a confusing array of metaphors at breakneck pace, a style unique among his extant correspondence. Alternately, the apostle is a beleaguered yet wise traveler (1:8–2:13), a wandering herald of a foreign god (2:14–17, and again in 4:7–12, 6:11–13, and 7:2), a courier of a divine letter (3:1–18), a philosopher contemplating the journeys of life and death (4:16–5:10), and a divine ambassador organizing a new, worldwide empire (5:11–21 and more broadly in chapters 8 and 9). In many cases, Paul's rhetoric itself takes on a marginalized, excluded quality, as his innovations of known tropes exceed or defy expectations, as he asserts his own novelty by considering, then rejecting, the status quo. This rhetorical marginality, however, attempts to structure the social project in which Paul is engaged. Biblical scholars have long looked for a unified theory of a single social contingency to explain the vague images—floating detached from historical referents—that make up the letter. My argument takes a different route: What if the variety that characterizes Paul's discourse in 2 Cor 1–9 mirrors the diversity of the community to which he appeals? Paul embraces and reframes his wanderings in the letter, not just through its travel-based content but through its wandering rhetoric, a style that sends out and recalls a series of apostolic images like heralds of a new empire. These wandering signifiers address suspicions about Paul's apostolic form of life and the diversity of subject positions among his community in Corinth.

Recent theories of social formation, change, and stability similarly view vagueness, variety, and multivalence as the hallmarks of the discourse of social cohesion. A particularly clear exposition of the role of variegated rhetoric in new social movements is found in the writings of Ernesto Laclau, who has long occupied himself with our central question: How do different social actors, parties, and individuals unite toward a common purpose despite their varying interests and contexts? For Laclau, unity is expressed through a common sign or symbol, usually a single party or demand among disparate, marginalized parties that comes to represent the whole. In order to represent diverse and (at times) opposing interests, the representing signifier must be specific enough to be meaningful but (paradoxically and yet most importantly) general and vague enough that it can mean different things to different parties and, moreover, continue to adapt to new eventualities in the hegemonic struggle; that is, the success of a new social movement depends on its ability to create vague or "empty signifiers," representing the needs of the new movement by expressing that which the current hegemonic domain excludes or fails to take into account. When used as a general banner under which critique or alternative is offered, an empty signifier unites various parties *insofar as they feel excluded.* In order to continue to function as a representative for a series of specific interests, however, an empty signifier must constantly respond to changing circumstances among the parties it represents or as occur in the course of struggles with the dominant regime. Following poststructuralist theories of language, Laclau explains that the signifier must react both to its own inability to represent fully and perfectly the movement and to new situations. Thus, the empty signifier must also be a *"floating"* signifier. Such signifiers "float" when people articulate them in new ways that respond to new situations. Thus, the work of social construction is fundamentally rhetorical, as the articulation of floating signifiers attempts to account for the different demands, expectations, and values represented in the new community, the polysemy of the community's relation to the world outside its ever-changing, ever-articulated boundaries. The signifier floats across the community's discursive landscape, making only strategic, "transient" attachments to specific ideals and demands.[23]

Laclau hesitates to describe in any general way, however, how such signifiers are floated or who among the new movement is responsible for creating such transient attachments between rhetoric and social demands. Instead, he prefers the more organic terminology of signifiers "coalescing" or "crystallizing" to create a new discursive regime. In the case of Paul's letters, however, we find a hegemonic actor deploying apostolic images at a rapid pace, the leader of a new movement in the process of rhetorically forming transient and ever-changing connections among his communities and between his communities and himself. In 2 Cor 1–9, Paul races to account for the inevitable semantic excess of his tropes, the sheer diversity of subject positions among his audience, and the shifting eventualities of his mission and his Corinthian congregation. As philosopher Giorgio Agamben notes in his commentary on Paul's letter to the Romans, all discursive attempts to create a new community, a new era, will fail to account fully for their social targets; new social movements such as Paul's group of communities produce semantic and social remainders. Paul's efforts at defining new communities—that is, of dividing them from the rest of the world as an elect "remnant"—exemplify the types of rhetorical work that build new social movements. Members of new communities in particular constantly must redefine their identity with respect to the larger world. Attempts at naming or labeling themselves with categories borrowed from the world outside the group can serve only as temporary self-expressions insofar as they inadequately encompass the new reality the members experience. Categories such as "Gentile" from the old era, for example, no longer adequately define God's new creation through Paul. For Agamben, "the remnant is therefore both an excess of the all with regard to the part, and of the part with regard to the all."[24] That is, the remnant as new social group exceeds the semantic codes of the old world, while the semantic efforts of the new group cannot adequately express the newness of its situation. As I will argue, remainder and excess are central themes and strategies in 2 Cor 1–9. Jacob Taubes, a Jewish legal philosopher who lectured on Paul and strongly influenced Agamben's readings, notably interpreted 1 Corinthians as a meditation on the Greek word *pan* ("all"), on the concept of completeness and wholeness. Following Taubes's lead, I view Paul as taking a new rhetorical itinerary in 2 Cor 1–9 by pairing his wandering motifs with a focus on the concept of *perisseia*, or "abundance." In 1 Corinthians, both the diversity of the community and the rapidity with which situations threatened Paul's leadership exceeded the rhetorical scope of the central "body of Christ" metaphor. In 2 Cor 1–9, then, Paul deploys a rhetoric of excess, a style that tirelessly traverses the varied ideological terrain of its audience.[25]

The international network of Pauline communities exemplifies a new social movement unified around the image of the leader, generated by its leader—the Traveling Apostle as Wandering Signifier. In both his rhetoric and his lifestyle, Paul issued a nomadic self-image, affording itself of all the adaptability and risk necessary to spread a fledgling movement. And as we will see, his identity as traveler or wanderer became a driving force behind the ethic he hoped to imbue in his worldwide communities. Paul offered his journeys as a representation for his followers of the ways in which they found themselves, by choice or circumstance, outside the normal boundaries of social status and cultural definitions during Augustus's new age.

Paul's letters offer a glimpse of a new social movement for which the figure of the leader—the apostle—centered and oriented the diverse subject positions comprising his communities. In order to examine how common expectations about travel informed Paul's self-construction and how ancient literatures deployed traveling figures, Chapter 1 surveys an array of ancient wanderers who were adopted in a variety of contexts throughout the centuries surrounding Paul's mission. As one among a long list of ancient itinerants—Dionysus, Odysseus, Anacharsis, Polyneices, and Socrates—Paul as Wanderer evoked a long history of travelers as figures of both social innovation and stability. The chapter ends with a discussion of clues from Paul's early correspondence to the role of travel in his apostolic form of life.

The subsequent five chapters analyze 2 Cor 1–9 as the paradigmatic case of both Paul's use of travel motifs and his rhetoric of social formation and change. I follow Paul as he marshals to his defense a series of wandering figures with a rhetorical pace driven by apocalyptic urgency in the face of the judgment of God. Beginning with the standard epistolary topic of travel plans, he innovatively introduces philosophic discussions of death and self-killing—the final journey—combining two topoi of self-revelation in the face of vacillating circumstances. From this point of departure, Paul cycles through other wandering signifiers: the captive messenger in the procession of a foreign, divine ruler; a letter carrier sent by God, in some sense comparable to Moses descending Sinai; a self-consoling philosopher, contemplating death as a final journey home; and an ambassador sent by God the Emperor, paradoxically offering reconciliation to the wayward. The final, ambassadorial image introduces Paul's presentation of his international network of co-workers and communities in a discursive remapping of the Mediterranean, offering an alternative, Jerusalem-centered empire.

I end by focusing on the legacy of travel in Paul's thought and later mission by examining briefly his letter to the Romans. The rhetorical lessons learned in the composition and reception of 2 Cor 1–9 cut paths through Paul's most famous letter—though the paths are sometimes obscured by the well-beaten thoroughfares of centuries of theological interpretation. Ultimately, it is likely that Paul failed in accomplishing his plans to spread his message to the western edges of the known world; it is certain, moreover, that his apocalyptic approximations that "the time is growing short" proved incorrect. Yet the motion of rhetorical excess that he initiated in his letters, the many paths of his wandering signifiers, proved able to exceed even his own intentions and expectations regarding the new era, the new empire, of the living God. For believers and nonbelievers alike, Paul the Traveler persists in making transient attachments with our discursive attempts at social innovation.

Traveling Leaders of the
Ancient Mediterranean

As we can tell from the clues left us in his correspondence, self-presentation—the image of "apostle"—was of primary importance in Paul's preaching mission. To those who encountered him, Paul initially appeared as one of many wandering artisans taking advantage of the freer, safer, yet still risky travel afforded by the *pax Romana*. His claims to be God's envoy evoked tales of wandering strangers and foreigners whom people could welcome or reject, risking God's wrath if they turned away an authentic, divine messenger. Paul's success depended on his ability to control the semantic excess flowing from apostleship. He needed to arrange prevailing cultural expectations about travelers in order to define his leadership role and the international community he hoped to build around it. Rival visions of apostleship from other Christian preachers further complicated his task, as we can see from the letters contained in 2 Corinthians. In part, this evidence of suspicions and accusations directed at Paul's apostleship makes 2 Cor 1–9 a unique opportunity for studying Paul's self-presentation, the formation of the early Jesus movement as an international community, social change during the first century of the Roman Empire, and theoretical approaches toward the rhetorics of new social movements.

I contend that Paul deployed travel—more specifically, the image of the "Wandering Apostle"—as a floating signifier that traced the boundaries of his self-image and his community. The travel images he used evoked itinerant figures that in turn represented prevalent expectations among his audience. In the background summary below, I emphasize traveling "figures," famous traveling heroes or types of the legendary past, for two reasons. First, I take seriously Pauline scholarship that cautions against the bewitching force of Paul's rhetoric and the place of his letters in the New Testament canon, an effect that can lead readers to overestimate his role in the spread and formation of earliest, international Christianity. In this light, a project like mine, locating Paul's image among other ancient wandering figures, risks falling into the gravitational pull of traditional narratives of early church history. In response, my study focuses on *self-fashioning* in the face of a situation of marginalization. To put it simply, Paul struggles to make himself a more central facet of the worldwide movement, and he calls to mind famous travelers and the discourses they represent as a part of his rhetorical strategy. Second, throughout the following investigation, ancient meditations on the structure of society and the nature of the individual indicate the centrality for Greco-Roman thinkers of stock individual types or characters (in Greek philosophical terminology, *prosōpa*; in Latin, *personae*). For ancient thinkers, people (or to be precise, upper-class men, the only true political actors for this period) filled certain personae on the basis of their natural aptitudes, a sense of divine calling or purpose, or the vicissitudes of certain situations. In constructing his vision of the role "apostle," Paul needed to engage certain common leadership types, whether the strong and open leader who suffered neither falsehood nor shame (think Ajax or Cato the Younger), the clever demagogue who would stoop to any means to achieve his desired ends (of which Odysseus was the paradigm), or any of a number of other familiar figures.

Furthermore, attention to Paul's rhetorical strategy of increasing and expanding his communities by establishing himself as the movement's coordinating signifier helps address an aporia in the study of new social movements—the role of the leader or "hegemonic actor" in assembling novel hegemonic rhetorics. Like other ancient moralists, Paul felt a divine calling to his mission and thus asserted his leadership position with a sense of divine authority. Yet he also realized that his image as apostle would need to be taken up and spread by his followers if it were to function successfully as a central signifier of the larger community. "We write you nothing except that which you can read and also recognize," he tells the Corinthians at the outset of 2 Cor 1–9. "I hope that you will recognize until the end (just as you have recognized in part), that we are your boast just as you are our boast on the Day of the Lord Jesus" (2 Cor 1:13–14). Paul's self-image would be fully fashioned only by his followers, a process concerning which he felt considerable eschatological pressure. In Paul's mind, his communities would need to attest to his fidelity and authority before other potential adherents in this age and before Christ in the next. The success of Paul's rhetoric, as we know, occurred in a slightly different manner; his followers indeed took up his image after his death, producing the many pictures of Paul that made up his diverse legacy, including the Great Apostle of catholic Christianity.

The starting point for the journey of the apostle as wandering signifier can be found in Paul's epistolary interactions with his communities. Evoking traveling gods and their proclaimers, epic heroes, foreign moralists, famous exiles, and sages contemplating death as a final journey, Paul cleared new space for his communities through the image of the Wandering Apostle.

Dionysus (the Traveling God)

In Euripides's *Bacchae* (504–631), the Theban king Pentheus receives a visitor, a prophet of the god Dionysus. Poor, wandering, long-haired, and effeminate, the prophet is arrested on sight and brought before the king as a charlatan bringing corruption to the city and, in particular, its women, who are already under the hypnotic sway of Bacchic devotions. Little does the king know that, beyond being a legitimate envoy of the god, the prophet is actually Dionysus disguised. The literary conceit encapsulates the anxiety with which "foreign" deities and their itinerant preachers were regarded in the ancient world. Famously called "beggars and sorcerers" by Plato (*Resp.* 364B–365A), the wandering practitioners of Bacchic rites exemplify a wider, complex phenomenon in Greek and Roman cultic devotions: the notion of gods as "travelers" and the proper way in which to receive them as visitors.

Insofar as mythmakers and cultic practitioners could easily construe immortals as foreign to the human realm, tales of gods and goddesses interacting with people could also be interpreted as instances of divine travel. Most prominent among the itinerant gods was Hermes, who conveyed divine messages throughout the cosmos. Apollo also traveled—most notably, according to ancient depictions, in the precivilized world, an era characterized by wandering. Tales of the gods traveling in disguise often lay behind ancient injunctions concerning the virtue of hospitality toward strangers. Stories of Zeus and Hermes traveling as emissaries may even stand as the background of some early Christian tales, as when the Lycaonians in Acts mistake Paul and Barnabas for the gods Hermes and Zeus (14:8–13).[1]

Various ritual performances reinforced the notion of gods as travelers. Observing the presence of couches, tables, and decorations in various offerings, scholars have identified a specific cultic tendency among the Greeks termed *theoxenia*, or "hospitality for the gods." Other rituals welcomed gods not from heaven but from other geographic locales, as when Greek cities celebrated the arrivals (*katagōgiai*) of deities. *Katagōgia* festivals tended to coalesce around certain deities characterized by their mythic travels, including Dionysus, Apollo, and Demeter and Persephone. The Athenian "City Dionysia" or "Great Dionysia," a festival featuring a procession and the performance of tragedies, commemorated the arrival of "Dionysus Eleuthereus" (the god's particular manifestation that originated in the city of Eleutherai). According to the legend, the Athenians had once rejected an Eleutherian statesman who arrived with a cult statue of the god. In retribution, Dionysus struck male Athenians with an unspecified malady of the genitals. An oracle from Apollo advised them to welcome the god with a periodic rite featuring sacred phalluses. The ritual served to appease the once angered deity. Other *katagōgiai* across Greece and Asia Minor celebrated local institutions of Dionysus's cult. In each case, he was regarded as an outsider welcomed into the community.[2]

Writers emphasized the foreignness of arriving deities. Cybele was always Phrygian, Syrian, or generically Asian, and Isis always retained the trappings of Egyptian culture. Apuleius's *Metamorphoses* witnesses to the continued Egyptianness of Isis while expressing her accrued universality. After appearing to Lucius, an impetuous adventurer turned into an ass by a magic spell, Isis explains her many names and guises in various cultures but asserts that "those who are enlightened by the earliest rays of that divinity the sun, the Ethiopians, the Arii, and the Egyptians who excel in antique lore, all worship me with their ancestral ceremonies and call me by my true name, Queen Isis" (11.5). The Isis procession in the city (Corinth, no less) the next day commemorates the beginning of the navigation season, a fact that may contain a historical kernel of Isis's Mediterranean migrations. The goddess who arrived in various towns with foreign merchants comes to express her universality through her divine patronage of all maritime activity. In some contexts, Isis retained her geographic particularity—for example, in one of Propertius's *Elegies* (2.33a), in which he humorously laments his lover's participation in a multiday feast to Isis, a rite requiring celibacy. Out of his resulting deprivation, the poet curses Isis's decision to take the long and uncomfortable trip from Egypt to Rome.[3]

So persistent was the "foreignness" of these deities—especially that of Cybele and Dionysus—that their rites and mythologies were often confused and combined. This syncretism is reflected in ancient literature: Euripides's *Bacchae* describes Dionysiac rites as being similar in nature and origin to those of the Great Mother, and Strabo picks up on these descriptions (as well as more oblique evidence in Pindar's *Hymn to Dionysus*) to explain the common "Asiatic" character of the rites of each deity, as well as those celebrated in Orphic devotion (10.3.10–18). The same sense of "foreignness" or "Easternness" was often attributed to the God of Israel and Judean cultic practices. Even some Jewish authors seemed to see similarities between Jewish and Dionysiac rites. For example, Jdt 15:12 and 2 Macc 10:7 describe among the Jewish worshippers the use of *thyrsoi*, a ritual prop best known for its role in Bacchic celebrations. Bacchic (and even Euripidean) connotations would certainly fit the plot of Judith: a *female* devotee of a foreign cult kills a king with her own hands and then celebrates her victory "with all the women of Israel . . . and some of them performed a dance for her, and she took *thyrsoi* in her hands and gave them to the women with her" (15:12). In the following hymn, Judith exhorts the crowd to praise God with "drums" and "cymbals"; to a certain extent, all percussive music was considered "Asiatic" and "Bacchic" (see, for example, Strabo 10.3.15–16). The passage in 2 Maccabees, in fact, describes Judas Maccabaeus's rededication of the Jerusalem Temple by referring to his use of *thyrsoi*. Outsiders sometimes confused Yahweh with Dionysus: Ptolemy IV Philopator's decree that Alexandrian Jews worship Dionysus may be partly due to this perception, while 2 Maccabees claims that Antiochus IV Epiphanes instituted Bacchic rites in Jerusalem. The Ptolemaic ruler Ptolemy IV Philopater is portrayed in 3 Macc 2:29 as forcing Jews in Alexandria to brand themselves with "the ivy-leaf mark of Dionysus." Plutarch explains the general confusion of the two deities with reference to the harvest feast of Sukhoth and its resemblance to Dionysiac rites. In Greco-Roman discourse, then, the lumping together of Eastern deities shows that their foreignness was a crucial aspect of their ideological function, worth distilling through the rhetorical act of conflation.[4]

Katagōgia celebrations honored and reperformed specific, legendary instances of the arrival of a foreign deity and its wandering preacher. On an everyday basis, however, itinerant cultic practitioners must have received more varied receptions. Plato's accusation that Bacchic advocates were con artists preying on the rich with false cures and promises of eternal life echoes through antiquity. Suspicions of falsifying cultic knowledge for petty gain characterized non-Bacchic rites as well. In an earlier exploit in the *Metamorphoses*, Lucius-turned-ass is bought by traveling "Syrian" priests of Magna Mater. The head priest is introduced as "one of the most common and impure of all people, who, through streets and towns, playing cymbals and castanets, carries around the Syrian Goddess and compels her to be a beggar" (*mendicare compellunt*; 8.24). The band of eunuchs who force Lucius to carry a statue of the goddess fits nearly every Asiatic stereotype: they are effeminate, play percussive music, and are susceptible to manic frenzy in their spiritual ecstasy to the point of self-mutilation. The priests carry out their performances to their fullest extent in front of the house of a rich man, the inhabitants responding by tossing hoards of money and food to the "greedy souls" (8.28). For Apuleius, their only motive is to "plunder" the towns they visit (8.29). To this end, they "devise a new money-making method for themselves" by composing an intentionally ambiguous oracle, a suitable response to anyone who queries the goddess for advice (9.8). Eventually, angered townspeople track down the priests and arrest them for "stealing a golden cup . . . secretly from the sacred seats of the very Mother of the Gods" (9.9). The eunuch priests of *Metamorphoses* 8 and 9 are stereotypical examples of hucksters of Eastern cults.

Conflation and stereotyping of foreign devotions can in part be attributed to fear of cultural novelty. For example, despite the official admission of the cult of Magna Mater into Rome in 204 B.C.E., her priests, who were imported from Asia to spare Romans the shame of castration and Asiatic behavior, were allowed to leave the sacred precinct of the temple only once a year. Such fear of the foreign also characterized Roman reactions to Bacchic devotions outside of the official worship of Liber (the god's Latin identification). Livy offers a highly reactionary account of the Senate's decision to crack down on Bacchic mysteries in 186 B.C.E., reportedly begun by a "sacrificer and sorcerer" (*sacrificulus et vates*) who came to Etruria from Greece. An inscription found in southern Italy records the senatorial decree regulating and limiting the growth of the mysteries.[5]

In reaction to the simultaneous popularity and scandal of foreign rites, practitioners and municipalities alike conceived of strategies for deploying traveling gods in socially productive ways. As already described, city festivals enacting the rejection and acceptance of wandering deities enshrined the dual nature of the gods as strange but welcome, potentially destructive but ultimately life-giving. The rise of Alexander the Great, moreover, would usher in a new era of Dionysian fervor at a political level, as Hellenistic propaganda portrayed the conqueror of the world from Greece to India as a new Dionysus, traveling the earth and taking captive each city he encountered. As I discuss more fully in Chapter 3, succeeding Hellenistic and Roman leaders would avail themselves of Dionysian imagery (in particular, the god as head of the triumphal procession) both to secure a connection to Alexander and to justify the novelty of their proposed power. Such rulers would rely on existing groups of mystery devotees (groups called *thiasoi*) to support their new reigns. The trend of kings appealing to Dionysus would halt briefly with Augustus, who foreclosed on such rhetoric in response to the Bacchic pretensions of his rival, Mark Antony. No Roman emperor would don the garb of Dionysus until Nero, just years after Paul's correspondence to the Corinthians.

Given the complex matrix of reactions to traveling gods, it would be surprising, then, if Paul's initial audiences did not understand him in light of wandering practitioners of Eastern divinities. After all, he spoke of a god who had interacted with a people, the Judeans, whose rites were often conflated with those of other "Eastern" nations. He promised either eternal life or judgment and death, depending on the reception his god received. And he presented this god (despite the god's ethnic roots) as a universal king who should be welcomed in advance of the final revelation of his power. The decision over whether to welcome the Wandering Apostle hinged on factors entirely comparable to those pertaining to prophets of Cybele or Dionysus.

Odysseus (the Wandering Hero)

While traveling gods served to demarcate the boundaries between a city's native values and foreignness (and later, between a new king and old regimes), the myths told in antiquity also deployed human travelers to explore the outer reaches of what it meant to be Greek, Roman, a citizen of a particular city, or generally "human." The wanderers of Greek and Roman epic, of which Odysseus was the paradigmatic forerunner, traced ideological paths and borders through and around the self-understandings of various ancient societies.

Scholars have long observed that behind the mythic journeys of Greek epic, depicted in verse and on vase, lay the experiences of the first Greek explorers and colonists. In functioning as collective self-representations, the epic tales of the *nostoi*—those "returning home" from the Trojan War—were a curious means through which to reflect on colonization, as François Hartog notes. Those who set out to establish a new city, after all, had no intention of returning. The repeated returns of Odysseus and the other *nostoi,* according to Hartog, express the eternal process of communal self-understanding, of philosophical "anthropology." The returns can be explained in less existential and more social-constructivist terms, however: that the *nostoi* always return to their homelands not only reflects the Greek colonial mercantile experience, but reinforces the connection and stability of the culture in colonial diaspora despite the separation of distance and the novelty of social creation.[6]

Although traveling heroes were revered by the cities who claimed them as founders, epics such as the *Odyssey* put forth travel as a curse worse than death. In part, the epic traveler's curse stems directly from the extreme dangers he faced. First and foremost, the hero feared death at sea, occurring outside one's homeland. In book 5, on a raft bound from Calypso's island to the Phaeacians and safety, Odysseus endures yet another setback in the form of a storm sent by Poseidon. In his distress, the hero wishes he had died in battle at Troy, like his fellows: "A hero's funeral then, my glory spread by comrades—now what a wretched death I'm doomed to die" (5.344–45).[7]

The epic wanderer is more deeply cursed in light of his removal from his homeland as his sphere of meaning and identity, often depicted as a departure from the regions allotted to humanity. As Silvia Montiglio explains, "wandering" for ancient Greeks could only truly take place apart from the realm of civilization, as evinced by the concentric geographic structure with which the *Odyssey* unfolds, moving from human habitations to more and more otherworldly realms, including the islands of the Cyclops, Calypso, and the gates of Hades themselves. Hartog, on whose reading Montiglio builds, interprets the *Odyssey* as tracing not just geographic, but also anthropological boundaries: "Defined as mortal, and feeding on bread and the flesh of sacrificed animals, human beings mark out their territory, always ephemeral, ever needing to be reconquered, in between the gods and the beasts. Odysseus strives always to maintain not only the distance separating humans from animals but also that which must separate humans from the gods." Homer explores what it means to be human through basic characteristics—eating and sacrificing, to be sure. But above all, humans are defined as social creatures. In opposition to the space of human society, the nonhuman outer world is "devoid of cultivation or sociability, isolated without detectable boundaries." The fear of travel— that is, the fear that travel will become wandering, without return—is a fear of loss of social ties, the loss of converse with one's society and one's gods.[8]

The notion of travel-as-curse is perhaps nowhere better expressed than in the prediction of Odysseus's final days made by the ghost of the seer Tireisias. The prophet foresees that the hero will endure one last journey before his death—a journey not narrated later in the tale:

> Go forth once more, you must . . . carry your well-planed oar until you come to a race of people who know nothing of the sea, whose food is never seasoned with salt, strangers all to ships with their crimson prows and long slim oars, wings that make ships fly. And here is your sign—unmistakable, clear, so clear you cannot miss it: When another traveler falls in with you and calls that weight across your shoulder a fan to winnow grain, then plant your bladed, balanced oar in the earth and sacrifice fine beasts to the lord god of the sea, Poseidon—a ram, a bull and a ramping wild boar—then journey home and render noble offerings up to the deathless gods who rule the vaulting skies, to all the gods in order. And at last your own death will steal upon you . . . a gentle, painless death, far from the sea it comes to take you down, borne down with the years in ripe old age with all your people there in blessed peace around you. All that I have told you will come true. (*Od.* 11.139–57, ellipses from translator)

The prophecy sets a clear ideological limit: Odysseus must journey until he finds a culture that has never even heard of the cursed practice of travel, a people who do not know what an oar is, who know nothing of salt and other wares of maritime trade. Only then can he die in his homeland with his family and his own people, the ideal death in Greek ideology. Peace can be found only in a culture self-sufficient enough to have never partaken in—indeed, to have never heard of—travel.

In the classical period, Greek colonialism became more and more of a mythic memory, and writers and politicians deployed the epics to reflect on new social situations. With the impending threat of Persian conquest, writers mapped the struggle between Achaia and Troy onto the contemporary international scene. As scholars as early as Thucydides have noted, the "Greek/barbarian" division of humanity so common to later thinkers is absent from Homer, "because in his time, the Hellenes were not yet known by one name, and so marked off as something separate from the outside world" (1.3.3). It is only with the clashes accompanying Persian expansion and the Panhellenic-Persian wars that Greek thinkers begin to castigate the non-Greekness of the great empire of the East, producing a notion of a unified Hellenic culture in the process. Just as the Persians were the enemies of Greek civilization, the *Iliad* and cognate myths were reinterpreted to present the Trojans as the "barbaric" enemies of Hellenism. Athenian artists, playwrights, and other writers strove to frame mythic Trojans as barbarians in the service of anti-Persian propaganda. A major side effect of this ethnic and political rhetoric was the establishment of a Europe-Asia geographic divide. Although "Greeks" technically lived on either side of the Hellespont, throughout antiquity writers could fix the strait as a historical and ethnic dividing line. Herodotus explains the Europe/Asia, Greek/barbarian line as a difference in political imagination, between the polis and tyranny. Barbarians, under the rule of kings, cannot help but live lawlessly and thus under the strict control of a sovereign.[9]

Throughout the war-plagued fifth century B.C.E., Athens in particular felt its polis structure threatened from within and without. The perceived threat increasingly led Athenian writers and orators to denigrate Odysseus. Such denigration linked the internal threat of wandering and demagogic sophists in Athens to the journeys and vacillations of the epic hero. Playwrights castigated Odysseus's smooth rhetoric and self-interest; in Euripides's *Troades,* the hero's long journeys are foretold as a punishment for his demagoguery. In subsequent centuries, sophists and Cynics would appropriate not only Odysseus's rhetorical style and populist manner, but also his penchant for travel. Against these wandering personalities, the forces of tradition in the polis felt a need to defend themselves, warning against the wandering ways of demagogues.[10]

Anacharsis (the Foreign Social Critic)

Ancient Greeks and Romans used tales of mortal wanderers to trace out their own identities. Odysseus could be deployed to valorize virtues of endurance and cleverness or to put down demagoguery and deceit. The tales of another legendary traveler, the Scythian Anacharsis, are similarly interpreted by Hartog, for whom competing and contradictory accounts of the foreign sage show "the malleability of the figure . . . a signifier travelling the world, through the centuries, charged willy-nilly with reflecting to the Greeks an image of themselves that they both do and do not want. Anacharsis was to be an observer observed, fashioned by the Greeks for their own use."[11]

Accounts of Anacharsis's life differ from author to author, each trying to explain the legend of the stranger from Scythia—to Greeks, a stereotypically barbaric nation—who arrived in Athens to learn about Greek culture. Herodotus gives two versions, the first that Anacharsis was a world traveler who, like Solon the Athenian sage, had gained and displayed much wisdom, even among the Greeks. Having picked up the worship of Magna Mater on his journeys, he is caught practicing his devotions upon his return to Scythia and is killed for introducing foreign practices (4.76.1–5). Herodotus also notes that some described Anacharsis as having been sent by the Scythian king to learn Greek customs. He reported back that the Greeks were always speaking wisdom but that only the Spartans knew how to speak well (4.77.1). Centuries later, Diogenes Laertius claimed that Anacharsis's mother was Greek; the Greek language he learned from her served as a ticket into the culture he was sent to study (1.101). Moreover, his access to Greek society is often explained and expressed in his friendship with Solon, the architect of Greek statecraft, laws, and customs. Diogenes Laertius relates an anecdote depicting how Anacharsis impressed Solon with his wit. When Solon initially tries to avoid association with the foreigner, claiming that people usually make friends with people "in their own homeland," Anacharsis asserts that since Solon is presently "in his own homeland," he should be more friendly (1.102; other versions of the story appear in the pseudonymous Cynic *Epistles* attributed to Anacharsis [2.18–28] and in Plutarch, *Sol.* 5.1). Lucian of Samosata, in a short dialogue (*Anacharsis*), displays a debate between the two friends about the sense behind the Athenian custom of wrestling in gymnasiums. The practice quickly becomes a metonymy for the Athenian constitution. Both in Lucian's work and in Plutarch's life of Solon, Anacharsis's typical reaction to the great lawmaker's reforms is laughter and mockery: wrestling Athenian youths resemble animals, not humans—or, if people, crazy people; and the prizes they strive for in the games of Olympus and Isthmia are ridiculously paltry (*Anach.* 9). In Plutarch's account, the Scythian jokes that Solon's laws have all the strength of spider webs, while the courts merely constitute fools judging the wise (*Sol.* 5.2–3). Anacharsis is permitted to mock the revered Solon; thus, through Anacharsis, Greek writers are allowed to criticize their own culture. Anacharsis's ability to cross boundaries grants him unique access to Greek culture in the literary tradition. In some accounts, he is numbered among the Seven Sages of Greek lore, most notably in Plutarch's *Dinner of the Seven Sages.*[12]

Yet the literary tradition also cautions against the figure of the wise savage Anacharsis. His travels across space and culture, after all, result in his demise, as he permeated and blurred one too many boundaries. In part reflecting his end, Anacharsis the traveler becomes the wise man who despises travel, even questioning whether travelers still inhabited the ranks of the living. Diogenes Laertius preserves other antiwandering maxims of the Scythian:

> Having learned that the hull of a ship was only four fingers thick, he said, "That's how far many people are from death." (DL 1.103)
> "How come," he said, "that those [the Greeks] who make lying illegal clearly lie through their mercantile activities [*en tais kapēleiais*]?" (DL 1.104)
> Having been asked which ship was the safest, he said, "The ones pulled up on shore." (DL 1.104)
> When Anacharsis was asked which were more in number, the living or the dead, he said, "In what category would you put those traveling by ship?" (DL 1.104)
> Some say that during his life he invented the anchor . . . (DL 1.105)

The sage whose travels produced knowledge about disparate cultures is made to condemn the practice of boundary-crossing. Travel is dangerous not merely because seafarers are so close to the tumultuous waters, but because leaving one's homeland and entering another is an essentially dangerous proposition. Greek tales of Anacharsis use the sage to step outside their own culture and critique it; simultaneously, they warn against ideological transgressions.[13]

Greek intellectuals who followed in Anacharsis's footsteps became similarly ambivalent figures, objects of great respect and sharp scorn. The Cynic philosophers, in adopting Anacharsis as one of their own, reject Greekness in a scathing and performative critique of the very notion of culture. Cynics also took Odysseus as an exemplar, pointing to his homelessness, his wanderings on the outskirts of civilization, and his willing endurance of poverty, abuse, and shame. Despite later representations, it seems unlikely that Cynics were world travelers; the cultural curiosity that extensive voyages would entail seem counter to the Cynic ideal. True, Diogenes the Cynic was an exile from his native land of Sinope. In general, however, any legacy of Cynic itinerancy seems tied to their *homelessness.* But through their appropriation of legendary itinerants, Cynics could express disapproval of common travel, insofar as citizens tended to take to road and sea following commercial pursuits. Thus, in the "Cynic epistles" attributed to him, "Anacharsis" chastises those who journey (or receive foreigners) out of financial interests. While the Athenians laugh at Anacharsis's foreign ways, they "buy without hesitation from non-Greeks, if they sell for a suitable price" (1.13–14). In *Epistle 9*, framed as a letter to the tyrant Croesus, the sage provides a decline narrative surrounding the rise of trade: primitive humans "sought the treasures of the earth in various ways, and deemed their search a wonderful thing" (9.21–22). Later, he depicts the dangers of chasing after riches through a parable:

> Through the land of the Scythians there flows a great river, which is called the Danube. On this river, some merchants ran their ship aground on a reef. Since they could not budge it in any way, they went away lamenting. So, when robbers, without understanding the problem of these men, sailed up with an empty ship, they freely loaded cargo, and at once transferred the cargo from the strange ship, unaware of the calamity as they made the transfer. For as the one ship was emptied, it started to float and became seaworthy. But the ship taking on the other's cargo quickly sank to the bottom because of the robbery of the foreign goods. (9.18–27)

The passage, within the context of the letter, not only frames trade as a potentially calamitous enterprise, but also questions what is truly "foreign" or strange to a person, presenting a philosophical critique of externals through a critique of trade and travel.[14]

On the whole, Cynics stayed in urban centers in order better to perform their intellectual assault on society. Through their rhetoric and actions, they demanded access to the heart of the city, even knocking on doors to beg and preach. Later travelers, however, especially exiles, appropriated the Cynic ideal in order to put a positive spin on their enforced wanderings—most famously, the orator Dio Chrysostom, who temporarily played the Dog when exiled from Rome.[15]

Cynic itinerancy became an ambivalent cultural motif in its diverse appropriations, as did the rest of the movement's provocative traits. Though many writers complained about the boorishness and laziness of the Cynics, the ideal was rehabilitated and domesticated among many Roman moralists in order to adopt its stance of radical, uncompromising critique. Any schoolboy who learned to read and write knew of the exploits of Diogenes through the *chreiai*—short memorable anecdotes suitable for instruction in writing and composition.[16]

Viewed through the writings both of and about Cynics, then, the figure of the wandering cultural critic simultaneously provided an outsider vantage point for interrogating cultural norms (or even the notion of culture as such) as well as a caution against transgressions of societal boundaries. Other philosophical traditions similarly warned against the allure of travel, creating a stock motif through which attachment to externals could be critiqued. As seen in the Cynic tirades against mercantilism and the antisophistic passages of the Platonic corpus, philosophers denigrated travel in order to denigrate the futile search for happiness outside one's self. Among the philosophical schools, perhaps none criticized attachment to externals and extolled the virtue of self-sufficiency more than the Stoics, for whom things apart from an individual's rational, ethical choice were ethically unimportant, or *adiaphora*. Such externals only blinded a person to the real source of vice and pain, a defective rational faculty not operating in accordance with nature. For Epictetus, one's station in life, including his locale, had been decided by God and should be embraced. " 'Where would you like me to be? In Rome, Athens, Thebes, or Gyara? Just keep me in mind when I am there. Should you send me to a place where people have no life according to nature, I will depart, not disobeying you, but as if you had sent me a signal to retreat. I do not abandon you—by no means!—but I perceive that you do not need me" (*Diatr.* 3.24.100–1). The Stoic will endure the travails of any travel or location unless he comes to understand that God no longer wishes him to remain—in which case, he returns home through suicide. The journeys of the sage, though ostensibly shameful, are divinely guided.[17]

While travel motifs could provide an author or speaker a vantage point from which to engage in cultural critique, such appropriations of travel were often accompanied by references to travel as shameful (especially as an expression of greed) or by connections between travel and death. Even when traversing the boundaries of the cultural imagination, such transgressions had to be constrained by various ideological controls. The lines between civilization and nature still required reinforcement.

Polyneices (the Exile as Civically Dead)

Among Greco-Roman travel discourses, treatments of exile highlight the connection between travel and death by distilling the general ancient fear of leaving one's homeland. From the advent of consolatory works dealing with exile (usually traced to the third-century B.C.E. Cynic Teles and his *Peri phugēs,* "On Exile"), writers observed that the individual physically and legally removed from his civic status suffered social oblivion. Much of the ignominy associated with exile flowed from its use as a punishment since archaic times. The miasma associated with murder and other serious crimes required societies to expel the guilty party—or, in some cases, allow the criminal to escape punishment at some time before or after sentencing. In this way, the worst criminals eventually faced exile or execution as interchangeable fates. Similar penalties existed in Roman law and seem to be related to the archaic figure of the *Homo sacer,* the criminal who is not executed but can be killed by any citizen with impunity. In this case, the man is called "sacred" because he exists utterly outside of any social framework or jurisdiction, human or divine. Flight would have been the only survival option for such a criminal. Giorgio Agamben relates the Roman notion of the *Homo sacer* and related concepts (including exile, funerals for emperors in the later Empire, and military *devotio*) to his analysis of sovereign power based on the state of exception (also known as the sovereign ban, state of emergency, or martial law); for Agamben, sovereignty is based in the power and potentiality of the ruler (or government) to suspend the law whenever he chooses (thus defining the basic situation in which the law is applicable) and assert his total authority over his subjects. In many ways, sending someone into exile exhibited a ruler's power more clearly than did mere execution. As we see most clearly in the writings of exiles under the late Republic and early Empire (including Cicero, Ovid, and Seneca), the exile was expected to wait on or even campaign and beg for the ruler's clemency, finding himself in a state of social limbo, a member of society so completely excluded as to evoke notions of death.[18]

Centuries of literature lamented exile as entailing total exclusion from the rights and status of social life. Most influential for later writers was Euripides's *Phoenissae,* in which Polyneices mourns his exile and its attending disenfranchisement—in particular, his lack of *parrhēsia,* the right of bold, free speech as a prince. When his mother, Jocasta, asks him to relate the worst parts of being an outcast, he enumerates other ills: suffering the stupidity of those who retain power, being hungry, lacking shelter, not having the ability to rely on one's former status. Mother and son conclude that nothing is more precious than one's own country. In the later tradition of philosophical works of consolation on exile, Polyneices would be the exile par excellence, and his complaints would provide the standard list of exilic evils. So reconstructions of the now-lost treatise by Teles, *On Exile,* comprise a similar list of exilic misfortunes, each refuted by the author. Later works, such as Plutarch's *On Exile,* employed Euripides's Polyneices as a straw man against which to argue the indifferent nature of banishment. Other writers praised exile as an escape from the hustle and bustle of upper-class life. Interestingly, as we will see throughout this book, similar arguments were made about death as a heavenly escape from life's political and social travails. For the Greek or Roman man of affairs, exile could be construed as an almost heavenly retreat.[19]

Alternately, writers on exile could continue to frame banishment as a sort of "civic death" because of the disenfranchisement it entailed. Most famously, Ovid's mournful poems from exile transport from epic memory archaic fears of dying apart from one's homeland. The helplessness of his situation led him to depict himself as already dead. An even more creative set of responses can be found in Cicero's writings on his exile among his letters, speeches, and treatises. Here, he follows a strategy of defying consolatory arguments, a generic innovation that Jo-Marie Claasen refers to as "anti-consolation," sequentially raising and refusing rationalizations of his situation. In other contexts (especially after the reinstatement of his citizenship), he portrays his exile in other terms: far from being excluded from the Republic (since he saw his banishment as unjustified), Cicero asserts that the Republic was banished with him as its only true representative and defender. One could easily read this through Agamben's analysis as a reversal of sovereign power. Instead of the ruler deciding that a man's actions require his exclusion from societal rights and protections, Cicero rhetorically wrests the sovereign power to banish whom he chooses and names himself the only true citizen. Cicero, faced with the loss of his civic persona, preserves it by denying the validity of the government that banished him.[20]

Finally, authors rationalized away the distinction between being at home and being in exile. For Seneca, exile was no different from travel—"in truth, a change of place" (*Helv.* 6.1). At base, life itself is a state of exile, of constant motion, of separation from the soul's divine origin and destination. After all, the state or society was such a fickle, human invention that one could scarcely feel "at home" simply for being in one's homeland. Humanity is changeable and migratory in its very nature because of the divinity of a person's soul. As Seneca expounds further, the planets themselves are on endless courses, and our souls are composed of kindred stuff (*Helv.* 6.6–8). Implicitly, the only true homecoming from exile can be death itself: "For all those people storm-tossed by setting forth and sailing the sea, there is no port except death" (Seneca, *Polyb.* 9). Only when the wise man gains perspectival distance from his exiled situation, conceiving himself as an impartial and critical outsider to the human situation, can he realize that all of life is equally a state of banishment from perfection and wholeness, mythically conceived as a postmortem journey to the divine. Consolations on exile and death similarly appealed to depictions of life and death as journeys.

Socrates (the Homeward-Bound Sage)

Throughout Plato's account of the trial and execution of Socrates, the condemned sage discusses his impending fate by comparing his death to a journey home. After his sentence is read, Socrates compares the realistic alternatives concerning the postmortem fate of the soul. First considering that the soul is dissolved completely, he moves on to the alternative:

> But if, on the other hand, death is some sort of journey [*apodēmēsai*] from here to another place, and it is true what they say, that all those who have died are there, what greater good could there be than this, judges? For if someone arriving in Hades, having left behind those who say they are judges, finds those who are truly judges, the very ones they say judge there—Minos and Rhadamanthus and Aeacus and Triptolemus, and all the others among those just demigods who were just in their own lives—would this really be such a terrible journey [*phaulē . . . apodēmia*]? (*Apol.* 40E–41A)

Subsequent centuries of reflection on death and dying would return to the persona Socrates occupied—that of a philosopher contemplating the uncertainty of death with rationality and composure. The genre of *consolatio mortis*, "consolation on death," would come to address the topic with a variety of stock approaches, among which was the notion of life and death as journeys—situations fraught with risk and danger but also opportunities for showing one's true character of dignity and strength.

In portraying death as a journey, Socrates (and Plato) had eminent forebears. The pre-Socratic philosopher Empedocles reportedly taught the Orphic and Pythagorean doctrine that all human souls were wandering exiles from their heavenly home. His teachings may have corresponded to his own status as an exile from his native Agrigentum in Sicily, a status he incorporated into his self-image. He proclaimed to the inhabitants of cities he visited that he was "an immortal god roaming about among you" (DK 112 D). Empedocles exemplifies the exploitation of a traveling and exilic lifestyle to explain the origin and fate of the soul—or conversely, to defend one's ignominious wanderings by expounding divine knowledge. Though Empedocles lived well before the emergence of the consolatory tradition, he provided fodder for later consolatory authors.[21]

Following the example of the sages who came before, the various followers of Plato developed the *consolatio* genre, the first examples dealing with death. Although the Platonic successor Crantor's *On Grief* was most influential (and is still usually cited as the earliest example of the genre), Aristotle's *Eudemus, or On the Soul* (now available only in quotations from later authors) was also widely read. The most significant fragment for our purposes is found in Cicero's *Div.* 1.53, where Cicero recalls an anecdote to testify to the legitimacy of divination through dreams. In it, Aristotle's friend Eudemus of Cyprus journeys to Pherae in Macedonia, at the time ruled by the tyrant Alexander.

Here, Eudemus becomes gravely ill but dreams that a young man makes three predictions to him: he will soon recover his health, Alexander will soon die, and Eudemus will return home in five years. The first two predictions are fulfilled in the subsequent days. However, in five years Eudemus finds himself joining in battle at Syracuse—a battle in which he is killed. "Due to this," the story concludes, "the dream was interpreted thusly, that when Eudemus's soul had departed the body, then it would seem to have returned home."[22]

Similarly (and obviously) influenced by Platonic texts on death and dying is the *Axiochus,* falsely attributed to Plato. While imitating Socratic dialogues in style and content, the *Axiochus* shows the influence of the later, Hellenistic schools, including Epicureanism, Stoicism, and Cynicism. In addition, the *Axiochus* borrows terms and concepts from the mysteries, especially Orphic and Pythagorean teachings and cult practices. In the dialogue, Socrates is urgently summoned to the bedside of Axiochus, who is ill and anxious about death. Socrates's initial arguments degrade life as a paltry and temporary abode, calling the notion "a commonplace, everybody's talk, that life is a brief stay in a foreign land" (365B). Later, he combines the Orphic notion of the body as a "prison" with the metaphor of the body as "tent" (*skēnos*), that is, a paltry, material existence (365E–366A). As in the Platonic works, the *Axiochus* portrays Socrates as putting forth ancient tales of the postmortem journey of the soul as uncertain but comforting explanations of dying, popular and widely held myths clung to as having a kernel of truth.[23]

Also influenced by the Platonic tradition of consolation was Cicero's own *Consolatio* on the occasion of his daughter's death. Though the work is now lost, the author gives hints as to its composition in another piece written soon after, the *Tusculan Disputations.* The dialogue comprising book 1 deals exclusively with the question of death and thus is driven by the same type of musings over the uncertain nature of the soul and its fate found in Plato's Socrates. After outlining various opinions on the soul and its destiny after death, Cicero notes in *Tusc.* 1.23 that "which of these opinions is true is for a god to consider; which is more probable is a question of great import." Throughout the discourse, he bases his views on the opinions of those philosophers who do not think the soul ceases to exist at death; such thinkers "offer hope . . . that souls, when they depart from bodies, can arrive in heaven as if in their own home" (*quasi in domicilium suum;* 1.24). Similarly, Cicero frequently describes death as a journey, often evoking the final journeys of famous travelers such as Hercules and Jason, as well as the death of Socrates. In turn, the notion of death as a journey home leads to the depiction of life as a temporary trip or exile. In 1.51, Cicero claims that he finds it much easier to imagine the soul separate from the body than in its interactions with the body; earthly, human existence seems to him as if the soul is living "in a home which is foreign to it" (*sit tamquam alienae domui*), while he can immediately picture the postmortem soul flying through heaven, "as if it had come to its own home" (*quasi domum suam venerit*). Near the end of the book, Cicero exhorts his interlocutor to take joy in death as the end of a long journey: "In fact, let us consider it [death] as harbor and refuge prepared for us [*portum . . . paratum nobis et perfugium*]: would that we be permitted to travel there under full sails [*velis passis pervehi*]! If, however, we are driven back by opposing winds, we will necessarily return to that very place a little later" (1.119). With this "epilogue" (*epilogum*), Cicero seems to hope for a quick death, perhaps even suicide. In any case, the nautical imagery is a concise yet fitting metaphor for the troubles of life and the hoped-for benefits of death.[24]

Among ancient authors, Seneca is particularly fond of the "journey" motif for death and the fate of the soul in his consolatory treatises and letters. In *Ad Marciam de consolatione*, he consoles the grieving Marcia concerning the death of her son. At the beginning of the work, he compares Marcia's fortunes to the fickle weather at sea (5.5, 6.3); he also compares life to "a stay at an inn" (21.1). His most extensive use of a travel metaphor for life occurs in 17.2–18.8, a section that seems to be inspired by Aristotle's *Eudemus* (discussed above). In showing Marcia that sorrow and misfortune are universal aspects of human nature, he compares life to a journey to Syracuse (the location of Eudemus's foretold death): though one will see great natural and manmade marvels on this journey, one will also encounter many hardships, including hot summers (17.4), a tumultuous and rocky shoreline (18.6), and, not the least, the tyrant Dionysius (17.5). In the background of this consolation, then, is one of the earliest comparisons of travel and death. As in such a trip, both the pleasures and evils of life must be accepted if one chooses to live it.[25]

Seneca, moreover, had no trouble advocating an early and voluntary voyage home through suicide, a choice he often framed as noble, and one he himself would choose after falling into disfavor with Nero. Thus, he also recalls the political suicide of Marcia's famous father, Cremutius Cordus, in order to indicate the extent to which she is already practiced at dealing with grief. Seneca recounts that her father tried to hide his suicide from his daughter. After he had spent days of solitude in his bedroom, Marcia inferred his plan and begged him to change his mind. Seneca approximates the father's response: "I have entered upon the road to death [*iter mortis ingressus sum*] and am now almost half-way there; you cannot and you ought not to call me back" (22.6). Similarly (as Seneca ends his discourse), Marcia's son, through his virtuous life, has escaped the mortal bonds of the body ("has fled and departed in whole," *fugit et totus excessit*) to meet not only the famous "Scipios and

Catos," but also his grandfather Cordus, who teaches his grandson about the ways and movements of the heavenly bodies: "just as a stranger is grateful for a guide through an unknown city, so your son, as he searches into the causes of celestial things, is grateful for a kinsman as his instructor" (25.2). Since the *animi* of Marcia's father and son have escaped earthly, physical bonds, Seneca turns the travel motif for death into a contrast between earthly and heavenly journeys: "Throughout the free and boundless spaces of eternity they wander [*dimissi sunt*]; no intervening seas block their course, no lofty mountains or passless valleys or shallows of the shifting Syrtes; there every way is level, and, being swift and unencumbered, they easily are pervious to the matter of the stars and, in turn, are mingled with it" (25.3). In this way, Seneca deploys travel motifs to give a more accurate description of the fate of the soul as explained through Stoic cosmology and physics and thus to console Marcia by referring to this blessed existence being enjoyed by her father and son. Insofar as Seneca's Stoic cosmology still yields a Socratic-Platonic view that the human soul during lifetime, through reasoning and virtue, begins the process of its separation from the body to be consummated at death, Seneca extends the notion of death as a journey to include the notion of life as a journey toward death.[26]

Paul (the Apostle)

"Sent" by definition, the *apostolos,* or "apostle," braved the dangers of travel to spread his or her message. In the traditions preserved in the Synoptic Gospels about Jesus's commissionings of his *apostoloi,* the hardships of itinerancy are readily apparent:

> He summoned the Twelve and began to send them out [*apostellein*] two by two, and he gave to them authority over unclean spirits. And he ordered them to take nothing with them for the journey except only a staff—no bread, no bag, no coins in their belts, but that they should strap on sandals; "And do not wear two tunics." And he said to them, "In whatever region you enter a house, stay in that house until you leave that region. And should a place neither receive you nor listen to you, when you journey from that place, shake the dust from your feet as a testimony against them" (Mark 6:7–11).

New Testament scholars are more likely to see these words as reflecting the self-understanding of the first Palestinian preachers of the gospel after Jesus's death than the historical situation of Jesus and his first followers. For the first itinerant proclaimers of the Jesus movement, radical dependence on the material provisions of those to whom they preached characterized apostleship. In turn, those who welcomed apostles were thought to play a key role in the spread of the message and the restoration of the kingdom of Israel.[27]

Paul also invested his arrival and acceptance in a new city with great theological significance. His rhetoric, read closely, makes clear that his joy at finding an audience for his proclamation was not confined to the spread of the gospel but to the happy fact of finding shelter after his travels. Unlike his Palestinian predecessors, however, Paul usually took pride in supporting himself through his own work. "We could have been a burden on you, as apostles," he claims in his earliest extant letter, 1 Thessalonians. "Instead, we were gentle among you, like a nurse comforting her own children" (2:9; cf. 1 Cor 9, 2 Cor 12:14–15). Some reconstructions of Paul's situation in the cities he visited have surmised that he eventually would have rented an artisan shop with an adjoining apartment. Moreover, as I discuss below, one theory sees the discrepancy between Palestinian and Pauline missionary strategies with regard to accepting material support as providing a source of conflict among the earliest, international apostles. Yet at least upon Paul's original arrival in a city, new followers benefited him by providing him temporary lodgings. Evidence for his reliance on hospitality abounds in the Corinthian correspondence. He calls a certain Gaius, who was (to the best of his recollection) one of the only people he baptized in Corinth (1 Cor 1:14), his "host" or "foreign friend" (*xenos;* Rom 16:23), almost certainly a reference to Gaius having welcomed Paul into his household. The phenomenon of Paul as itinerant and relying on hospitality may, in fact, lie behind one of his repeated expressions for evangelization: the "open door." The phrase first occurs in 1 Cor 16:9, where Paul explains that he will stay in Ephesus because "a great and active door has been opened to me." It occurs again in the travelogue at the beginning of 2 Cor 1-9, where Paul explains his arrival in Troas by saying that "a door opened for me in the Lord" (2 Cor 2:12). Although this term certainly means that Paul found people receptive to his message, the metaphor also has a literal component. For Paul the traveler, one of the benefits of converting people to the gospel was that those people would almost certainly "open their doors" to him if they had the means.[28]

While the welcome and support Paul received in cities may seem quotidian enough, the language with which he framed his arrival and its effect on those who received him drew upon grandiose cultic and political imagery. From his earliest letter, 1 Thessalonians, he explains how the message (the *euangelion,* "good news" or "gospel") he proclaimed presaged the arrival or presence—the *parousia*—of Jesus Christ, an event for which the Thessalonians' "hearts must be established as blameless in holiness" (3:13; see also 5:23) and at which

Paul and his community must "boast" in each other (2:19). Paul goes on to describe the event in detail:

> This we say to you with a message of the Lord: we who remain living until the arrival [*parousian*] of the Lord will by no means precede [to welcome and join him] those who have died; the Lord himself, with the command and cry of an archangel and with the sounding of God's trumpet, will descend from heaven, and the dead in Christ will rise up first, then we living who are left behind together with them will be taken up in the clouds for the greeting [*apantēsin*] of the Lord in the air. And in this way we will be with the Lord always. (4:15–17)

The passage has attracted much critical attention as a vivid picture of the eschatological scenario Paul envisioned. The account, however, owes at least as much to Greek and Roman ideologies of kingship as it does to Jewish apocalyptic. The terms *parousia* and *apantēsis* derive not from apocalyptic, but from Greco-Roman political discourse, the first denoting "the arrival of a king or emperor" and the second being a technical term for the ritual welcome offered by a city. This particular mixture of apocalyptic and imperial politics appears to be distinctive to Pauline usage. Paul's followers will greet Christ as a conquering emperor journeying from heaven.[29]

Such travel metaphors provided ideal raw materials for Paul's rhetorical strategies. Despite his focus on the apostolic act of proclamation, travel was one of the main characteristics of his vision of the apostolic lifestyle. For example, the geographic aspect of his mission anchored his self-definition as apostle. Paul was convinced that God had apportioned out the world to his emissaries, to the extent that the arrival of an apostle in a region constituted the arrival of God's spirit. If a community welcomed an apostle and his proclamation, their acceptance had been made possible through the power of God, who had thus established the apostle as authority over that community, as its "father." Paul's geographic understanding played a central role in the controversies with his Corinthian followers, prompting the letters preserved in 2 Corinthians. In 2 Cor 10–13 (an agitated letter sent, as I reconstruct it, after 1 Corinthians and before 2 Cor 1–9), Paul rebukes other teachers he terms "false apostles" who have come to Corinth. Paul implies in 10:10 that the apostles accused Paul of being deceptive and vacillating: " 'His letters,' they say, 'are substantial and strong, but his bodily presence [*parousia*] is weak, and his speech contemptible.' " In response, Paul condemns the teachers as violating his geographically construed apostolic authority:

> Let such a person consider that however we appear, though absent, in word through our correspondence, we will also be in deed while present. For we

are not so bold as to judge or compare ourselves with those who commend themselves; rather, when they measure themselves with respect to themselves, or compare themselves with themselves, they show a lack of understanding. We, on the other hand, will not boast beyond what is measured out to us, but only according to the measured boundary God has measured out for us, to reach even to you. For we do not extend beyond ourselves, as if we did not reach you; for we arrived first among you with the gospel of Christ. (10:11–14)

When Paul reached Corinth as its founding apostle, his acceptance signified God's allotment of the community to Paul's paternal auspices. Indeed, Paul's geographic principle of apostolic authority was so foundational that he extended the privilege to other regions. In Rom 15:15, he apologizes to the community in Rome—a community he did not found—in case he had overstepped his regional, apostolic bounds with the boldness of his advice.

I argue in this book that Paul variously resembled other legendary travelers of Greco-Roman lore in a way that evoked notions of shame and death associated with wandering. Yet it is important to note initially that the physical distance between Paul and his worldwide communities entailed a communicative distance bridged only with difficulty. True, Paul worked with a close network of emissaries whom he dispersed in his stead with his letters and recommendations. But the related activities of travel and correspondence created a basic semantic gap between message and messenger. From a distance, the orality of proclamation is devoid of power. The discrepancy between the presence of proclamation and the absence of the Traveling Apostle stands as a specific instance of the larger, early Christian paradox that Christ's word comes to the world through the decidedly human and finite efforts of his messengers. To push this gap a little further: the dilemma of apostolic proclamation is a subtype of the distance between intended meaning and the semantic shifting of language.

Ancient epistolographic practices worked to close the distance between correspondents using linguistic formulae and conventions of letter delivery. As I discuss in more detail in Chapter 4, Paul availed himself of—and even adapted to his own purposes—the customary forms of writing and sending epistles. In his letters, Paul frequently and fondly recalls his initial visits to his communities as the events in which God's spirit entered their hearts and the relationship between church and apostle began. Future travel plans pervade the frames of his letters, as he promises to visit soon and commends the co-workers who deliver the letters as authorized representatives of himself and of Christ. Despite these provisions, the distance opened up by Paul's traveling lifestyle also created space for suspicion among his followers.

To be sure, Paul's own particular style of itinerancy offered even greater opportunity for his communities to doubt his authenticity. While other apostles accepted material support as their divine right, Paul avoided handouts whenever possible, preferring to earn his own keep. He had many reasons for insisting on working a trade. He took pride in not being a "burden" on his followers (1 Thess 2:9). He also seems to have believed that offering the gospel "free of charge" would increase his reward from God, even while acknowledging that material support is his right:

> The Lord ordered that those who proclaim the gospel should live out of the gospel. But I myself have not made use of these rights. I do not write these things so that I may get the same treatment [i.e., receive material support]. For I would much rather die than . . . let no one make my boast an empty one! For if I preach the gospel, it is no reason for me to boast, since I am under a compulsion to do so; woe is me if I do not preach the gospel! For if I do this willingly, I receive a wage; if unwillingly, I have been entrusted with a stewardship. So what is my wage? That, when preaching the gospel, I offer it free of charge so that I do not make full use of my authority in the gospel. (1 Cor 9:14–18)

As he often does with "the Lord's commands," Paul sees himself as going above and beyond existing understandings of the apostolic lifestyle. Instead of availing himself of the allowance God grants his servants, Paul abstains from support in the interest of winning more adherents and winning a greater "wage" or "reward" (*misthos*) from God. For Paul, gaining followers, increasing communities, and connecting them into a worldwide web of Gentile believers in Christ ultimately guarantees his reward.

Paul may have been particularly concerned, however, with rejecting support from the Corinthians. As discussed in the introduction, most of 1 Corinthians seems to target directly the "strong" faction and their reliance on their own socioeconomic status, knowledge, and authority. Some among the strong ran households, owned slaves, and presumably patronized clients in their business dealings. Scholars have long suspected Paul's fear that if he were to accept money from the strong in Corinth, he would fall into the role of intellectual client—a veritable "house philosopher"—beholden to the needs and whims of his patrons. At the outset of the letter, Paul emphasizes that, far from being on the dole of the strong, he is their intellectual "father" (1 Cor 4:15) who could visit them "with the rod or with love and a gentle spirit" (4:21). Refusing material support allowed Paul to maintain a role of independence and authority.[30]

Paul struggled to balance his assertions of leadership in Corinth with the importance of maintaining a devoted community in this most crucial city. Set on the isthmus joining the Greek mainland and the Peloponnese, Corinth and its two ports served as a major crossroads for the Roman Empire, a gateway between the western and eastern Mediterranean. Eschewing the antiquity and reputation of Athens, Paul made Corinth, with all its cultural diversity and commerce, his headquarters in Achaia (see 2 Cor 1:1). In 1 Corinthians, Paul attempts to maintain authority over the community without ostracizing the strong and their spiritual support. He strives for unity among the strong and weak by encouraging the strong not to rely on their perceived wisdom—not to despise those among the weak, for example, who do not practice celibacy (chapter 7) or who abstain from eating meat, fearing it may have been sacrificed to idols (chapters 8 and 10). He also rebukes a member of the community for his sexual relationship with his mother-in-law (1 Cor 5:1). In order to retain the power to instruct both strong and weak in Corinth, Paul rejects financial ties with the strong. Refusing their financial contributions must have been a necessary and calculated risk.

This is not to say that Paul never asked Corinth for money. For Paul, the primary sign of the unity among his communities and their devotion to the God of Israel was their financial contribution to the church in Jerusalem, a community headed by the disciples Peter and John, as well as James, the brother of Jesus. Paul's account of his first meeting with these leaders perhaps alludes to the collection, insofar as he claims they asked him to "remember the Poor" in his ministry (Gal 2:10). At the closing of 1 Corinthians—the same letter in which he explains his refusal of his apostolic right to personal financial support—Paul instructs the community to set aside weekly donations to Jerusalem. "When I arrive," he explains, "I will send with letters whomsoever you approve to bring your gracious gift to Jerusalem. And if it seems fitting for me to go, too, they will travel with me" (16:3–4). He then promises to make a lengthy visit with them after crossing through Macedonia, though he suggests that his co-worker Timothy, with whom they were well acquainted, may come first.[31]

Paul's plans for the collection and his future journeys may well have touched off the subsequent controversy between the apostle and his community in Corinth. It seems as if Paul did not adhere to the arrangements set forth in 1 Cor 16; either he did not come as soon as he had implied, or he sent Titus (heretofore unknown to the community) instead of Timothy, or he and Titus arrived not for a lengthy journey but asked to stay a short time with some accommodating host. Perhaps in response to his changing plans (and probably at the insinuation of his rival apostles), the Corinthians began to suspect Paul of fraud. After all, he ostensibly refused material support yet gathered money from all members of the community for a mysterious collection to the far-off province of Judea. What differentiated Paul from the stereotyped con man who wandered from town to town, peddling invented devotions to Dionysus,

Magna Mater, or any other foreign deity? More generally, Paul's lifestyle itself left him open to such suspicions. How could a poor, menial worker and vagabond seriously claim to be a messenger of the divine? Both sides frame the dispute as a question of Paul's sincerity, of the concordance between his words and deeds. In response to his accusers, Paul asserts his authenticity: "Let such people [who accuse me] understand that whatever we communicate through letters when we are absent, we will also do when present" (2 Cor 10:11). In general, the dispute figures the issue of Paul's sincerity as one of his presence and absence—an indication of the role his wandering apostleship played in fostering suspicions against him. Paul tended, in opposition, to assert his sufferings and wanderings as guaranteeing the truth of his message, the gospel of the crucified Christ. For some in Corinth the distance between travel and glory, weakness and power, death and life was difficult to overcome.[32]

Just as the Corinthians' misgivings toward a wandering messenger of the divine stemmed from cultural resonances associating travel with shame and death, so too could Paul draw on centuries of legendary figures deployed to explore the rough but fertile terrain opened up by discourses on travel. In the letter preserved in 2 Cor 1–9, Paul evokes notions of the traveling god, the wandering hero, the foreign social critic, the exile, and the dying sage as homeward-bound soul in a series of floating signifiers meant to take head-on the Corinthians' mistrust. At the same time, he distances himself from traditional travel roles in order to fashion a new vision of the leadership position "apostle"—and, in turn, to fashion both the local and worldwide Christ-believing community in his apostolic image. To borrow from Laclau, the attachments Paul makes to wanderers of the past are merely "transient," severed almost as soon as they are made, a rhetorical strategy that accounts for the quick pace of imagery that makes 2 Cor 1–9 so unique among the Pauline letters. It is this pace that allows Paul to rearrange common expectations about travel and leadership in ways that more clearly draw the contours of apostleship. Paul defines his new social role in reference to personae of the past, but he also differentiates or disidentifies with those same positions in order to set forth the superiority of his persona.

In what follows, I trace the travel motifs that wander in and out of 2 Cor 1–9 in order to discern how Paul constructs a new leadership role. One should always be careful to posit in too much detail the mind of the author behind a text. But I suspect that 2 Cor 1–9 is the product of Paul's realization that his itinerant lifestyle was a particularly volatile aspect of his mission, one he needed to exploit properly in order to repair his relationship with Corinth and continue building a worldwide community of Gentile Christ-believers.

2

Travel, Suicide, and Self-Construction

Generations of interpreters have viewed 2 Corinthians as the most emotional and self-revealing of Paul's letters. Among early readers, its beginning was a go-to passage for examples of how Paul's rhetoric could pull on the heartstrings of his audience. And yet, the letter's unexplained allusions and vague imagery confound modern readers, impeding exegetical pursuits of Paul's meaning. Assessments among scholars have described the letter as both intimate and opaque. Adolf Deissmann's description is succinctly representative, calling 2 Corinthians "the most personal of the 'greater' Pauline epistles . . . It is as a whole the least well known to us, just because it is so entirely letter-like, so entirely a personal confession, full of allusions which we cannot now fully understand. Paul begins deep in emotion; for God has once again graciously saved him out of a terrible risk of death . . . Paul lays bare his inner and outer life for his Christian brethren to see."[1] For Deissmann, Paul "lays bare" his life in 2 Corinthians—though, paradoxically, his self-disclosure results in a letter that is "the least well known to us." The apostle of 2 Corinthians is at once revealed and hidden.

The letter's language evokes a strong emotional response designed to bridge the gap that had opened between Paul and his followers in Corinth. Following the epistolary opening and address, Paul launches an effusive and markedly repetitive blessing (1:3–7) expressing God's "comfort" (*paraklēsis*, occurring

47

five times in the five verses) in the midst of "affliction" (*thlipsis,* occurring four times) and "sufferings" (*pathēmata,* three times). Interpreters usually explain the passage as an attempt to ground his disclosure (in 1:8–11) of an instance of affliction. The disclosure itself, however, communicates little about the nature of Paul's recent troubles. Second Corinthians 1:8–11 begins with a formulaic epistolary expression often called a "disclosure formula" by scholars ("we do not want you to be ignorant"), supplying information as a basis for the letter contents to follow: "We do not want you to be ignorant, brothers, of our affliction that occurred in Asia—that we were exceedingly burdened beyond our capacity, so that we despaired even of living. Rather, we ourselves had a death sentence among ourselves, so that we had no confidence in ourselves but, rather, in the God who raises the dead" (1:8–9). Although 1:8–11 certainly expresses the severity of some particular instance of Paul's suffering, the strange and vague wording of the disclosure leaves readers to guess at the nature of the incident behind the statement. Many early Christians, appealing to the Acts of the Apostles as a reliable historical source, suggested that Paul refers to a riot in Ephesus and its aftermath (Acts 19:23–20:1). Modern commentators, rejecting Acts as a source for clarifying the reference, posit alternate theories, though usually admitting the speculative nature of their reconstructions. Paul's nondisclosing disclosure forces the reader to resort to educated guesswork.

Interpretation of the events lying behind the beginning of the letter is complicated further by the ostensibly diverse number of issues with which Paul deals in the first chapter and a half. Modern commentators have had difficulty explaining the transitions from one topic to another, rendering the section a hodge-podge of contingent situations to which Paul responds using a handful of theological premises. For example, at 1:15–2:4, after his vague disclosure, he begins to explain why he reneged on an earlier plan to visit—a change of plans that called into question the apostle's trustworthiness and sincerity. Then, in 2:5–11, Paul interrupts the explanation of his travels to advise the Corinthians to relax their punishment against a member of their community who had somehow distressed Paul. Finally, at 2:12–13, he again returns to his "travelogue," only to launch into a figurative description of his apostleship as a triumphal procession led by God at 2:14–17, creating in the minds of some contemporary readers a clear redactional seam, leading them to set aside 2:14–7:5 as a separate letter fragment. Since the topics of Paul's discourse change so rapidly, it becomes difficult to discern a propositional unity.

Throughout history, however, other readers have sought not propositional, but rhetorical coherence at the letter's outset. John Chrysostom (specially attuned to issues of Paul's rhetoric and self-presentation) provides a particularly illustrative example in his first *Homily on 2 Corinthians*. For Chrysostom, Paul's main reason for writing 2 Corinthians was to explain his failure to visit as promised—raising the issue, however, of why Paul begins the letter proper in 1:3 by blessing "the God of comfort" for rescuing him from affliction. What does Paul's curious blessing have to do with the travel plans that follow? Chrysostom writes:

> Observe: it very much grieved and troubled them [the Corinthians] that the apostle had not arrived there, since, even though he had promised, he spent the whole time in Macedonia and seemed to have chosen others over themselves. Because of this, situating himself against this feeling, he explains why he has not arrived. But he does not set the cause before them directly; he does not say, "Yes, I know I promised to come, but since I was impeded by afflictions, forgive me, and do not condemn me for any sort of disdain or indifference towards you." Rather, in another way, he arranges his language with more nobility and trustworthiness, elevating the matter with consolation, so that afterward they would not ask why he was late. He does this as if a person who promised to come to someone he longed for, then, coming after myriad dangers, would say, "Glory to you, God, that you showed me the face for which I have longed! Blessed be God, that you rescued me from such dangers!" For this doxology becomes a defense to anyone intending to make accusations and will not allow him to complain about the delay. For it would make such a person blush with shame to drag before the jury someone thanking God for a rescue from evils, and demand an explanation for his lateness. (*Hom. 2 Cor.* 1 p. 385, 21–43)

Here, Chrysostom focuses not just on the topics Paul discusses, but on the overall strategy their concurrence could indicate. Paul manipulates the emotions of his audience from the outset in order to prepare the way for his defense of his failure to visit.[2]

My analysis in this chapter follows the general trajectory of Chrysostom's reading: far from being a tangle of loosely related issues, the beginning of 2 Cor 1–9 comprises a delicate rhetorical strategy framed as an explanation of failed travel plans, a common epistolary topic in the Greco-Roman world. Paul adapts generic conventions of the travel apology, however, in order to refashion his self-presentation as apostle and rehabilitate his relationship with his Corinthian community. Specifically, Paul juxtaposes travel and death (particularly death by suicide) as complementary discourses of self-revelation. Both discourses portend to reveal the writer's persona by removing it from the normal domain of civic life and logic. This is not to say that Paul's main point is to defend the fact that he has not yet visited. Rather, he chooses to address the issue in order to repair his relationship with the community by manipulating both emotions and status relationships. And as part of a larger strategy in the letter, Paul lays a foundation for variously depicting his self-sacrificing apostleship through a series of travel motifs.

Thus, I identify the epistolary situation of the letter represented in 2 Cor 1–9 by focusing on Paul's innovative use of a common epistolary topic—travel plans. By modifying letter formulae to suit his purposes, Paul establishes an explanation of his failure to visit as promised as a starting point for a figurative depiction of his apostleship through travel motifs. Through a consideration of his generic innovations to epistolary forms in light of both literary and papyrus letters, I examine the emotional and social effects of Paul's rhetoric. Namely, Paul attempts to counter the possible perception that his failure to visit represents weakness and vacillation by asserting instead that his travels indicate his role as a leader guided by God. In order to reveal his inner disposition and sincerity, he implies that he once contemplated making the ultimate journey back to God through suicide (drawing upon the cultural cache of self-killing among first-century upper-class Romans), though he finally proves his tireless devotion by committing himself to continue on his earthly journeys. Moreover, Paul claims that he engages in these troublesome travels for the spiritual benefit of the Corinthians, thus creating a sense of emotional and social debt on the part of the audience.

The Revelatory Rhetoric of Travel Plans: Conventions and Violations

In framing his letter as an explanation for his failure to visit, Paul follows a common ancient epistolographic practice of communicating or clarifying travel plans. Ancient understandings of letters—as well as cultural conventions of letter delivery—emphasized travel plans as an important topos, insofar as the practices surrounding correspondence strove to make letters adequate replacements for the presence of their authors. Works of epistolary theory and evidence from actual letters support this observation. Demetrius, in his work *De elocutione* (written sometime around the turn of the Common Era), claims that "everybody reveals his soul in his letters. In every other form of composition it is possible to discern the writer's character, but none so clearly as in the epistolary" (227). Cicero, in many of his own letters, speaks of letter-writing as a nearly adequate replacement for being present with the correspondent. "Though I have nothing to say to you," he writes Atticus, "I write all the same, because I feel as though I were talking to you" (*Att.* 12.53). The view of letters as providing the *parousia*, the presence or arrival, of the author also emerges in the quotidian, personal correspondence among papyri preserved in the deserts of Egypt. In one example, a letter writer implores his friend to continue writing him because, when he received his prior letter, "I rejoiced very, very much, as if you were present" (*P.Mich.* 8.482).[3]

When a writer could not visit as planned, he might employ standard ways of explaining and apologizing. In most cases, one did not simply inform the addressee(s) of the impossibility of a visit but framed this information as a disclosure of an intention, hope, or desire to visit. Consider a letter of the mid-first century B.C.E. from an author whose name has been effaced by time from the papyrus: "E[. . .] to my brother Apion, greetings and, above all, be healthy. I wanted [*eboulomēn*] to have indicated the state of your household in person. For just as I left to make it tidier, I was prevented by the porter" (*BGU* 8.1881). In another example, a certain Horion informs Heron of his intention to send his son in his place: "Horion to Heron, most beloved, greetings. Since my son, Dionysios, who is with me, wrote you, I intended [*mellontos*] to come to you, but was not able to because of my so-so health. So I have sent you his brother, Didymos, to carry out my affairs immediately, as if I were there with you" (*P.Lips.* 108).[4]

The expression of one's intentions and emotions with regard to travel plans is commensurate with the closeness (or desired closeness) of relationship between sender and addressee. In business letters, writers tend to be terser in their travel plans, often omitting mention of intention or desire. In familiar letters, however, language of internal disposition becomes more explicit and often repetitive. So, in a letter from Saturnilus to his mother, Aphrodous, the devoted son repeats his desire to visit three times:

> Satornilus to Aphrodous, his mother, very many greetings. Before all things I pray for your health and prosperity. I wish you to know that [*ginōskein se thelō hoti*] I sent you three letters this month. I have received in full the monthly allowances which you sent to me by Iulius and a basket of olives by the lad of Iulius. I wish you to know that [*ginōskein se thelō hoti*][5] another male child has been born to me, whose name is Agathos Daimon. The gods willing, if I find an opportunity of putting my plan into effect I am coming to you with letters. I wish you to know that [*ginōskein se thelō hoti*] it is now three months since I came to Pselkis, and I have not yet found an opportunity to come to you. I was afraid to come just now because they say: that the prefect is on the road, lest he take the letters from me and send me back to the troops, and I incur the expense in vain. But I wish you to know that if another two months pass and I do not come to you before the month Hathyr I have eighteen more months of sitting in garrison until I enter Pselkis again and come to you. All those who come will bear witness to you how I seek daily to come. If you wish to see me a little, I wish it greatly and pray daily

to the gods that they may quickly give me a good chance to come. Everything in the army runs with the favorable chance. If I have the opportunity I am coming to you. (*P.Mich.* 3.203)[6]

Saturnilus tells his mother five times that he is trying to visit her. His repeated assurances serve the epistolary interest of revealing his inner disposition. In fact, near the end, he attempts to correlate his own emotions with his mother's: "If you wish to see me a little, I wish it greatly." Saturnilus not only constructs his role in this one-sided conversation, but attempts to form his mother's desires as well. This highlights another function of the epistolary expression of internal dispositions: by revealing emotions and setting up one side of the dialogue, the author hopes to evoke a reciprocal response and thus mold the inner disposition of the addressee.

Examining travel plans among the papyrus letters helps us see how the trope functions as a rhetoric of self-revelation and authorial presence. A clearer picture of the contours of the practice, however, comes to light through a *violation* of that rhetoric in what we may justifiably call a para-epistolary corpus, Horace's verse *Epistles*—not "epistles" per se, but rather poems relying on letter-writing topics and conventions as a frame for popularized philosophical meditations. Horace's (sometimes extreme) adaptation of epistolary conventions highlights subtle tendencies within the epistolary form and helps us trace the boundaries of the genre. In fact, I find Horace's intentional departure from common epistolary formulae an ideal entrance for examining the rhetorical and social logics of the epistolary travel apology, and for this reason I consider at length recent interpretations of one of his *Epistles*. Just as excluded social positions reflect in negative the universality of the whole, so do explicit genre violations reveal the inner rhetorical workings of literary forms. After examining the mechanics of Horace's epistolary innovations, I draw analogies to Paul's manipulation of epistolary travel apologies at the outset of 2 Cor 1–9.

Many of Horace's verse epistles seem to take generic inspiration from the philosophical epistles of Plato, Aristotle, Epicurus, and the Cynic movement, missives filled with moral maxims and exhortations to the virtuous life. Yet among these lofty ideals, we find an invitation to dinner (*Ep.* 1.5), letters of recommendation or introduction (1.9, 1.12), and humorous instructions to a courier (1.14)—all, in part, aesthetic exercises as poetic musings, taking their impetus from the everyday concerns of the common familiar letter. The variety of topics and techniques (perhaps intentionally) creates tensions among varying ideas and apparent intentions encoded in the poems. Nowhere is such tension more apparent than in *Ep.* 1.7, as Horace uses his refusal to visit Maecenas as an opportunity to dwell upon the nature of social and philosophical freedom within Roman intellectual patronage practices.

Epistle 1.7 begins with a statement of a promise upon which Horace has gone back. Most scholars have read this "refusal" as a generic adaptation of the poetic *recusatio*, a standard type in which the poet rhetorically declines to compose a poem for which the patron has asked under the guise of false modesty: the writer claims to be inadequate to the task of glorifying so great a figure in paltry verse, thus obliquely increasing the praise rendered in the work. In light of the discussion of epistolary travel plans above, it seems just as likely that Horace is also riffing on the epistolary convention so common to familiar letters, as exemplified in the papyri. So, the poem begins with an explicit mention of the prior intention to visit: "Although I promised [*pollicitus*] you I would be in the countryside five days, I, a liar [*mendax*], have been missing the entire sixth month. But if you would have me live sound and healthy, the favor you grant me when I am sick you will grant me when I fear I will be sick" (1.7.1–5). The initial participial phrase surrounding a verb of intention or promise (*pollicitus*) reads like a common epistolary acknowledgment of a prior intention to visit. The poet gives his patron a plausible excuse for his delay: he fears the urban environment of Rome will make him sick and wants to summer in the country and winter at the seashore. He promises to return to Rome in the spring (lines 5–13). Immediately following this explanation, however, Horace launches a curious and obscure set of tirades against what he portrays as Maecenas's unreasonable demands. Most of these tirades take the form of fables, which make the poem not just an odd complaint against the gifts of his patron, but also a circumlocutionary musing on the nature of social obligations among Augustan intellectual circles.[7]

In lines 24–28, Horace prefaces his first fable with an explicit complaint against the obligations that seem (at least in Horace's eyes) to accompany his patron's beneficence. He claims that if Maecenas expects him to be at his side at all times, he must somehow restore the poet's youth and health in return (lines 25–28). Horace illustrates his wish in the following fable: a female fox enters a bin of grain through a thin crack, gorges herself, and naturally finds herself trapped by her new corpulence. A passer-by weasel offers some advice: slim down to the size of the entrance. The moral Horace provides is emphatic: "If I am arraigned by this picture, I give back everything" (34). A few lines later, after the poet recalls his oft-praised "modesty," he again claims he could happily renounce the favors he's been granted: "See if I can happily return these gifts" (*inspice, si possum donata reponere laetus;* 39).[8]

The final fable takes up the second half of the poem. A lawyer named Philippus sees an auctioneer, Menas, loitering in downtown Rome. Philippus sends his slave to ask who Menas is and what he does. Learning that Menas is a humble but content man, Philippus invites him to dinner, assumedly making overtures to hire the man as a sort of client. Menas initially refuses, but Philippus tracks him down the next day, and the auctioneer accepts. Soon, Menas is working for Philippus and has entered the patronage system of upper-class Roman society. One day, on a trip to the countryside, Menas marvels at the Sabine climate; in response, Philippus provides Menas with money and encouragement to buy a Sabine farm of his own—the paradigmatic gift of the *Epistles* (see below). It does not take long, however, for Menas to realize that he is unsuited to country life, and he begs Philippus to restore him to his former lifestyle. The poem ends here with an overall moral: "The one who recognizes, at last, how much affairs that were abandoned are better than those sought, let him return in time and seek again what was left behind. Each person should measure themselves by their own standard" (*Ep.* 1.7.96–98).⁹

Epistle 1.7 is confusing for a variety of reasons. For years, scholars attempted to read the poem autobiographically and questioned the extent to which it reflected a rift between poet and patron. Recent treatments have approached Horace's tirades through the complementary lenses of rhetorical and social theories. Likewise, in a book that more explicitly treats the Roman patronage system as a social context for understanding Horace's writings, Phebe Lowell Bowditch analyzes the *Epistles* written to Maecenas "as poems that aesthetically refashion the patronal relationship into one of a more egalitarian friendship." In the process of her analysis, Bowditch lays out a rigorous theoretical description of patron-client societies construed as "gift economies." Her approach heavily draws on Pierre Bourdieu's description of "gift economies," particularly the mechanism of encoded "misrecognition" embedded within ideologies of giving, obligation, and reciprocity. Simply stated, in societies where benefaction is valued, parties are always engaged in spontaneous and culturally instilled calculations of debt and repayment. Simultaneously, the explicit ideology expressed (and even thought) by these parties conceals calculations by emphasizing generosity and deemphasizing expectations of return. Misrecognition allows social structures that preserve order and support hierarchies to continue, insofar as the ideology overlaying these structures conceals expectations of obligation and reciprocity and induces people to participate in predetermined social relations. The theory helps describe social actions in a surprising number of societies across space and history: anyone who has received a gift at a birthday party or wedding shower and said "You shouldn't have" to the giver has played this game.¹⁰

The phenomenon of misrecognition in gift giving was central to Roman society. As recent scholarship on Roman patronage has indicated, language of "patron" and "client" was rare—because avoided—in ancient texts, replaced with the beneficent and obscuring "friend" (*amicus*). Ancient analyses of misrecognition are evident especially in what may profitably be viewed as ancient works on social theory, such as Cicero's *De officiis* ("On Duties") and Seneca's *De beneficiis* ("On Benefits"). Seneca explains that, though calculation of beneficence and debt is inevitable, the ideology of giving is ensured by the socially inculcated dispositions of the individual: "In benefits the bookkeeping is simple—so much is paid out; if anything comes back, it is gain, if nothing comes back, there is no loss. I made the gift for the sake of giving." On the other hand, the recipient of a benefaction should always strive "to surpass in deed and spirit those who have placed us under obligation, for he who has a debt of gratitude to pay never catches up with the favor unless he outstrips it" (*Ben.* 1.2.3). Since the ideology of beneficence obscures reckoning of debts outstanding and made good, the recipient of a gift experiences constant uncertainty as to his obligations toward the giver at any given time. Obligation persists in the recipient as an emotive remainder, a socially conditioned response to the expectation of expressed or enacted gratitude and the simultaneous ideological effacement of reciprocal reckoning.[11]

For Bowditch, *Ep.* 1.7 is a meditation on patronage, obligation, and misrecognition. In the poem, Horace seems to chafe at the persistent sense of obligation clinging to his patronage relationship with Maecenas. He considers the possibility of sacrificing benefactions in order to regain freedom from debt. In the *Epistles*, "Horace both threatens to rend the veil completely, revealing—even exaggerating—patronage in all its naked economic interestedness, and at the same time 'repairs' the fissure, the gap between ideology and objective structure, by aligning it with different levels of audience."[12]

Why does Horace choose the epistolary topos of travel plans as a frame for his investigation and manipulation of his patron-client relationship with Maecenas? What sort of ideological cache does travel provide the poet? Bowditch, building on the work of Stanley Stowers, notes that the epistolary form Horace adapts in the *Epistles* conveys for the reader a sense that the author is revealing his true self. In *Ep.* 1.7, however, Horace may deploy the notion of travel in order to explore the difference between real and presented self at the heart of epistolary production, or more generally, the disconnect, inherent in all language, between an author's intention and his composition. In most epistolary explanations of failed travel plans, the writer emphasizes that despite his best intentions, he was prevented from visiting by external circumstances. Unexpectedly, Horace simply states that despite his promise (*pollicitus*), he is a liar (*mendax*). Thus, his intentions are not concurrent with his language.[13]

One additional factor in the use of travel in *Ep.* 1.7 is the locales involved in this specific instance of proposed travel: Rome and the countryside—in particular, the "Sabine farm" to which Horace retreated, itself a gift from his patron. Philosophical discussions of travel and location frequent the *Epistles: Ep.* 1.11, in which Horace lectures his friend on his constant travel, teaching him that location is an external, irrelevant for the inward cultivation of virtue, is a prime example of the topic. Standing in tension with the philosophical rejection of the importance of place is another recurring theme: the Epicurean ideal of philosophical retreat from worldly affairs, figured in Horace's farm. The importance of place creates special tension in *Ep.* 1.7; for if the Sabine farm exemplifies the power of benefactions to bind through obligation, Horace introduces profound implications for patronage and status by threatening to return it. By making Horace a rural landowner, Maecenas had conferred upper-class status upon his client, the very social position that grounds the Epicurean-style intellectual authority upon which the *Epistles* are based. As Bowditch further points out, the tension is more than just literary or aesthetic: the leisured philosopher of Horace's self-presentation in the *Epistles* cannot give back the gift upon which his identity is grounded any more than an aging man can go back in time to his youth. Although Horace rhetorically threatens to sever patronage ties with Maecenas, he is more likely creating the discursive space to shift social positions, moving from the role of crafter of lyric at the service of Augustan ideology to philosopher-poet beneficently granting wisdom to his public audience.[14]

Approaching *Ep.* 1.7 through social theories of benefaction helps explain Horace's puzzling rhetoric in it, especially his violation of epistolary conventions regarding travel plans. When the poet transforms the travel apology, a trope of self-revelation and sincerity, into one of mendacity, he toys with expectations of relationships and obligations. Far from expressing a desire to be near his patron, he rhetorically pushes away to create distance both geographic and social. By turning the travel topos on its head, Horace reveals how rhetoric of self-disclosure such as epistolary travel plans simultaneously serves interests of self-fashioning and social manipulation.

Studying the ways in which Horace manipulates the epistolary travel apology in order to pull the strings of the Roman patronage machine helps illuminate the ways in which Paul's generic innovations at the outset of 2 Cor 1–9 help him manage his relationship with his Corinthian community. I understand Paul's focus on travel plans, as in *Ep.* 1.7, in relation to the ambiguous issues of status obtaining in this relationship. Of course, there are obvious differences between Horace and Paul on these accounts. Aside from their radically different social circles, backgrounds, and vocations, the rhetorical strategies also differ in each case. Whereas Horace attempts to move from one social location (lyric poet devoted to bolstering imperial ideology) to another (leisured philosopher granting wisdom), Paul fashions a novel vision of a new social role by manipulating and reacting to the status implications of his actions as perceived by the community. In Bourdieu's terms, Paul is attempting to "regularize his situation" with regard to Greco-Roman ideological expectations, "win[ning] the group over to his side by ostentatiously honouring the values the group honours."[15] Paul cannot simply tell the Corinthians to erase all their expectations of an itinerant, foreign moralist and servant of the divine. Rather, he must rhetorically mold their culturally encoded reactions to his apostleship in order to create in them a picture of what "apostleship" is. By using travel as a floating signifier, and by expanding and displacing conventional understandings of leadership and authenticity, he creates a discursive space in which to delineate his social role by selecting and shaping cultural common sense associated with travel. All of Paul's successes and failures in dealing with the Corinthians can be explained as successes and failures in the endeavor to manipulate social expectations.

As I discussed in the introduction, many of the problems Paul experienced with the Corinthians can be explained as a discrepancy between his refusal of material support and his request for money for the Jerusalem collection. Paul's perceived mendacity was reinforced by the recurring observation that his physical presence did not seem to match the strength of his letters (see 1 Cor 4:18–19, and especially 2 Cor 10:10–11). While some of the answers Paul gives to these problems occur earlier in the Corinthian correspondence (especially the oft-observed "power in weakness" theme, appearing at least as early as 1 Cor 1:22–2:5), Paul in 2 Cor 1–9 once again tries to redefine the status implications of apostleship by building upon the epistolary topic of travel plans. Some of the ways travel plans address the controversies in Corinth may already be apparent. First, the practical vicissitudes of travel necessitate a certain amount of support and hospitality from those to whom Paul preaches. The discussion of travel could thus function as a reminder of the real financial needs of apostleship.

Paul's travel apology also serves to assuage suspicions about his inner disposition. As discussed above, travel apologies among friends and family expressed the writer's sincerity of intention. Similarly, in 2 Cor 1:15, Paul explicitly expresses his wish to visit with a standard formulation: "I wanted [*eboulomēn*] to come to you first." Paul assures his community of his continued interest in them and his relationship with them. Since travel plans make more explicit the attempt to bridge the gap between physical and epistolary presence, the topic provides Paul with an opportunity to express his desire and concern for the community despite the recent rift in their relationship.

Moreover, insofar as the apparent discrepancy between Paul's epistolary tone and physical presence was a point of contention, travel plans were an ideal starting point for his engagement with doubts concerning his sincerity, the concurrence of his words, deeds, and intentions. Paul's assertions on this front come to the fore in 1:12, when he puts forth "the testimony of his conscience"; 1:13, when he assures the Corinthians that he "writes nothing except what you read and recognize"; and especially 1:17, where he explicitly addresses the possible charge that he was "vacillating" with respect to his travel plans. Paul addresses the charge in conventional epistolary style, using the language of his intentions to visit: "So, in wanting [*boulomenos*], surely I wasn't vacillating, was I? Or, the things I plan [*bouleuomai*], do I plan [*bouleuomai*] them according to the flesh, so that, with me, it's 'Yes yes,' and 'No no'?" (1:17). As in the familiar letters surveyed above, Paul explicitly focuses on revealing his inner disposition through a travel apology. Indeed, Paul exaggerates the topos by his repeated use (in vv. 15 and 17) of the verb *boulesthai*, to "want" or "intend" to do something, and the related *bouleuein*, to "consider" or "plan." In contradistinction to Horace, Paul reinforces conventions of travel apology in order to secure his relationship with his community. His manipulation of his social role will come not through violation of travel-plan conventions, but through a reinforced application of the trope, combined, as I discuss below, with its juxtaposition with another discourse of self-revelation: a self-depiction as impassively facing and rationalizing his own death.

Self-Killing and the Construction of Personae

As I discussed at the beginning of the chapter, the first hint of the epistolary situation of 2 Cor 1–9 (in the sense of the external circumstances prompting Paul's writing) occurs in 1:8–11, introduced by a "disclosure formula." As readers such as John Chrysostom early discerned, Paul's reference to an ambiguous "affliction" at least partially serves to anticipate his travel apology. Other features of his "disclosure," however, have puzzled commentators. First and foremost among these difficulties is the paradox that this disclosure formula actually discloses very little: Paul mentions an unspecified affliction experienced somewhere in the Roman province of Asia, and that this affliction was so intense that it caused him to "despair [*exaporēthēnai*] of living." More metaphorically, Paul claims that "we ourselves had the sentence of death among ourselves," an expression which has yet to be deciphered by exegetes. In this case, "disclosure formula" seems a misnomer. Nevertheless, the passage corresponds to the wordings and placements of so-called disclosure formulae in non-Pauline ancient letters, especially those found among the papyri. John Lee White has found that such formulae predominate in transitions between letter openings (address) and bodies of letters, as well as between the body and letter closing.[16] Second Corinthians 1:8 occupies just such a transition at the beginning of the letter.

The vague statement is especially curious in light of other occurrences of the same disclosure formula throughout the undisputed Pauline corpus, where, in every case, Paul is far more specific about the information disclosed. He uses the formula "I do not want you to be ignorant" in many different contexts, not just at transitions between epistolary greetings and body openings. On occasion, it seems as if Paul uses it to denote particularly significant information, both logistical and theological. So, in 1 Thess 4:13, Paul introduces a clarification of the main issue troubling the Thessalonian community: What would happen to those who had died before Christ's return? So also in a climactic section of Romans (11:25), Paul introduces the "mystery" of Israel's redemption with the same formula. The phrasing was not unknown to the Corinthians either, who had heard it from Paul at least twice—in 1 Cor 10:1 (introducing the apostasy of the exodus generation as a cautionary tale) and 1 Cor 12:1 (commencing a lengthy discussion of spiritual gifts).

For our purposes, the most significant Pauline use of the formula is in Rom 1:13, where Paul explains that he has been unable to visit Rome despite his best intentions. Following a thanksgiving period, the disclosure leads directly into the thematic statement of 1:16–17:

> I do not want you to be unaware, brothers, that I have often planned to come to you (but have thus far been prevented from coming) so that I might have some harvest even from among you, just as from among the rest of the Gentiles. To both Greeks and Jews, the wise and the ignorant, I am a debtor; thus my desire to preach the gospel even among those of you in Rome. For I am not ashamed of the gospel: for it is the power of God for salvation for everyone who is faithful—Jew first and also Greek. For the righteousness of God is revealed in it for faithfulness from faithfulness, just as it is written: "The righteous one will live from faithfulness." (Rom 1:13–17, quoting Hab 2:4)

Here, Paul reveals no concrete impediments to his intended journeys west; he simply asserts his frequent "plans" to visit. In comparison, he is similarly reticent in 2 Cor 1:8–11 to communicate specific obstacles to his itinerary.

As discussed above, generations of readers have speculated about the event lying behind Paul's "affliction in Asia," with most assuming some form of external suffering—arrest, beatings, encounters with beasts, an illness contracted on the road. Many interpreters, both ancient and modern, explain the passage's ambiguity by asserting that, for Paul, his emotional reaction to the affliction was far more significant than the event itself. To depict his reaction, Paul chooses an intense yet ambiguous verb, *exaporēnai*, denoting either confusion, lack of resources, or despair. More figuratively, he states that he felt like he had received some sort of internal "sentence of death" (*apokrima tou thanatou*). Paul chooses to disclose his inner disposition rather than an event.

Against the vast majority of readers, I contend that Paul's affliction was a purely internal bout of turmoil, not an external incident—that Paul's focus on his emotional and cognitive state in his disclosure stems from the nature of the affliction itself. I see at least two factors as contributing to this reading. First, as New Testament scholar David Fredrickson has recently and compellingly argued, a long tradition of Greek philosophical literature employed the trope of self-condemnation as an expression of internal regret. The metaphor served as an apt depiction of philosophical notions of regret as resulting from a conscience being divided against a person's will, making accusations of wrongdoing. So, in his *Eudemian Ethics*, Aristotle shows the folly of regret, through which a person "puts himself to death" (7.14.6–15.1). Later, the Christian writer Clement of Alexandria, well acquainted with philosophic discourse, described true repentance as "utterly to root out of the soul the sins for which a man has condemned himself to death" (*Quis. div.* 39). The image of self-condemnation that Paul deploys had long been used to express inner affliction. In 2 Cor 1:9, it expresses personal regret over the recent trouble between himself and Corinth.[17]

A second factor in reading Paul's turmoil as internal involves identifying a specific social and discursive context for Paul's revelation of regret, despair, and self-condemnation. Most interpreters see Paul as easily overcoming his emotional reactions by an appeal to God: "We had no confidence in ourselves but rather in the God who raises the dead, who saved us from such a death and will continue to save us" (1:9b–10a). What are we to make of this complex of despair (and the sense of the verb *exaporēnai*), a self-imposed death sentence, and hope in a God described as one who "raises the dead"?

We may find help pinning down the contextual meaning of the verb *exaporēnai* by examining how some early Christian translators rendered it into other languages. What did the letter's first readers make of Paul's state of mind? Early Latin versions in particular cast some light on the problem: almost all early Latin translations of 1:8 and the vague Greek statement *exaporēnai hēmas kai tou zēn,* "we even despaired of living," render *taedoret nos etiam vivere*—the verb *taedere* being a form of the word *taedium,* denoting not just "despair" but "weariness," yielding, "we tired even of living." The phrasing gives us a glimpse of how many readers understood Paul's language and opens for us a new avenue for interpretation. *Taederet vivere,* converted to its nominal form, *taedium vitae,* "weariness of life," was a stock Latin phrase for a general motivation for suicide. We find the formulation in Cicero's correspondence, Seneca's *Moral Epistles,* Pliny's *Natural History,* epitaphs on tombstones, and later Roman legal codes. In the minds of some ancient readers, then, Paul was experiencing *taedium vitae;* he was "sick of living," so he may well have considered his appropriate responses.[18]

Some may balk at the notion of St. Paul contemplating suicide, an act defined by centuries of Western ethics (conditioned by Christian teaching) as sin. The interpretation is not as outlandish as it may initially seem, however. Scholars have highlighted that credit for the stigmatization of self-killing should be attributed to Augustine. Before this period, discourse on self-killing differed significantly from that in the post-Augustinian West. Neither Greek nor Latin knew a single term equivalent to "suicide," an early-modern neologism that most ancient speakers of Latin would have construed as meaning "pig murder," not "self-killing." Contrary to what came to be regarded as a normative prohibition of suicide, ancient intellectuals engaged in a vigorous debate over the situational ethics of a voluntary departure from life, with the Stoic philosophical school advocating suicide as an ultimate expression of the individual's free will. The debate influenced political thought on status and nobility in Rome at least as early as the late Republic, when Cato the Younger, modeling himself after Socrates, famously killed himself rather than submit to Julius Caesar's rule. By the mid-first century C.E., imperial officials increasingly turned to self-killing when falling into the emperor's disfavor, establishing an era that classicist Arthur Darby Nock famously termed "the Stoic cult of suicide." In an ostensible paradox to modern sensibilities, first-century self-killing could be seen as a method of self-preservation. Or, to put in terms common both to ancient and to more recent discussions, the way an upper-class man faced death—including the choice to kill himself—revealed the true nature of his character.[19]

The question of whether or not Paul contemplates killing himself is not a new one and has, in fact, received much treatment in recent years. Most discussions of Paul and Roman discourse on suicide focus on Phil 1:19–26 (in which an imprisoned Paul states that, when faced with life and death, "he does not know what he will choose" [v. 22]) and a similar passage at 2 Cor 5:6–10 (where he states that "we prefer to be journeying away from the body and be at home with the Lord" in v. 8; see the discussion in Chapter 5). Interpreters debate the finer points of Paul's word choice and syntax in hopes of revealing the sense of his statements with regard to his own death. But dissecting Paul's language misconstrues the broader social and rhetorical context of discourses on self-killing. Ancient readers would not have assumed a modern, "perish-the-thought" attitude toward the notion of Paul contemplating a self-inflicted end. The Latin versions of 2 Cor 1:8 cited above only force us to confront the ancient social reality that, for a person facing "despair" or "weariness" of living, suicide was an open issue. As I will show, understanding 2 Cor 1:8–11 as Paul performing the contemplation of suicide brings more rhetorical cohesion to the immediate context of the letter. By juxtaposing the language of epistolary travel plans with that of self-killing, Paul joins two tropes of self-revelation, laying a foundation for the succeeding exposition of apostleship. In the broader context of the letter, linking travel with suicide at 1:8–11 prepares the way for their explicit union at 5:1–10 (as mentioned above, a more traditional locus for debates about Paul and self-killing), where Paul considers "journeying home to God."

If Paul contemplates suicide in 1:8–11—even as a rhetorical device—what would be his ostensible motivation? Modern thought on suicide has been more occupied with its psychological impetus than were ancient writers, who saw internal factors in self-killing to be diverse and often multiple. A complex of grief and regret could be the impetus behind Paul's consideration of suicide; in 2 Cor 2 and later in 2 Cor 7, Paul seems distraught at the pain he may have caused the Corinthians in his dispute with them. Alternatively, he could be considering the same recourse as numerous Roman leaders of his day— avoiding the shame of failure or even escaping the punishment awaiting those who broke the law or displeased the emperor. Avoidance of an impending trial frequently emerges in Roman literature as a motive for suicide. The Roman legal corpus bears witness to the accreted statutes surrounding the practice. For imperial jurists, the salient issue was whether suicide in anticipation of a trial was an admission of guilt, citing (as discussed above) *taedium vitae* as a catch-all category for the motivation for this type of self-killing. Paul's use of the phrase "we were even sick of living" in 1:8, rendered *taederet nos etiam vivere* by Latin readers, may point to his raising this possibility.

But why would Paul raise the rhetorical possibility of suicide to avoid a trial? By trial, does he suggest final judgment at the eschaton? The Corinthians might have heard this possibility in Paul's death wish, especially in light of statements he made earlier in the Corinthian correspondence. For example, in 1 Cor 3:10–15, Paul figuratively compares his apostolic community-building to the laying of a building's foundation: "The work of each builder will be made visible; the Day will make it clear, because it will be revealed in fire. And fire will test what sort of work each has done. If the work which someone has built up remains, he will receive his reward. But if someone's work is burned up, he will be punished (though he will be saved, but as through fire)" (3:13–15). Paul believes his work will be tested and that he will receive reward or punishment based on its quality. If the Corinthians are found to be a faulty building, as it were, Paul as contractor will also face the fire. If the Corinthians had in fact rejected Paul for false apostles, then in Paul's mind, he himself would have been subject to punishment on the last day.

If Paul raises the possibility of avoiding the trial through self-killing, however, he quickly discounts it. He believes such judgment to be unavoidable, and reminding the Corinthians of its inevitability is one of the functions of his strategy in discussing suicide. In each place where Paul expresses his death wish, he quickly reminds the Corinthians of the impending trial that all humanity—he and the community included—must face. So, in 1:13b–14, after his assertion of confidence in "the God who raises the dead," he reminds the community that he and they must testify on each others' behalf at the final trial: "I hope that you will recognize us until the end (just as you have also recognized us in part), that we are your boast just as you are our boast, on the day of our Lord Jesus." Ultimately, Paul rejects the available exit of self-killing because all are eventually accountable to judgment.

Another possible motive for suicide in 2 Cor 1–9 is Paul's feeling shame over potentially losing his leadership position over the Corinthian community. In the preceding letter (2 Cor 10–13), Paul targets his anger at those in the community who rejected his apostolic authority in favor of new, false apostles. "For we have not overreached our bounds like those who did not reach you; for we came even as far as you in the gospel of Christ" (10:13). As I discussed in Chapter 1, Paul emphasizes his firm belief concerning the particular mission field assigned by God to each apostle and the reward promised for the apostle's work. Similarly, as Anton van Hooff explains in reference to the epic hero Ajax: "an ancient leader is expected to end his life if he has been defeated or for some other reason can no longer face his people. An individual with Ajax's personality had to commit suicide when he had experienced the deadly disgrace of not receiving Achilles's weapons. Ajax remained one of the models of heroism."[20]

That Paul broaches the topic of self-killing is not surprising in light of ancient theories of motives for suicide. Nor is it a departure from the travel frame of his rhetorical strategy. The topic fits for at least three reasons, each of which I consider in detail below. First, discussions of self-killing during the peak of the "cult of suicide" revolved around how a voluntary departure (or at least its deliberate consideration) ultimately revealed the true character of the individual. The whole of philosophy was, from this point of view, a "preparation for death."[21] The self-disclosing aspect of considering suicide thus works hand in hand with the revelatory nature of the epistolary travel apology.

Second, contemplating self-killing in a reasoned and deliberate manner bore considerable status implications in the mid-first century; Paul, however, with his expression of personal despair and reliance on God, may well turn this tradition on its head. Third, a prevalent figure for suicide was, in fact, that of departure or traveling to one's true home, as is made especially clear in the writings of the famous Stoic, Roman official, and proponent of suicide Seneca.

For many philosophers (especially the Stoics), self-killing was a way for the wise man to show the power of his free will—or, to be more specific, the consonance of his will with that of God. Basing their thought on the model of Socrates's voluntary death, Stoics taught that one should wait for some "sign" or "compulsion" from God as an indication that one was being called home. So, in Plato's *Phaedrus,* Socrates sees his unjust trial as "compulsion" (*anagkē*) signaling him to depart from life (61B–C). Zeno, founder of the Stoics, famously fell and broke his toe in his old age and cried out, "I am coming; why do you call me?" In response to the perceived sign, he killed himself by holding his breath (DL 7.28). His later successor, Cleanthes, was said to have starved himself upon discovering an inflammation of his gums (DL 7.176). In many cases, then, self-killing was about preserving the moral strength and dignity that could be compromised by external constraints such as failing health. He who is trained in philosophy should be able to discern the divine recall insofar as the wise man's will should be in harmony with God's.

Later in the Roman period, agreement between the mind of the sage and that of God became expanded to include the duty of the Roman upper-class man to discern how his character best fit his *persona*—a sort of naturalized view of his social role—and what style of death was appropriate for him. As recent scholars have shown, philosophical notions of *persona* grounded discussions of suicide in the late Republic and early Empire. When Cicero, in *De officiis,* discusses Cato's suicide, he deploys Stoic theories on the social relevance of *persona*. For Cicero, it is a moral imperative that the Roman gentleman discern his particular endowments and live accordingly (*Off.* 1.110). As Cicero explains, the issue of *decorum* (that is, what is "fitting" or "proper" to a certain character type in a certain situation) has direct bearing on the issue of self-killing: "Did Marcus Cato find himself in one predicament, and were the others, who surrendered to Caesar in Africa, in another? And yet, perhaps, they would have been condemned, if they had taken their lives; for their mode of life had been less austere and their characters more pliable. But Cato had been endowed by nature with an austerity beyond belief, and he himself had strengthened it by unswerving consistency and had remained ever true to his purpose and fixed resolve; and it was for him to die rather than look on the face of a tyrant" (*Off.* 1.112, LCL trans.). For Cicero, Cato's suicide was an example of self-preservation insofar as, if Cato had supplicated to the tyranny against which he had fought so hard, he would no longer be Cato. Yet as Timothy Hill indicates, the Self preserved by *decorum* is not an essential Self but a social *persona*, filling a specific function within Roman society: "The rigidity of Cato's character meant that his voluntary death could only serve to demonstrate the absolute incompatibility of Caesar's rule with the ethical ideals of the Republic. The manner of Cato's death therefore not only continued to express the ideals he had exemplified in life; on a rhetorical level, it granted him victory over Caesar." With the advent of the Empire, suicide increasingly became one of the few options open to the Roman upper class for fulfilling their *personae* and making their mark in political discourse, helping to explain the Roman cult of suicide.[22]

Figures who opted for suicide in the face of restrictions against their political freedom—particularly Socrates and Cato—were widely valorized in the centuries straddling the advent of the Common Era. For Roman thinkers, the strength of such heroes' characters had been revealed in the way they faced their deaths. Reasoned confrontation with death became such a sign of wisdom, courage, and social status that eventually the mere ability to contemplate one's options for dying became as much a marker of nobility as actual suicide. The phenomenon is made clear in one of Seneca's *Epistles* (30) dedicated to his deceased friend Aufidius Bassus, an adherent of the Epicurean school, a group that rejected suicide. Despite Seneca's disagreement with his friend on the utility of self-killing, Seneca praises his ability to contemplate his end in the face of grave illness. In Seneca's words, Bassus was "a great pilot of his ship[who] still navigates with a torn sail" (30.3). For the Stoic, it was a pleasure to converse with his old, sick friend, who, out of sheer strength of character, was still able to "pass his sentence on death" (*ferentem de morte sententiam;* 30.9).[23]

In line with the growing tradition framing upper-class approaches to death, Paul depicts himself as being confronted with a decision, and the manner in which he in turn addresses that decision confers upon him the status of a noble, virtuous, intelligent, and even self-sacrificing leader. To be sure, in rejecting the fashionable option of self-killing, Paul more resembles Aufidius Bassus then his Stoic friend Seneca or the legendary exemplars Cato and Socrates. Yet it is striking to note how all five figures participated in the discourse of suicide—or, to be more specific, of nobly facing death—as a status-conferring discourse of self-revelation. Paul's apocalyptic background, however, is what finally distinguishes him from his upper-class Roman contemporaries. In the end, Paul rejects self-killing for trust in "the God who raises the dead" and who, imminently, will judge all humanity (2 Cor 1:9–14). For

Paul, the message of impending judgment radically questions self-killing as a fashionable response to shame, regret, and status.

Still, Paul's language shares much with the meditations on death produced by his contemporaries, especially those who undertook dying as a political act. Again, Cato is the preeminent example here, as a stalwart aristocrat and defender of tradition whose *persona* could not allow him to sacrifice his freedom and submit to Caesar's tyranny. In the ensuing centuries of Roman imperial rule, writers used death scenes to explore the place of the upper classes in relation to the absolute power of the emperor. For such writers, it rarely mattered whether a particular Roman noble was ordered by the emperor to commit suicide, anticipated the emperor's sentence by killing himself, or simply reacted to a general sense of the emperor's displeasure. What was important for Roman writers was not precise motivations, but the commentary on imperial power one's method of dying conveyed. Even if the power to live or die were the only right retained by an upper-class Roman, he could exercise that right in a way that limited the emperor's authority and reasserted his own agency. In a time of social change and uncertainty, trajectories of communal power were played out through discourses of subject formation. How a Roman asserted his "true character" at death established him as a potential paradigm for the role of upper-class leader in an age of empire.

Similarly, Paul's confrontation of death effected an attempt at rebuilding a crucial part of his international community by "revealing"—or more precisely, constructing—his own leadership role in the face of suspicions over his character. Despite his "despair of living" and self-imposed "death sentence" in the face of his broken relationship with Corinth, he relies on "the God who raises the dead" to sustain his own sense of authority. As a reminder, he asserts that the Corinthians would also do well to focus on God in light of the imminent return of Christ and final judgment. In doing so, he performs the type of deliberation expected in leaders of the time. Paul's alternative answer, however, evokes yet another trajectory in the Greco-Roman tradition of thinking about death and leadership, one that contributes to a portrayal as a self-sacrificing apostle: in opposition to the figure of leader as stalwart and open man of traditional virtue and strength, Paul presents himself as a demagogue.

In ancient political and philosophical discussions, the contrasting pair of traditional leader and demagogue was often figured in the mythic characters Ajax and Odysseus. As mentioned above, Ajax was famously depicted as killing himself out of shame when the weapons of Achilles were given not to him but to Odysseus. The contrast of the two characters is at least as old as the fictional speeches of each epic warrior, written by the companion of Socrates, Antisthenes. In each speech (known simply as *Ajax* and *Odysseus*), the hero makes his case to the Greek army why he and not his rival should receive the prize. In Ajax's mind, his noble manner of fighting in the open, in full sight of the enemy, and his clear superiority to most men make him the obvious choice over the sneaky, deceptive Odysseus. In response, Odysseus puts forth his shifty nature, his willingness to endure shame, as a sign of his commitment to his troops, his dedication to protect them and ensure their prosperity by whatever means necessary. He even foretells that Ajax's noble intransigence would one day lead to his rash departure from life.

The two stock characters endured for centuries in ancient discussions of leadership. In *De officiis*—the same work in which he considers Cato's revelation of character through suicide—Cicero deploys the pair in a discussion of contrasting leadership *personae*: "How much Ulysses endured on those long wanderings, when he submitted to the service even of women (if Circe and Calypso may be called women) and strove in every word to be courteous and complaisant to all! And, arrived at home, he brooked even the insults of his men-servants and maid-servants, in order to attain in the end the object of his desire. But Ajax, with the temper he is represented as having, would have chosen death a thousand times rather than suffer such indignities!" (*Off.* 1.113, LCL trans.). For Cicero (as for other Roman writers), Ajax and Odysseus figured opposing *personae* available to upper-class men—the first unwavering, open, and noble, the other vacillating, hidden, and self-sacrificing. Since the days of Socrates, philosophers had built upon the implicit contrast between Ajax and Odysseus found in the legends of the Trojan War. As mentioned in the previous chapter, Cynic thinkers in particular deployed the pair, adopting the cunning and adaptable Odysseus as one of their own. Odysseus endures travels, poverty, insults, beatings—all considered evils—in order to attain benefit and "gain" for the people he represents. In the late republican and early imperial discourse of *persona*, travel and death, figured by Odysseus and Ajax, played central parts.[24]

Paul the Demagogic Traveler

The pairing of Odysseus and Ajax offers us another lens through which to view Paul's contemplation of suicide in 2 Cor 1. For in joining the rhetoric of self-killing with an exaggerated travel apology, Paul defines his leadership role in the terms of a well-known political contrast. After his deliberation over death and its resolution in 1:8–14, Paul includes an extended explanation for not visiting (vv. 15–22)—as discussed above, a trope designating self-disclosure of sincerity toward the letter recipients. Yet the topos as Paul deploys it also addresses a common accusation against ancient demagogues, "vacillation" or "light-mindedness" (*elaphria*, v. 17). Similarly, Odysseus's willingness to sneak, spy, and deceive was seen as a mark of populism and vacillation, a trait externally and figuratively expressed through his epic wanderings.

Paul, in fact, extends his travel apology to explain that his change in plans was ultimately for the sake of the Corinthians themselves:

> I call upon God as a witness upon my soul that it was to spare you that I did not yet come to Corinth—not because we act as lords over your faith, but because we are coworkers with you for your joy. For you walk in faith. For I decided this for myself—to not come to you again in pain. For if I cause you pain, then who is there to cheer me up except the one who was pained by me? So I wrote this way, lest I come and experience pain from those who ought to give me joy—being confident that my joy is all of you. (1:23–2:3)

Paul explains his apparent vacillation concerning his plans to visit the Corinthians as a deliberate change in strategy in light of their tumultuous relationship. He is "sparing" them "pain," deciding not to appear to "act as lord" (*kyrieuomen*, a verbal form of *kyrios*, "lord" or "master") over them. Here is a description of the demagogic mode of leadership explicitly contrasted with the patriarchal model of the noble, intractable "lord." Instead of escaping through suicide the shame of his potential failure in Corinth, Paul pursues a wandering course of action for the sake of his community.

Paul reinforces his rhetorical strategy by narrating his erratic paths since last corresponding. He had searched in vain for his messenger, Titus, with news from Corinth and crossed the strait between Macedonia and Asia to find him. "When I came to Troas for the gospel of Christ and had a door opened for me in the Lord, I had no respite in my spirit since I did not find Titus my brother. Rather, having taken my leave, I left for Macedonia" (2:12–13). Paul's continued affliction causes him not just internal pain, but leads him to persist in the dangerous and ostensibly ignoble business of traveling, a situation alleviated only when people accept his message and "open a door" of hospitality to him. As discussed in the previous chapter, the occurrences of the "open-door" phrase in the Corinthian correspondence (1 Cor 16:9 and 2 Cor 2:12) both elucidate travel plans and most likely include the notion that Paul has been welcomed into someone's home. Paul thus describes his distress over the Corinthians as overriding his relief at finding shelter.

More significant may be the placement of Paul's travelogue from Asia, through Troas (that is, Alexandria Troas, a city founded by Alexander the Great near the ancient cite of Troy) to Macedonia and eventually Greece. The path from East to West, from Asia to Europe, embarking from Troy, evokes Odysseus, hero of Troy, the most famous traveling demagogue. As I have already mentioned, ancient writers deployed the strait between Asia and Europe as a cultural boundary, often building upon its epic role separating the two sides in the Trojan War. Paul's normal practice in referring to locations on his international routes is to refer to cities (Ephesus, for example) as opposed to regions (Asia). By mentioning Asia and Troas, Paul evokes a host of traveling leaders who crossed the boundary between continents in order to found new worldwide regimes, from the legendary Greeks fighting Troy, to Persian invaders, to Alexander the Great. Additionally, Paul breaks off his travelogue before narrating his arrival in Macedonia and reunion with Titus. Much like Odysseus, his return is deferred, resulting in wandering. The juxtaposition of a contemplated suicide in Asia and a wandering journey from Troy is Paul's way of communicating that an apostle is a slave of God and God's people, enduring all manner of dangers and humiliations—even tireless travel—for the sake of gaining and saving more followers for Christ. By trading noble death for suspicious travel, Paul begins his attempt once again to define what sort of leader he is, what sort of *persona* he exhibits to his communities.

In this investigation of social contexts for the initial motifs of 2 Cor 1–9, I have argued that Paul evoked and juxtaposed at least three ancient discourses: epistolary travel apologies, reasoned deliberation and political self-formation in the face of self-killing, and the vacillating and self-sacrificing demagogue. All served the interest of forming a new leadership role, that of the Wandering Apostle. By drawing on multiple antecedents for Paul's rhetoric, my interpretation may itself be subject to accusations of wandering. But the accusations instead highlight the necessary strength of Paul's rhetoric of social change, his use of floating signifiers to create transient attachments to cultural expectations and draw new definitional boundaries for a new, diverse community. Just as he had appropriated the rhetorical tropes of travel apologies and self-killing, he situates himself on a cultural map marked by well-worn paths and overdetermined boundaries. In doing so, Paul establishes a point of departure for further rhetorical journeys in the letter. By adopting the motifs, he avails himself of the status implications of various leadership discourses; by adapting, challenging, and even dropping these motifs in favor of others, Paul depicts himself as an outsider capable of pulling the strings of the ancient social economy, a wanderer with the power to intersect and bypass the roads laid by leaders who came before him.

3

The Wandering, Foreign God of Israel

Members of Jewish apocalyptic groups such as Paul's Christ-believing followers eagerly awaited the arrival—the *parousia*—of God and/or his messiah, conquering the world and granting Israel worldwide and eternal dominion. As radical as eschatological expectation may seem to some today, the language of arrival and conquest was not unique within the ancient world. In myth and ritual, deities were thought to arrive and rule in various cities in different eras. The Israelite prophet Zechariah expected Yahweh to return during the Persian period to restore rule in Jerusalem and expand it over the nations: "Rejoice exceedingly, Daughter Zion! Proclaim, Daughter Jerusalem! Look, your king comes to you, righteous and bringing safety; he is humble and riding a donkey, a young colt" (LXX Zech 9:9). In some cases, a human agent of the divine signaled the god's triumphant arrival. The authors of the Gospels thus used the above verse from Zechariah to frame the story of Jesus's entry into Jerusalem days before the crucifixion. The great kings of antiquity were also understood to arrive in the presence of the gods. Isaiah 45:1 declares Cyrus the Great of Persia to be the "messiah" of Yahweh in light of the expected liberation of Judah from Babylonian rule. Contemporaneously, citizens of Babylon, tired of their own emperor, declared that the god Marduk "made him [Cyrus] set out on the road to Babylon going at his side like a real friend . . . All the inhabitants of Babylon as well as the princes and governors (included) bowed to him and kissed his feet . . . Happily they greeted him as a master through whose help they had come (again) to life from death."[1]

Greek and Roman lore similarly depicted a wide range of gods and goddesses as arriving triumphant in a city, distinguishing among good and evil people—or in many cases between those who accept the god's arrival, pledging loyalty, and those who refuse. As with the Jewish eschatological notion of the "Day of Yahweh," Greek and Roman deities arrived periodically in order to judge a city's inhabitants. Yearly civic festivals commemorated their initial visits and welcomed them anew into municipal life. As I highlighted in Chapter 1, texts and rituals frequently figured such deities as foreign travelers. While any god could be considered a foreigner—a citizen of heaven touring the mortal realm—many of the most prominent traveling gods were thought to have originated in particular geographic or ethnic contexts. A central and common idea, however, was that the god had been exiled in the East, only to return in a grand triumphal procession to reward his or her devotees and destroy those who had cast him or her out. No matter the mythic background understood, however, the god's essential foreignness instilled a power difficult to control in a civic context. Traveling gods, as outsiders with the perspective to question the very foundations of a society, defied attempts to confine their meaning.

Paul, as a wandering preacher of another foreign god (that is, Yahweh, from Judea) and a proclaimer of a new age, also faced suspicions stemming from his foreignness, his transient lifestyle, his voluntary poverty, and his apparent lack of physical and oratorical impressiveness, as his letters to Corinth indicate. In light of his appearance, then, it is puzzling why Paul begins to defend his authority in Corinth in 2 Cor 2:14–17 with a reference to the God of Israel as a "triumphing" (*thriambeuonti*) God. In response to his revelation of affliction, his travel apology, his lament over having caused the Corinthians pain, and his travelogue of his desperate attempt to find Titus in his crossing from Troas to Macedonia, Paul thanks God for leading him in triumph. The thanksgiving seemingly interrupts his travelogue, since it is not immediately clear what the triumphing God of Israel has to do with the more mundane details of Paul's recent itinerary. Moreover, the fact that Paul is "led in triumph" connotes the shameful position of a humiliated captive in a king or general's victory procession. Finally, Paul concludes his peculiar thanksgiving with another sudden interjection, a protest that he is "not like the many who huckster [*kapēleuontes*, related to the noun for 'trade,' *kapēleia*] the message of God" (2:17). Many readers have surmised that, lacking any immediate motive in the text for the interjection, Paul must be referring to the opponents who had disrupted his relationship with the community, accusing them of deceptive preaching.[2]

Such a choppy interpretation, however, disregards the breadth of the constellation of meaning surrounding the concept of a triumphing, foreign God. Within a first-century Greek context, the triumph of a traveling deity conveyed simultaneous meanings of victory and shame, sincerity and fraud, stability and wandering, power and servitude. With the image, Paul enters the world of cultic itinerants and practitioners, especially as exploited by Hellenistic and Roman leaders. As with any evocation of foreign gods, royal appropriation of the triumph drew upon the divide between Europe and Asia, since the gods both of itinerant prophets and of processing kings were most often "traveling deities" voyaging westward, demanding hospitality and exacting judgment. The dualistic nature of traveling gods yielded volatile material for propaganda and populist rhetoric, and political leaders who availed themselves of their power often lost control of the semantic range such deities covered. Carefully treading this well-worn ideological path, Paul tries to tap and control the rhetorical force of the triumphing god by contrasting references to "triumphing" (*thriambeuein*) and "huckstering" (*kapēleuein*). Briefly evoking Dionysus in all his ambivalent, wandering might, Paul hopes to further build his image of "apostleship" over and against his community's suspicions of an itinerant preacher of an Eastern god. After taking a close look at the interpretive difficulties presented by the short passage 2 Cor 2:14–17, I flesh out a broad semantic range for Paul's "triumphing–huckstering" axis in order to provide a background for understanding the import of this snippet of Paul's rhetorical strategy.

Paul's Shameful Triumph

In 2 Cor 2:12–13, Paul claims that, though he had found shelter among new believers in Troas, his lack of "respite in his spirit" caused him to cross over to Macedonia in search of Titus and news from Corinth. He then continues with a sudden and paradoxical thanksgiving in the face of the shame of continued travel:

> But thanks be to God who always leads us in triumph [*thriambeuonti hēmas*] in Christ, and who makes known through us in every place the odor of the knowledge of him. For we are the fragrance of Christ toward God among those who are being saved and those who are perishing—for some, an odor from death to death, for others, an odor from life to life. And who is sufficient for these things? For we are not like the many who huckster [*kapēleuontes*] the message of God; rather, we speak out of sincerity, as from God, speaking before God in Christ. (2 Cor 2:14–17)

Only recently have scholars interpreted the ostensibly embarrassing image of Paul as a captive in a triumph as a metaphor well-suited to his argument. First of all, although the Greek verb *thriambeuein* almost always indicates a military triumph leading conquered prisoners, the idea of the military triumph found many figurative contexts—especially in Latin texts employing the term from which the Greek is derived, *triumphare*. By extension, the triumph could be used as a metaphor for shame apart from actual triumphal processions. So, in Seneca's discussion of obligation and benefaction in *De beneficiis*, a man whose friend saved him during a time of political turmoil tires of how his friend lords the benefaction over him and wishes he had been led in triumph after all: " 'Give me back to Caesar!' How long will you keep repeating: 'It is I who saved you, it is I who snatched you from death'? . . . I owe nothing to you if you saved me in order that you might have someone to exhibit. How long will you parade me? . . . In a triumph, I should have been made to march but once!" (2.11.1, LCL trans.) The triumph provides an obvious metaphor for shame, in that the captives are subjected to public display.[3]

The ideal prisoner in a Roman triumph was one who had lost the most in terms of status—a general or, better still, a ruler. In Plutarch's depiction of the Roman general Aemilius Paullus's triumph over the Macedonian ruler Perseus (167 B.C.E.), the fallen king begs of the general clemency to exclude him from public spectacle. Paullus, "ridiculing, as was proper, his lack of bravery and love of life, rather said, 'But this at least, as it had been for him earlier, also is possible now, to do whatever he wished,' making clear that death could take the place of shame. Yet the cowardly man could not submit to death, but being made effeminate by certain hopes, became part of his own spoils" (*Aem.* 34.2). Plutarch comments that Perseus's unwillingness to kill himself to avoid the shame of the triumph constitutes a sort of "effeminacy." In his expectations, suicide is preferable to procession as captive. In my reading, it is precisely such an expectation that Paul reverses in the demagogic self-portrayal of 2 Cor 1:8–2:17. The juxtaposition of political self-killing and politico-military triumph serves as a main trajectory of this section of the letter. The triumphal procession seems to be at least one important referent for Paul's use of the verb *thriambeuein*.

Perhaps most relevant for our purposes is the recent observation (made by Roger David Aus) that when Paul claims that God "always" (*pantote*) leads him in triumph, a first-century reader could hardly fail to recall the Roman assertion that Augustus was an "eternal triumphator." Here, Paul draws a quick but telling comparison between the deified emperor and the God of Israel, a God engaged in a worldwide and eternal triumph. As interpretations like that of Aus indicate, Paul's use of *thriambeuein* certainly bears politico-military connotations. The reading of 2 Cor 1:8–2:13 presented in Chapter 2 strengthens the case (and reinforces the compositional link between the two sections in terms of thematic trajectories): Paul's rejection of face-saving suicide in light of the shame and possible divine condemnation in the wake of his trouble in Corinth would understandably lead to images of a captive Paul forced to walk in shameful procession.[4]

Although the triumphal prisoner signified social shame, the figure simultaneously connoted other aspects of Roman political thought. Discourse on triumph as found in its literary and artistic depictions served as a means by which Romans thought about their foreign neighbors, conquests, and (increasingly during the late republican and imperial periods) their fellow Romans of other nationalities. The triumph was a main route by which the foreign entered Rome—at the very least, through the prisoners, spoils, and even graphic geographical depictions of lands conquered, all of which were common elements of the ritualized procession. After his grand triumph of 61 B.C.E., Pompey constructed a massive theater complex decorated with the imagery and styles of the peoples he had defeated. As a symbol of foreign conquest, the triumph signaled that the city's domain was expanding, encompassing the foreign into its sphere, inevitably changing Roman customs and notions of identity. After Julius Caesar's triumph over the Gauls, many joked that he had led the Gauls to Rome in two distinct but related ways, as captives and as citizens, since Caesar had also opened the rolls of citizenship to many from these northern peoples. As Mary Beard has recently synthesized in a study of the Roman triumph, republican and imperial writers alike used notable triumphs to reflect on how Rome often seemed to be conquered by the very nations it led in triumph.[5]

The perceived relationship between the Roman triumph and the foreign leads us to a second, related, and no less important antecedent for Paul's image in 2 Cor 2:14—the Dionysian triumph as depicted in myth, festival, and political propaganda. Paul's vocabulary certainly recalls the Roman military triumph, but we must also observe that the *triumphator* in Paul's case (namely, God) is not a general per se, but a god, a foreign god, an Eastern god. In this second backdrop for Paul's triumph image, I see the apostle as evoking at least three different appropriations of Eastern—and more specifically, Dionysian or Bacchic—devotions, practices, and myths: the celebrations and stories of Greek cities welcoming foreign gods, wandering practitioners of Bacchic and Orphic mysteries, and Dionysian self-presentations of a host of Hellenistic rulers (and, in turn, their late-republican Roman opponents and successors). By evoking these dual antecedents—military and Dionysian triumphs—Paul can address the shameful aspect of his apostolic form of life only to transform it into a divine mission of a powerful, foreign, traveling deity.

Various elements of 2 Cor 2:14–17 point in the direction of the cultic aspects of the triumph motif: the verb *thriambeuein* itself; the occurrence of "fragrance" (*osmē* in v. 14 and twice in v. 16, as well as *euōdia* in v. 15), representing the incense used in such processions; and the occurrence of *phanerein*, to "appear" or "become manifest," in 2:14, connoting divine epiphany. The most compelling argument for the presentation of a deity's procession, however, is the most obvious evidence: the triumph in 2:14–16a is not a human triumph (neither Paul nor any other mortal is figured as a general here) but one led by the God of Israel. It is hard to imagine that a Greek audience would not compare such a journey with those told of other deities such as Dionysus, Magna Mater, and Isis.[6]

In effect, then, Paul has retained both politico-military and cultic senses of the triumphal image. By choosing Greek terminology usually reserved for the political sphere (in which he had already been operating with his allusions to political self-killing and juridical imagery), he connects this section with what came before. Yet he also moves in a metaphoric direction extensively explored by Greek and Roman cultures, depicting a god as participating in victorious procession. In effect, Paul reconstructs a well-known metaphor in order to transport his audience to more figurative locales. Moreover, he makes the discursive journey smoother with a common denominator missed by most exegetes—travel. In effect, Paul shifts from imagery of *literal, human* politico-military triumph to that of *metaphorical, divine* triumph.

In sum, it is only by examining various possible backgrounds of Paul's triumph image that we can explain the semantic movements of the passage. Instead of pulling on just one of his audience's expectations concerning the triumph, Paul evokes multiple preconceived notions. By noting how he strategically evokes these expectations, we can see the trajectory of his rhetoric in the passage and how it may have re-formed the Corinthians' understanding of apostleship as a new leadership role.

"Eastern" Gods: Cult, Proclamation, and Royal Self-Definition

As discussed in Chapter 1, many ancient writers conflated Judean worship with rites to other "foreign" gods, including Dionysus. As a subject of this colonizing gaze, Paul exploits his Easternness in the interests of self-fashioning. To be specific, Paul's communities worshipping the God of Israel and his Messiah constituted the arrival and installation of a new, foreign deity in Greek cities. The same cities celebrated similar, legendary installations with yearly festivals, such as the Athenian "City Dionysia," commemorating the arrival (after an initial rejection) of Dionysus from Eleutheria. For the Corinthians, accepting Paul's message amounted to the acceptance of a foreign, traveling deity like Dionysus—or at least the god's herald. Yet such divine welcomes had accrued specific political connotations as well. In the four centuries before Paul's arrival in the cities of Asia, Macedonia, and Greece, Dionysian processions had played a crucial role in royal self-fashionings, both Hellenistic and Roman. Specifically, Paul's choice to describe his travels not just as a "procession," but as a "triumphal procession" bears Dionysian connotations. As Paul Brooks Duff points out, Greeks and Romans viewed Dionysus as "the triumphator *par excellence* as well as the inventor of the triumphal procession."[7]

This perception was largely due to propaganda disseminated in the wake of Alexander's conquest of the East and the claims of his various successors. Alexander's triumph is thus reflected in later recountings of Dionysus's myth, such as the one found in Diodorus Siculus:

> He also led about with himself an army composed not only of men but women as well, and punished such men as were unjust and impious. In Boeotia, out of gratitude to the land of his birth, he freed all the cities and founded a city whose name signified independence, which he called Eleutherae. Then he made a campaign into India, whence he returned to Boeotia in the third year, bringing with him a notable quantity of booty, and he was the first man ever to celebrate the triumph [*thriambon*] on an Indian elephant. And the Boeotians and other Greeks and the Thracians, in memory of the campaign to India, have established sacrifices every other year to Dionysus, and believe that at that time the god reveals himself to human beings. Consequently in many Greek cities every other year Bacchic bands of women gather, and it is lawful for the maidens to carry the thyrsus and to join in the frenzied revelry . . . in this manner acting the part of the Maenads who, as history records, were of old the companions of the god. (4.2.6–3.3, LCL trans.)

Dionysus's path in this account roughly parallels the Macedonian conquering of Greece and the East as far as India. Note the god's behavior in the course of his march, as he "punished such men as were unjust and impious," just as Paul claims God's procession provides life for the saved and death for the perishing. Dionysus is also portrayed as having liberated various locales, and one of the cities he erects, Eleutherae, has a name meaning "independence" or "freedom." Such actions were anciently attributed to Dionysus, as reflected in polis festivals to the god, including the Athenian Dionysia, as well as in tragic depictions such as Euripides's *Bacchae*, in which it is repeatedly stated that the Bacchic mysteries are not for the impure (see 70 and 474). Later in 2 Cor 1–9, Paul will assert that God grants "freedom" to those who receive him (3:17). Additionally, the above passage from Diodorus explains the licit worship of Dionysus in relation to his triumph: because of Dionysus's initial triumph through the Greek world, his cult among female devotees is considered "lawful" at approved times. Despite the dangerous cult's wandering, suspicious nature, Greek cities domesticated it, confining it to certain festivals. Paul may similarly be attempting to domesticate the more troubling aspects of his ministry.[8]

The linking of Dionysian processions to Alexander and his successors put a regal spin on a style of worship that had long been associated with travel and foreignness. As I discussed in Chapter 1, the Dionysian mysteries in their earliest known forms were spread by itinerant practitioners, as shown by recent discoveries of funerary texts promising life after death to initiates, courtesy of Orpheus, Demeter, and Dionysus. The traveling proclaimers were derided by Plato (*Resp.* 364B–365A) as *agurtai kai manteis,* "beggars and sorcerers," who travel "to the doors of rich people" seeking financial support in exchange for their bogus rites. Hellenistic and Roman rulers sporadically restricted and even banned Bacchic rites as licentious, foreign, and inauthentic. Yet at times, governments would also sponsor Dionysian and related foreign practices, finding resources for propaganda in the idea of a god who both conquered and liberated the world. For would-be kings, Dionysus proved to have populist appeal, if only his many facets could be rhetorically controlled.[9]

As a god of dualities—technology (viniculture) and inebriation, order and chaos, Greekness and foreignness, reward and punishment, life and death—Dionysus threatened the notion of a society based on a stable production of rules and meaning. Yet inhabitants of locales across the Mediterranean found in the god a figure fruitful for social change. At the very least, civic rites to Dionysus enshrined a city's ability to adapt to new situations or, alternatively, to periodically and ritualistically perform the founding of the city's regulative domain. By acting out the destructive and creative forces of Dionysus, a city provided an outlet for the expression (and purgation) of the dualities the god encapsulated. The civic harnessing of Dionysus subjugated him to the interests of the status quo. At times of social upheaval, however, the triumphing, resurrected Dionysus could provide rich (if risky) rhetorical resources for guiding a populace into a new era. So, during the age of kings and emperors ushered in by Alexander the Great, a series of powerful and charismatic leaders took the cities of the Mediterranean by storm in the guise of the "New Dionysus." Bacchic myths and rites, in all their forms, bore considerable popular appeal as they promised a challenge to prevailing notions of virtue and political control. Dionysus, as an outsider, provided a vantage point from which regulative domains of common sense could be questioned. The foreign god of reward and punishment, of order and chaos, of life and death, served as an ideal rhetorical conduit for social change.

The early identification of Alexander with Dionysus allowed his successors—especially the Ptolomies in Egypt—to harness the power of the myth of the outsider triumphing universally in order to secure their reigns. Memories of Ptolemy II Philadelphus's massive parade stood for centuries as a particularly conspicuous example of the royal deployment of Bacchic propaganda. The spectacle featured evocations of many deities, but the central part of the procession was devoted to Dionysus, as described in a fragment of the historian Callixenus recorded in Athenaeus (5.196a–203b). The parade portrayed Dionysus in his many mythic manifestations and cultic functions, including Indian triumphator, patron of the local Bacchic mysteries or *teletai,* and benefactor through his gift of wine. The beginning of the procession comprised Dionysiac attendants, the *Silenoi* and *Satyroi,* followed by marchers clad as Victory and bearing incense. In fact, many participants in the procession are said to have borne incense in one form or another. The procession included poets, athletes, and Dionysian theater workers. The Bacchic mysteries and sanctuaries were also well represented by priests, priestesses, "all types of mystery-clubs" (*thiasoi*), initiates, and Maenadic women in their various forms and titles (5.28).

After a number of floats displaying copious amounts of wine (5.29–30), depictions of the god's myths came, including the bedchamber of his Theban mother, Semele (in which she was impregnated by Zeus); the cave in which he was born; and his triumphal return from India. This last scene included the standard iconic elements: the god rode an elephant, followed by a heraldic satyr "sounding a golden goat's horn" (5.31). The triumphing Dionysus led an army, including satyrs in armor and chariots drawn by various beasts and driven by young boys. Following the chariots were carts full of foreign women dressed as prisoners (5.32). Next in the procession came the products of various nations: camels bearing fragrant spices, including frankincense, myrrh, cassia, saffron, cinnamon, and iris. Later, images depicted both Alexander the Great and Ptolemy I, triumphators in the Dionysian tradition. In fact, after processions to other gods, a separate procession honored the triumphant Alexander, riding an elephant-drawn chariot and accompanied by Victory and Athena (5.34).

Callixenus and Athenaeus transmit the description of Philadelphus's procession as a sheer marvel of opulence, and it may well have been the king's partial intention to show strength through wealth. But the event also communicated an ideology of Ptolemaic kingship, drawing on the seemingly universal yet various meanings of Dionysus—as foreign and thus global in his reach and reign, as benefactor through his gift of wine, as patron of arts and local *thiasoi*, and, most importantly, as victorious.

Processions of this type, especially involving Dionysus, became an important aspect of royal ideologies in subsequent centuries. In Egypt, the use of Dionysian imagery also led kings to patronize and regulate the *thiasoi* themselves: Ptolemy IV Philopater (the same ruler that 3 Maccabees claims forced Jewish Alexandrians to brand themselves as devoted to Dionysus) established new regulations for the mysteries and even fashioned himself as a "New Dionysus." On the Greek mainland, however, the successors to Dionysus evoked other aspects of the god. An early Macedonian successor, Demetrius Poliorcetes, entered Athens insisting that he be admitted at once to the mysteries. Later, certain Athenians decided he be honored along with Dionysus and Demeter at the City Dionysia, with the attendant rites of foreign hospitality for a god. In his account, Plutarch frowns at this innovation and claims that omens expressed the gods' displeasure at the honors given Demetrius. Plutarch accuses the public figures responsible for granting such honors to Demetrius as, "in begging foolishness and shamelessness, appearing to imitate the proclivity toward the populous that characterized Cleon of old" (*Demetr.* 11.2–3). Especially among later writers, the Athenian statesman Cleon, who flourished more than a century before Demetrius, was the archetypical demagogue. Plutarch pejoratively associates the welcoming of a king as Dionysus with demagoguery.[10]

Athenaeus is equally dismissive of the Athenian reception of Demetrius and cites earlier historians portraying further how the Athenians welcomed the would-be king as a god. Quoting the orator Demochares, a contemporary of Demetrius, Athenaeus relates how the Athenians greeted him "not only burning incense and wearing crowns and pouring wine, but also with processional choruses and Bacchic performers [*ithuphalloi*], with dancing and singing" (6.62). These elements point to a Dionysian reception, especially the mention of *ithuphalloi*—literally, "erect penises"—referring to the cult object carried in such a procession but also to a musical style devoted to Dionysus. In her study of the City Dionysia at Athens, Christine Sourvinou-Inwood surmises that both Demochares and Plutarch point to Demetrius's procession as being modeled after the reception of Dionysus as a foreign god.[11] Moreover, Athenaeus broaches this topic as an example of the "flattery" of the Athenians and states that they were "flatterers of flatterers" when they honored Demetrius (5.62). Thus Demetrius and the Athenians are portrayed with the flattery that attends demagoguery.

In later centuries, both Greek and Roman aspirants to kingship availed themselves of the social type of the Dionysian demagogue in their processions and entries into Greek cities. Cicero reports that the cities of Asia Minor received Mithridates VI Dionysus (not surprisingly), after he conquered Asia Minor around 88 B.C.E., as "Lord, the very father and preserver of Asia, Euhuius, Nysius, Bacchus, Liber" (*Flacc.* 61). Perhaps more intriguing is the story recounted by the Stoic polymath Posidonius (again preserved by Athenaeus) concerning the Peripatetic philosopher Athenion who went to Athens as Mithridates's ambassador and became a brutal tyrant of the city. Posidonius portrays the Athenian citizen as a charlatan who "began to work as a sophist, preying after young students. Having worked as a sophist in Messene, Larissa, and Thessaly and made quite a bit of money, he returned to Athens" (5.48). Posidonius pejoratively casts Athenion's social type as the traveling, charlatan "sophist." He relates his rise to power under Mithridates; he was soon elected ambassador (*presbytēs*) to the Asian king, a position that allowed him to fall upon the king's good graces. In correspondence with his native city, he persuaded them that Mithridates would be their protector from Roman rule and financial ruin—that "not only, their debts being removed, would they live in concord with him, but also that they would regain their democracy" (5.48). Upon return to Athens, Athenion is led into the city on a silver-footed litter with purple linens. His arrival is met by the usual suspects:

> Then men, women, the elderly, and children ran to this spectacle, expecting fine gifts from Mithridates, when the beggar Athenion, who had given lectures for scraps, thanks to the king, behaving boorishly, processed [*pompeuei*] through country and city. The Dionysian artisans sang hymns to him as a messenger of the young Dionysus [*ton angelon tou neou Dionysou*], calling him to the public altar and its customary prayers and libations. And he who had formerly come from a rented house came to the house of a then rich man with processions from Delos, decorated with couches, paintings, statues and silver platters on display . . . and at the sacred precinct of the artisans they made sacrifices and libations in honor of Athenion's arrival [*parousia*] after the introductory proclamation of a herald. (5.49)

Much of Posidonius's mockery takes its cue from standard, antidemagogic rhetoric (though his impetus may be Athenion's brutal reign over Athens). Yet the pattern seen in the case of Demetrius holds here as well: a new ruler (or his representative), understood as a victor and savior, is welcomed as a new deity, often by crowds, especially including those who take their livelihoods from the Bacchic cults in their many forms. Athenion's "arrival" (*parousia*) is even described with the terminology usually reserved for kings (as discussed in Chapter 1). For later writers, Athenion is especially suspect as a traveling sophist elevated to a powerful station. Using the stock metonymy of the philosopher's cloak, Posidonius jeers that such a man "lay on purple linens, who had never seen any purple on his poor cloak before" (5.49).[12]

Mirroring their Greek counterparts, successive Roman generals and conquerors would also avail themselves of Dionysus's mask. Pliny, in his *Natural History*, deploys Bacchic tropes to portray Pompey's Roman triumph after his conquests in Africa: "The first harnessed elephants that were seen at Rome were in the triumph of Pompey the Great over Africa, when they drew his chariot; a thing that is said to have been done long before, at the triumph of Father Liber on the conquest of India" (8.2, LCL trans.). Pliny also claims that C. Marius fashioned himself after Dionysus by drinking from a cantharus (a vessel typically devoted to the god) after his final defeat of the German tribes in 101 B.C.E. in order to impress people with how far he had come from humble beginnings (33.53).[13]

Yet the most prominent use of Dionysian imagery during the Republic came at its end, in Mark Antony's struggles against Octavian. Antony adopted the Ptolemaic identification with Dionysus to his advantage to secure power in Egypt, Asia, and Greece, a decision that contributed to both his popularity and his downfall. Much of Antony's use of Bacchic imagery can be traced to his partnership with Cleopatra and the old Ptolemaic strategy of exploiting the identification of Dionysus with the Egyptian god Osiris, in the case of kings, and Isis with Aphrodite, in the case of queens. As outlined above, Dionysian propaganda also had considerable traction in Asia and Greece. The earliest evidence for Antony as Dionysus is Athenian, consisting of an inscription from 38 or 37 B.C.E. that seems to refer to the Panathenaic games of "the god Antony, the new Dionysus"(*[Antō]niou theou neou Dionyso[u]*), as well as coins depicting Antony as Dionysus.[14] In his *Life* of Antony, Plutarch relates the conqueror's arrival in Asia from Athens, contrasting his benevolence on the Greek mainland with his arrogance across the continental divide:

> While Caesar was in Rome worn out with conflicts and wars, he [Antony] living in great peace spun right back around through his passions to his accustomed lifestyle, with the Anaxenores harpists and the Xuthoi flutists and Matrodorus, a certain dancer, and a certain other cultic club [*thiasos*] of Asiatic musicians, surpassing in audacity and boorishness the noisy bees who with him from Italy, insinuated themselves and took over the court . . . Then, when he entered Ephesus, women dressed as Bacchae and men and boys dressed as satyrs and Pans met him, and the whole city was full of ivy, thyrsoi, harps, fifes, and flutes, calling out that he was Dionysus, Giver of Goodwill [*Charidotēn*] and the Gentle [*Meilichion*]. For, without trying he was this to some, but to many he was the Brutal [*Ōmēstēs*, literally, "Raw-flesh Eater"]

and the Savage [*Agriōnios*]. For he deprived well-born men of their possessions to grant favors to knaves and flatterers [*mastigiais kai kolaxi*]. (24.4.2–6)

As in his portrayal of Demetrius at Athens, Plutarch associates Antony's Dionysian entry into Ephesus with the demagoguery attending new rule. Appeals to the populous went beyond the attention and work given to Bacchic *thiasoi;* Antony and his entourage deprived the landed in order to grease the wheels of new, strategic social contacts. The contrast between the Dionysian connotations perceived by each social group tellingly draws on Dionysus's dual nature with opposing epithets ("Giver of Goodwill" versus "Raw-flesh Eater," for example), an essential part of his persona of old. Dionysus demands acceptance when he arrives and thus promises either salvation or doom, depending on the eye of the beholder. The dualistic Bacchic lens filtered perceptions and receptions of the arriving conqueror as "New Dionysus" and resulted in social bifurcation and upheaval.

As mentioned above, Antony's self-identification with Dionysus gained him much popularity in the East. But when word of his Bacchic affiliation reached Rome (probably with the help of Octavian's rumor mill), the foreign and licentious connotations of the god proved a liability. So un-Roman was Antony's Dionysian persona that, as Cassius Dio described it, many thought he had been bewitched by Cleopatra (50.5). Antony even felt compelled to pen an apologetic tractate, *De ebrietate sua* ("On his drunkenness"), to combat rumors of the assumed ill effects of his Bacchic lifestyle.

After his final defeat at Actium, Antony-as-Dionysus lived on in the literature of the Augustan period, this time as a foil to his former rival's now universal *imperium.* Although references and allusions to Dionysus abound in Vergil's *Aeneid,* none of them identifies Augustus with the god. In fact, in book 6, when Aeneas receives a prophecy about Rome's future, the culminating glory of Augustus's rule is portrayed as *surpassing* the glory of the achievements of "Liber, who, as conqueror, drove holding a yoke of ivy branches, leading tigers from the high peak of Nysa" (6.804–5). Vergil refuses to *identify* Augustus with Dionysus in the style of the Hellenistic and Roman conquerors who had come before. Rather, the new emperor exceeds the accomplishments of the victorious god and—more to the point—the leaders after Alexander who had availed themselves of Bacchic imagery, Antony being the last in a long line.[15]

Other Dionysian references in the *Aeneid* implicitly denounce Antony's Eastern decadence. In the story of Aeneas's sojourn with Dido in book 4, Vergil's description of Aeneas frequently deploys Dionysian imagery, leading some scholars to posit that Aeneas, who usually is a mythic forerunner to Augustus, represents Antony when in Carthage. The Roman ancestor falls under the spell of the foreign queen Dido just as Antony was bewitched by Cleopatra. Later, in book 12, in a battle on the Italian peninsula, Aeneas's allies kill a towering Italian soldier named Osiris, the Egyptian counterpart to Dionysus, with whom Antony had identified. At this point in the epic, Aeneas, now a stand-in for Rome and Augustus, defeats the Egyptian enemy, representing Antony and his foreign affinities. The imagery for Augustus sets itself over and against what had become the common Hellenistic practice identifying kingship with Dionysian triumph.[16]

Although Antony found Bacchic imagery successful for a period, the god simply contained too many various and even contradictory elements in his character to control as propaganda. In a penetrating analysis particularly relevant for my approach, Joseph D. Reed reflects on Antony's efforts to control the interpretation of propagandistic imagery:

> [T]his political masquerade relied on an awareness that the referent of every metaphor can itself be a metaphor; thus through linked chains of models Antony picked up qualities incidental to his immediate precursor. When he entered Ephesus as Dionysus he was not just Dionysus but also Alexander, projecting a different, but overlapping, set of attributes and inspiring different, but related, expectations in his beholders. Through Alexander he in turn invited comparison with other Roman generals who had taken Alexander as a model: Marius, Pompey, Caesar. In this respect his appearance before his soldiers as Bacchus was not careless, but shrewd, as long as they could draw the proper links between explicit and implicit models. But how does one limit one's interpreters, or call a halt to the racing linkages of meaning that one has set in motion? Antony's swarm of Dionysian personae proved too semantically volatile to control.[17]

It is precisely this semantic surplus that successful attempts at social change and claims to hegemony must restrain. Dionysus, the traveling god, constituted a wandering signifier whose rhetorical paths from Alexander to Antony proved difficult to guide. Outside of Egypt, Greek leaders deploying the god won the support of urban populations—in particular, the Bacchic *thiasoi* hoping to win royal support—but risked upper-class accusations of demagoguery, as the rich feared the potential for social upheaval inherent to regime change and the establishment of new patronage alliances. As I discussed in the introduction, agents of hegemonic change deploy traveling signifiers with the semantic range to unify diverse subject positions, though the images simultaneously threaten to outrun the intentions of the agents.

Contemporary theorists have begun to investigate the mechanics of how such signifiers are controlled. For example, Slavoj Žižek emphasizes the importance for subject formation not only of an individual's identification with a certain image, but also of a subsequent and implicit *dis*identification. Homologies drawn between an existing, common subject position and the one imagined by a hegemonic agent can help communicate and create the new subject position, such as a new leadership role. So, by associating themselves with Dionysus, conquerors imported numerous meanings that helped mold their images—promising benefits, a new life, social upheaval, and punishment for evildoers. But in order to distinguish himself from evoked cultural expectations, Antony in particular needed to disidentify with Dionysus, at least before certain audiences (his native Romans) or in terms of some of the god's less savory characteristics (drunkenness, licentiousness, foreignness). In general, new movements must strategically articulate a series of comparisons and disidentifications with regard to preexisting universalities in an attempt to rearrange the social framework. Antony's demise constituted a failure to control adequately the floating signifier of Dionysus before the diversity of an international audience. After Antony's death, no Roman leader would avail himself of imagery of the New Dionysus until Nero, just a few years after Paul's correspondence with Corinth. In the mid-fifties, Dionysus was still off-limits as Roman imperial imagery. I read Paul's style of ministry as reflected in 2 Cor 2:14–17 as an attempt to exploit this ideological vacuum by evoking Dionysian desires for a new social order among the inhabitants of a major Greek city.[18]

The Apostle among Captive, Herald, and Charlatan

Similarly, Paul's language in 2 Cor 2:14–17 quickly establishes and renounces a series of transient connections between his form of life and the image of being led captive in the international triumph of the God of Israel. Interpretations of the passage as a jarring interruption of Paul's travel narrative fail to appreciate the social import of that narrative. Changing travel plans reinforced suspicions against Paul of vacillation and mendacity because, through his itinerancy, he resembled a charlatan purveyor of an Eastern god. His framing of his itinerary and his quick refiguring of his travels as the eternal triumph of a foreign yet universal god address such suspicions. Paul's ministry as described in 2 Cor 2:12–13 uncomfortably resembles the wandering practices of Eastern cult practitioners: "When I came to Troas for the gospel of Christ and a door had been opened for me in the Lord, I received no respite in my spirit since I did not find Titus my brother. Rather, taking my leave of them, I left for Macedonia." While he potentially depicts himself as a wanderer dependent on the "open door" of hospitality, the trajectory of his journey from Troas (near the site of Troy) to Macedonia establishes the trip as a border crossing, transgressing the continental divide, East to West. Paul's path sets up the complex background of the image to come.

Paul's initial statement, thanking the God "who always leads us in triumph in Christ, and who makes known through us in every place the odor of the knowledge of him" (2:14) addresses the suspicions that Paul raises in his travel apology, transforming the stereotype of the Bacchic con man. The image alludes strongly to the epiphanic processions of foreign gods, rituals understood to reveal divine presence through images and incense. But his statement also draws upon the politico-military evocations of Dionysus that had characterized three hundred years of propaganda from Alexander to Antony through the image of the universal triumph, "always" and "in every place." Soon after, in verses 15–16, he draws upon the dualism common to both cultural anteced-ents, festal processions and demagogic political claims alike, stating that the "fragrance" of God's triumph has polarizing effects: "death" for "those who are perishing" and "life" for "those who are being saved." Like the herald of a god-emperor, Paul must be considered carefully by his audience, since acceptance or rejection of him leads to radically contrasting fates. The juxta-position of Paul's travels and the triumph of God may seem incongruous to modern readers, but an ancient urban audience accustomed to the reception demanded of heralds of foreign gods and conquerors could have easily made the connection. Paul implicitly disidentifies with the wandering behavior of Bacchic proclaimers, positing a far more impressive set of self-images. Though a prisoner in a triumph, Paul still represents a divine, worldwide king.

In the second half of verse 16 and in verse 17, Paul fleshes out his rhetorical movement between the two passages: "And who is sufficient [*hikanos*] for these things? For we are not like so many hucksters [*kapēleuontes*] of the message of God; rather, we speak out of sincerity, as from God, speaking before God in Christ." The issue of Paul's self-"sufficiency" characterizes much of his argument to come. For the time being, note how he marks for his community that they should not focus on his own apparent strength, but should interpret it within the broader context—both international and cosmic—to which he introduced them in his initial preaching. They should not categorize him as a charlatan preacher of foreign gods, as one of the itinerant "hucksters" or "traders" stereotyped in ancient discourse, despite his wandering apostleship. Instead, Paul claims "sincerity," insofar as he is "from God"—or, better yet, that he veritably speaks "before God," always in the presence of the One he proclaims. In some sense, where Paul is, there God is, too. Much as in the welcome of the herald Athenion to Athens, Paul-as-herald is to be received as a stand-in for his divine master. In this way, an explicit rejection of Corinthian suspicions comes at the end of the passage. By evoking the very doubts about his authenticity that conditioned his controversy with Corinth, Paul allows himself to subsequently disidentify with the image of the itinerant fraud. In its place, he appropriates the common cultic image of the triumphing god in a manner already employed by imperial propaganda since Alexander.[19]

Adapting the motif of the *parousia* of the triumphing god and emperor allowed Paul to transform his identity in Corinth in a way familiar to his audience. Yet his strategy also bore considerable risk. The God of Israel—for Paul, the one universal God—could not be too closely identified with Dionysus without beginning to compromise Paul's monotheistic message. Additionally, and as with Antony, Paul must avoid the licentious aspects of the Dionysian persona: foreignness, drunkenness, and promiscuity. While Paul self-identified as an ethnic Judean, his facility with Greek cultural idiom allowed his message purchase in the urban landscape of the Empire. He himself claimed to function as "all things to all people" (1 Cor 9:23). And while temperance only makes brief appearances in his letters (he castigates wealthier Corinthians for "getting drunk" while others go hungry at the eucharistic meal; 1 Cor 11:21), he may have felt a need to treat sexual matters with care. He frequently targeted the sexual laxity of Gentiles (see 1 Thess 4:3–8), particularly in Corinth. Certainly, sexual morality was a stock trope of Jewish literature. Yet Paul's professed celibacy (see 1 Cor 7:7), like his itinerancy, bore ambivalent connotations. While in some cases a sign of philosophical discipline and self-sufficiency, celibacy could be interpreted as a form of sexual deviancy.[20] In an age of low infant mortality, in which procreation was enforced by imperial and local statutes, sexual abstinence was considered dangerous. Recall also, from Chapter 1, how some charlatan, foreign preachers—particularly those of Magna Mater—were eunuchs, and that eunuchs were often cast as perverts. Deployment of Dionysus would prove especially volatile if Paul allowed it to wander (as it were) from his rhetorical strategy. The strategy required yet another disidentification, another transient attachment for the wandering signifier "apostle," one that continued to identify his travels with the arrival or *parousia* of God's Christ. In the subsequent passage, Paul defuses the volatility of the foreign, conquering god with a far more quotidian travel metaphor—the letter carrier.

4

Delivering the Spirit

Although Julius Caesar had pardoned and befriended him after his opposition during the Civil War, Cicero still felt himself on the wrong side of history—not to mention of the graces of the *imperator*—in 45 B.C.E. As a strategy for righting his position, Cicero took a letter of recommendation he was writing to Caesar on behalf of a certain Praecilius as an opportunity to improve his situation. In many ways, the letter became a self-commendation. As Cicero states, Praecilius himself "used to scoff at and scold me because I did not attach myself to you" (*Fam.* 13.15.1, LCL trans.). He then describes his error and current change of heart, employing a series of poetic quotations from Homer and Euripides, an uncommon practice in letters of recommendation. In closing, Cicero admits that he is well aware that his letter breaks with epistolary conventions: "I have adopted a new style of letter in writing to you, so that you may understand that this is no stereotyped recommendation" (*non vulgarem esse commendationem;* 13.15.3). Both out of consideration for the importance of his recommendation (because of his friendship and admiration for the recommended) and in the interest of repairing his relationship with Caesar, Cicero needed an extraordinary recommendation and thus relied on the established wisdom of the Greek poets.[1]

In Chapter 1, I examined how Horace's generic violations in his verse epistle to Maecenas corresponded to an attempt to alter his social role in relation to his patron. Similarly, Paul in 2 Cor 1–9 adapts numerous cultural and literary forms to mold his position as apostle and manipulate his standing in Corinth. In 2 Cor 3, he famously turns to an aspect of his own ethnic tradition, the Jewish scriptures, in a rapid and confusing array of citations and interpretations. The quotations from Jeremiah, Ezekiel, and Exodus focus on contrasting views or forms of the law of God, given either as writing on stone tablets or as the gift of God's spirit dwelling in the hearts of his people. Christian readers since the first centuries of the church have read Paul as depicting the severing of Christianity from Judaism, of the separation of a law of the spirit from the stony code that kills. In a similar vein, the passage has been interpreted as entailing a new, Christian hermeneutic of spiritual interpretation that sees past the literal words of the Hebrew Bible to God's work in Christ foretold.

In many ways (and I will discuss some below), the approach has failed to account for the section's more pernicious interpretive problems. Most glaring is widespread lack of attention to the topic opening the passage: letters of recommendation. According to Paul, he and his co-workers bear "no stereotyped recommendation," to borrow Cicero's phrase. The citations of scripture that follow serve, as did Cicero's citations of the ancient poets, to redefine the criteria by which Paul's addressees judge him. As a traveling courier of God's spiritual message, Paul claims to have succeeded in building God's community on earth in a way no prior envoy—not even Moses—ever had.

Paul's contention in 2 Cor 3:3 that his work constitutes a "letter of Christ" that establishes actual communities on earth mirrors the socio-rhetorical functioning of 2 Cor 1–9, an act of communication designed to change social expectations and roles. It is an act of language, a group of words, intended to create or *do* something. Theorists call "doing things with words" (to borrow the title of J. L. Austin's famous work) "performativity," a concept central to numerous approaches to the role of discourse in society. Foundational to investigations into performativity is the question of how language has the ability to evoke certain social contexts in order to alter them. By what social logics do people understand and heed acts of language such as a recommendation, a promise, a constitution? On the one hand, performative speech mimics prior, similar statements or acts; one knows an oath is being sworn by the formula "I promise." Yet each performative act strives to enact something new, unique, an alteration of the context in which the speaker is embedded.[2]

Jacques Derrida mediated the tension between "imitation" and "innovation" in performativity by casting it as a process of "citationality." "Could a performative utterance succeed," he asks, "if the formula I pronounce in order to open a meeting, launch a ship or a marriage were not identifiable as *conforming* with an iterable model, if it were not then identifiable in some way as a 'citation'?" Judith Butler later built upon Derrida's observation to show how citations of cultural conventions, when performed (in both speech and action) in certain contexts, could challenge and even begin to create anew the subject positions generated by discursive structures. Such subversive performances often take on a parodic quality, as with drag or queer forms of life taken on in the interests of sexual justice or the refashioning of sexual subject positions. Butler writes, "This kind of citation will emerge as *theatrical* to the extent that it *mimes and renders hyperbolic* the discursive convention that it also *reverses*." In a performative utterance, one evokes a known cultural convention yet creatively deploys it within a new context in order to change that context. The alteration is not a result of any sui generis intention on the part of the speaker/actor but of the innovative, even rhetorically excessive and provocative, manner in which he or she has linked heretofore unrelated social codes.[3]

In the same light, we can read the citations of ancient texts found in both Cicero and Paul as examples of "citationality" designed to manipulate social relationships. We might also observe how Paul cites not just Jewish scriptures, but other, broader social conventions of his time—here, the letter of recommendation and conventions of letter delivery. By depicting himself as a courier from God, delivering the Corinthian community as a spiritual letter from Christ, Paul situates the performative work of an "apostle" amidst a host of ancient expectations about the limits of language's ability to alter the world at hand.[4]

Letters of Introduction and Initiating Relationships

My line of interpretation on the social implications of Paul's self-depiction as messenger and "courier" within the context of the epistolary metaphor at the outset of 2 Cor 3 relies on a reconsideration of earlier work on letters of recommendation/introduction and the function of ancient couriers. The motif of couriership seems almost buried in the introductory verses of the chapter: "Are we starting to recommend [*synistanein*] ourselves once again? Or, rather: do we have need, as some do, of letters of introduction [*systatikōn epistolōn*], either to you or from you? You yourselves are our letter, written in our hearts, known and read by all people, and making known that you are a letter written by Christ which was delivered [*diakonētheisa*] by us, written not with ink but with the spirit of the living God, not on stony tablets but on tablets that are fleshy hearts" (2 Cor 3:1–3). Traditional interpretations read 2 Cor 3:1 as rejecting the common practice of using letters of recommendation, or, more specifically, as Paul rejecting the specific practice among his opponents. As with the brief mention of "the many" in 2:17, many scholars see the phrase "as some do" (*hōs tines*) in 3:1 as referring to Pauline rivals. Yet it is unlikely that Paul would reject the general practice. He himself employed epistolary introductions as a way of securing the welcome of his co-workers and couriers, as evinced by his recommendations of Timothy in 1 Cor 4:17 and 16:10–11, Epaphroditus in Phil 2:25–30, and Phoebe (a "servant [*diakonon*] of the church in Cenchreae," Corinth's eastern port) in Rom 16:1–2. Some have seen Paul's epistle to Philemon as a letter of recommendation for Onesimus (though a highly unique one, considering the circumstances). For our purposes, it suffices to note how the notion of recommendation suffuses Paul's rhetoric in 2 Cor 1–9, with which Paul must effusively recommend Titus and his anonymous companions in order to ensure reception of the letter (as well as his request initiating the collection) in 8:16–23. Since the Pauline mission was part of an international movement with numerous co-workers, epistolary introductions were an indispensable component of it.[5]

To fully appreciate Paul's reference here, we should observe that, in mentioning recommendation letters, Paul evokes not just their *commendatory* but also their *introductory* function. That is, he implies that he and the Corinthian community have no need of the epistolary convention initiating a relationship because they have long known and supported each other. Second Corinthians 3:1b could be paraphrased as, "Surely we don't need to be reintroduced, do we?" Such an interpretation is evident from the letter metaphor that follows, in which Paul figures the community as a "letter of Christ delivered by us" (3:3), depicting the founding of the community as the delivery of a letter written by Christ. The metaphor functions in part to remind the community of its relationship with Paul and his role as founder. Through an innovative metaphor, Paul tells the Corinthians that they themselves recommend Paul's authenticity by their very existence.[6]

As mentioned above, Paul makes an appeal to his initial preaching and founding of the community in many other contexts in his letters (see, for example, 1 Thess 1:5–7 and 2:1–12). In fact, such reminders are a common strategy throughout earlier sections of the Corinthian correspondence. At the outset of 1 Corinthians, Paul immediately appeals to his initial preaching activity. So, in 1 Cor 1–4, recalling the community's origin fills at least two functions: a shaming technique recalling the community's founding (suggesting that they have not yet improved spiritually since their first encounter with the gospel), and an assertion of Paul's authoritative role as founder. Paul first recalls their initiation into Christ by addressing Corinthian factionalism through a reference to their baptism in 1:14–16, then invites them to "consider your own calling" in 1:26. In 2:1–5, Paul even reveals the strategy he used in first approaching the Corinthians with the gospel: "And when I came to you, brothers, I came not proclaiming to you the mystery of God with authoritative-sounding speech or wisdom. For I decided to know nothing among you except Jesus Christ and him crucified. And I appeared among you in weakness, in fear, in great trembling, and my speech and my proclamation were not in a persuasive act of wisdom but in a display of spirit and power, so that your faith would not be in the wisdom of humans but in the power of God." Paul emphasizes that he emptied himself of the personal "power" of eloquence or wisdom in order to emphasize the work of God in his preaching activity—though he immediately emphasizes that "we speak wisdom among the perfected" (2:6) and that "I could not speak to you as spiritual people but as fleshy people, as babies in Christ. I fed you with milk, not solid food, for you were not yet able to stomach it. Nor are you yet now able to stomach it, for you are still fleshy" (3:1–3). The motif of beginning students as "babies who need milk" was common in moral pedagogy in the ancient world, often (as in 1 Cor 3:1–3 and Heb 5:12–14) as a shaming device urging the audience on to moral progress.[7]

Paul's appeal to the community's initial call in 1 Cor 1–4 also serves the explicit function of asserting his authoritative role as founder of the Corinthian community. After a sarcastic tirade in 4:8–13, Paul ends the first section of the letter with an admonition: "I write these things not to shame you but to admonish you as my beloved children. For though you may have ten thousand pedagogues in Christ, you do not have many fathers. For in Christ I fathered you through the gospel. So I exhort you: become imitators of me. For this reason I sent Timothy, who is my beloved and faithful child in the Lord, who will remind you of my ways in Christ, just as I teach everywhere in every community" (4:14–17). Despite his arguments against factionalism, Paul reminds (indeed, "admonishes") the Corinthians that he is their primary instructor in the gospel, figured as their "father," the one who sired them, as it were, in the teachings of the gospel. Paul reminds them of this fact so that they might obey his authority above all else—that they may even be his "imitators." Even his representative and courier, Timothy, is an authentic reflection of the Pauline lifestyle, insofar as Timothy is, like the Corinthians, a "beloved and faithful child" of Paul. The apostle takes the opportunity to assert his role as authority through his recalling of the community's founding.

A similar appeal recurs in the letter of introduction metaphor at 2 Cor 3:1–3 and serves the same two functions I highlighted above in my discussion of 1 Cor 1–4. First, the appeal to the initial formation and instruction of the community introduces the exegetical section in the remainder of 2 Cor 3, which (as I discuss below) largely repeats already learned material. Second—and more importantly for the immediate context of my argument—recalling the community's founding and the close relationship between Paul and Corinth acts as an admonition and even a gentle (at least, it is subtler than what we find in 1 Cor 4) shaming of the Corinthians for not holding fast to this close relationship with their apostolic father figure. Indeed, note that in 1 Cor 1–4 Paul strives to admit the importance of other proclaimers of the gospel (here, Apollos and Peter) and yet to emphasize his central role as founder and "father." A similar purpose can be inferred from 2 Cor 3:1–3, where Paul reminds the Corinthians of their relationship. He requires no recommendations for the Corinthians, *as so many other preachers would,* because he and his deeds are (or should be) well-known to them.

The "letter of Christ" metaphor, however, also propels Paul's rhetoric in other directions. Many scholars have sought to provide more social specificity to Paul's discussion of his *diakonia* (traditionally translated as "ministry") by focusing on the image of the Corinthians as "a letter of Christ ministered by us" (*epistolē Christou diakonētheisa huph' hēmōn;* 2 Cor 3:3), attending specifically to the sense of the construct *diakonein epistolēn.* Many have argued, by pointing to similar uses in other ancient texts, that the phrase should be translated as "to deliver a letter." In light of these parallels, it seems likely that Paul portrays his founding of the Corinthian community as a divine courier-ship. Since the letter mentioned in 3:3 is the same metaphorical letter from 3:1–2, Paul would be the deliverer of his own letter, since a person necessarily carries his own recommendation. In order to understand the metaphor, then, we need a fuller understanding of the nature of ancient letter delivery.[8]

Aside from institutionalized systems of governmental travel and correspondence, letter writers in the ancient world had to improvise to ensure the delivery of their letters, either sending or hiring slaves as letter carriers or relying on the responsibility and goodwill of those, friends and strangers alike, who happened to be traveling in the right direction. One could never be sure whether a letter would actually reach its addressee, a topic of considerable worry in extant epistles. As M. Luther Stirewalt explains, anxiety over the reliable delivery of letters could be interpreted as a subset of a more general "distrust of the written word and . . . the nature of the personal letter as a substitute for oral speech. It was generally thought that one might better send an oral message to an absent friend through an intermediary who could then continue the conversation."[9]

Mistrust of written language and physical distance led ancient letter writers and epistolary theorists to frame letters as substitutes for the presence of their authors (as discussed with reference to the ancient theorist Demetrius in Chapter 2). In this vein, many practices of letter delivery also strove to ensure that letters were sufficient stand-ins for their senders. In many cases, the courier not only delivered the letter and read it aloud, but also had authority to interpret it and answer any questions the recipient might have had. Acts 15:22–32 depicts an instance of the phenomenon when the Jerusalem elders send a letter to the community in Antioch concerning the results of the Jerusalem council. Along with Paul and Barnabas, the Antiochene community sends back two couriers, Judas and Silas, "leading men among the brothers" (v. 22). The letter explicitly specifies: "So we have sent Judas and Silas, who will report these same things through their own word" (v. 27). Upon delivery, "Judas and Silas, who were also prophets themselves, exhorted the brothers with many words of their own and strengthened them" (v. 32). In an organized and international (though still inchoate) group such as the early Jesus movement, a loose system of known and trustworthy messengers was an immediate necessity.[10]

An even more vivid example of the courier as proxy for the letter writer appears among Cicero's letters. In his collection of resources for ancient epistolary theory, Abraham Malherbe includes *Fam.* 12.30, in which Cicero chides his friend Cornificius for not writing him more often. "What could give me greater pleasure, failing a *tête-à-tête* talk with you, than either to write to you, or to read a letter of yours?" (12.30.1). Later in this same letter, Cicero seems to commend the mutual friend who delivered and read aloud Cornificius's most recent letter. "Your affection," he writes, "has been much more definitely impressed upon me by Chaerippus. What a man he is! I always found him congenial, but now he fascinates me. He did more than convey to me your thoughts and words; I swear to you, there was not a single expression of your face that he did not make vivid to me" (12.30.3, LCL trans.). Here, the courier Chaerippus seems to be doing a Cornificius impersonation as he reads the letter aloud. The cultural convention of standing in for the sender is performed, acted out, by the letter carrier. Thus, even improvised efforts on the part of couriers could strive to assert letters as replacements for the presence of their authors, while the letter introduced, recommended, and guaranteed the courier as a suitable agent (and even replacement) for the letter writer and his intended meaning.[11]

Another cultural convention of ancient epistolographic practice comes to the fore when reading any letter in which the actions of the courier are in view. Letters of recommendation often ask that the letter carrier, the "recommended," be treated well by the letter recipient, sometimes with the explicit modifier "as if I were present." Letters of introduction often made the vague request that the recipient "receive" the recommended, which could include providing lodging and hospitality or perhaps career services. Lodging can often be assumed as the most basic and necessary provision, however, because the recommended is in most cases traveling to a new locale. In some return letters, the writer comments upon the successful and even charitable reception of the courier. This seems to be the function of Cicero's gushing over Chaerippus in the letter cited above; Cicero may be expressing to Cornificius that he shares Cornificius's affection for the go-between. In many cases, whether in introductory or more general letters, a return acknowledgment that the favor of receiving the courier was fulfilled completed the communicative act. On both sides of the imagined dialogue constructed by epistolographic practice, letters and couriers were laden in their travels by ideological controls guaranteeing them as replacements for their senders.[12]

Evoking cultural norms of epistolography, the appeal to the figure of the courier in 2 Cor 3:1–3 furthers the rhetorical strategy of constructing Paul as "apostle" through a chain of travel motifs, arranging the social landscape to create a space for his new role. Paul sidesteps the ambiguity raised by the letter's earlier motifs—the travel apology, which put into question the true intentions of the writer, and the traveling devotee of the Eastern deity, plagued by shifting locales and shifty morality. In raising the figure of the courier, Paul disidentifies himself with respect to more suspicious travels and associates with a more neutral figure at once ambiguous and secure. A courier could be anyone, yet people placed their trust in him to carry their messages despite dangerous and uncertain circumstances. Moreover, a courier was understood as (because a courier was hoped to be) a legitimized replacement for the letter sender, a notion that does much to support Paul's self-depiction as an authentic representative of Christ. Paul thus domesticates and authenticates his identity as an apostle through the metaphor of "Christ's courier," an authentic stand-in for the one who sent him.

Paul's appeal to the social realm of epistolography (and its concern for the successful transmission of the letter writer's thoughts and feelings) also raises underlying issues of communication and meaning that plagued ancient theoretical discussions. The distance that separated author from audience highlighted the nagging yet often ignored "distance" between writing and authorial intention, between the external mark of the written language and the inner recesses of thought. Suspicion over the "epistolary I" was a subset of a more general anxiety concerning the written word and its relationship to human knowledge and communication. Epistolary provisions can be understood in light of more general anxiety over writing as a communicative medium.

Scholarship on the oft-observed "logocentrism" of the ancient world (and, indeed, the Western intellectual tradition), coalescing especially around the twentieth-century advent of poststructuralism, has been increasingly applied to Paul, with 2 Cor 3 serving as a central text in such analysis. Beyond historiography of Christian origins, most scholars have traced the logocentric critique of writing to the Socratic tradition preserved in Plato. Fingers are often pointed at the *Phaedrus,* particularly the story Socrates recounts of how the Egyptian god Theuth (or Ammon), inventor of many other fields of knowledge, offered writing to Thamis, then king of the land, as a tool for making Egyptians wiser and improving their memory. Thamis, however, rejects the god's view of the power of writing: "this art will yield, through lack of practice in memory, forgetfulness in the souls of those who learn it, because of trust in writing, an external thing, produced by things alien to them, not in their internal memories, produced by their very selves. Indeed, you have invented a drug not for memory but for reminding" (275A). Socrates goes on to compare written words to a painting, which cannot explain its meaning to an observer. The written word, "when treated badly or abused in an unjust way, always needs its father as a helper" (275D). The only authentic and effective type of writing (a "legitimate" son when compared with the "bastard" offspring that is the written word) is "that which is written with learning in the soul of the student, which can protect itself, having learned those to whom it should speak and those to whom it should keep quiet" (276A). Language, written or otherwise, must be accompanied by the soul that produced it in order for it to be protected from abuse, from erroneous interpretations, in order to assure its clarity and authenticity. The epistolographic practice of authorizing a letter deliverer to explain the meaning of the text and act as a stand-in for the letter's source is an almost Socratic solution to the Greek philosophic problem of language: the written word is providing a living soul to act as a chaperone for the letter's meaning, protecting it from harm.[13]

I argue that the "letter of introduction" metaphor in 2 Cor 3:1–3 encapsulates the tradition of suspicion against writing in preparation for Paul's scripture citations and self-comparison with Moses to follow. Since a letter carrier was authorized to explain the intentions of the letter's author and act as the author's stand-in, Paul depicts himself not simply as a suitable replacement for Christ, but as a courier for Christ's very spirit, transmitting knowledge of Christ (cf. 2:14) in unmediated form. A closer exegesis of 3:2–3 highlights the effect of the courier motif. After ridiculing the notion of needing letters of introduction to or from the Corinthians by means of the rhetorical question of verse 1, Paul suggests the metaphor that the Corinthians are his letter of recommendation: "you yourselves are our letter, written on our hearts, recognized and read by all people" (v. 2). Paul claims that his profession of the existence, faith, and strength of his community in Corinth is the best recommendation he could ever seek. By figuring the community as a letter he carries in his heart to commend himself to other communities, Paul implies that they are a constant presence despite their distance from him. What is more, they play an essential role in his mission as the chief proof of his apostleship. Despite his travels, Paul and the Corinthian community are always present to each other, working together in Christ's mission. The reciprocity mentioned at the outset of the letter arises again, both confirming Paul's sincerity and elevating the Corinthians' sense of status within the international Pauline movement.[14]

Paul continues the metaphor, however, in verse 3, all the while raising its stakes. He claims that the contents of his community-turned-letter make known the very nature of his mission: "[You] make known [*phaneroumenoi*] that you are a letter written by Christ which was delivered by us, written not with ink but with the spirit of the living God, not on stony tablets but on tablets which are living [*sarkinais*—literally, "fleshy"] hearts." Classical Greek *comparanda* (especially relevant portions of the *Phaedrus*) help shed light on the meaning of the metaphor of writing on human hearts. The dense imagery here is complicated further by its conflated allusion to various texts from Jewish scriptures. Much real ink has been spilt in an attempt to untangle these references to Exodus and the Major Prophets. The "echoes," though numerous, are not difficult to hear, and scholars have debated and prioritized a group of usual suspects. "Stone tablets" immediately calls to mind the Mosaic covenant, specifically described as being inscribed on "stone tablets" in Exod 31:18. The allusion prepares the way for the comparison of covenants in 2 Cor 3:6–18. In contrast, the notion of God writing on the human heart could evoke a number of texts: LXX Jer 38:33 has God assert, "I will give my laws in their mind, and upon their hearts I will write them." Insofar as this passage in Jeremiah refers to the "new covenant" (v. 31) that God promises to make with Israel, the verse may foreshadow Paul's mention of the "new covenant" he bears in 2 Cor 3:6. In addition, the phrase "tablets which are living hearts" in 2 Cor 3:3 may evoke Ezekiel's depiction of a divine promise to his people of a new spirit, also described as a new heart of flesh to replace their stone heart; the statement is found in two forms, in Ezek 11:19 and 36:26. Retreating from earlier attempts to determine which scriptural allusion "actually occupied the *determinative* role in Paul's thinking by providing the dominant image," many scholars have begun to see the passage as invoking a composite of similar allusions, as explained by Scott Hafemann. So Richard Hays, untangling the delicately woven pattern of intertexts here, helpfully highlights not just Ezekiel's contrast of stony and fleshy hearts, but also how the notion of a "new spirit" in God's people (an aspect already evoked by the spiritual composition of the community-as-letter) speaks to the notion of the "incarnation" of God's spirit through Paul's apostolic activity as an expression of the sort of "new covenant" found in Jer 38. Hays's notion of "incarnation" here perfectly describes the communicative limit case fashioned by logocentric discourses in antiquity and the desire for the transferal of meaning to entail the transferal of real, spiritual presence.[15]

Paul most ostensibly evokes the problem of writing and presence in his scriptural catena of 2 Cor 3:3b–6, but it is the metaphor of couriership that acts as an overarching rubric for the section and conditions Paul's comparison in 3:7–18 of his mission with that of Moses. Moreover, insofar as the motif of writing on human hearts was common to non-Jewish and Jewish literature alike, the quotidian imagery of letter delivery may have served Paul's Gentile audience as an accessible entry point into Paul's self-understanding with respect to the Hebrew prophetic tradition. The "echoed" texts in 2 Cor 3 all yearn for a special type of divine message, expressing a prophetic desire for a divine intervention that would not merely communicate God's will but would activate within believers the willingness or capacity to perform it. These formulations from the Hebrew Bible resonate with broader, underlying ideological concerns in the Greco-Roman world over the possibilities of communication. Indeed, the image of a divine courier is a fitting introduction and frame for Paul's complex allusions to prophetic texts. By raising the common practice of letter delivery, and then figuring himself as carrier of a divine and internally carried letter, the apostle evokes an entire constellation of metaphorical "heavenly messengers," grouping these images under the blanket term *diakonos*.[16]

Divine Diakonos as Traveling Intermediary

The logic of Paul's rhetorical strategy in 2 Cor 3 is remarkably similar to the one I indicated in 2:14–17; namely, Paul rebuilds a well-known metaphor in order to use it for his own purposes. In 2:14–17, he presented himself as being led in triumphal procession by God, a common metaphor for an Eastern deity that drew upon the notion of political triumph. With the verb *thriambeuein*, he evoked the Roman military and political practice and then applied it to an Eastern deity (the God of Israel) in much the same way it had long been used in association with Dionysus (in fact, up until the advent of the Augustan period). In this way, Paul leads his audience on a more familiar path, guiding them in a chain of identifications and disidentifications, creating the social location of apostleship. Controlling the semantic force of a figure with such a broad range of connotations as the triumph is a difficult rhetorical prospect, and Paul drops it momentarily in favor of a new identification.

So, too, does he rebuild the metaphor of divine messenger in 2 Cor 3:1–18. By raising the topic of letters of recommendation and then creatively depicting the Corinthian community as a letter written by Christ and delivered (*diakonētheisa*) by Paul, he reconstructs (in his own unique way) the notion of a messenger (*diakonos*) sent by God. Paul's use of the *diakon*-root uniquely marks 2 Cor 3 (and, indeed, 2 Cor 1–9 as a whole): out of eighty-five instances of the word group in the New Testament and thirty-three in the seven undisputed Pauline letters, fifteen occur in 2 Cor 1–9, with six in the section extending from 3:1 to 4:15. Understanding the shifting meaning of the word group as used in 2 Cor 3 is essential for understanding the section.

The most recent, exhaustive word study is by John N. Collins, and his work provides a foundation for my discussion. Collins argues that, though *diakonia* was often used to mean "service" (for example, waiting at table), a survey of ancient uses shows a frequent reference to commissioning as a "go-between," often conveying some sort of errand or message. The meaning emerges especially in Plato's *Politicus,* in which Socrates and the Stranger distinguish among social roles that are *hypēretikos* ("function as a subordinate") and *diakonikos* ("function as a *diakonos,* or go-between"). The key example in this passage is the discussion of prophets and priests (290C), the first vocations described using *diakon-* terminology. In Plato's words, "we know diviners are held to be interpreters for the gods to men."[17]

Use of the word group to denote *heavenly* messengers was widespread throughout antiquity, especially with respect to the ultimate "messenger of the gods" in Greek lore, Hermes. The god's ambiguous Homeric epithet, *diaktoros,* is often explained by ancient writers as a rough synonym for *diakonos.* In light of this connection, the *diakon-* word group recurs in connection to Hermes throughout Greek literature. Similarly, Jewish authors describe divine messengers and prophets as *diakonoi.* Most relevant for our exegesis of 2 Cor 3 is the depiction of Moses in Philo's *Vita* of the prophet: although Moses is nowhere called a *diakonos,* the function is implied in God's appointment of Aaron as a *hypodiakonos* ("assistant envoy"), implying Moses's role as divine *diakonos.*[18]

Characterization of divine messengers as *diakonoi* early entered literary expressions and philosophical conversations concerning language and communication. Collins highlights instances of the instruments of communication being described with the word group; a fictional epistle from Heliodorus's *Aethiopica* has the writer refer to written language as *to gramma diakonon,* "the mediating letter" (4.8). Philosophers could employ the term to denote the mediatory functions of human senses and speech. Ammonius, in his second-century C.E. commentary on Aristotle's *Categories,* calls the human voice a medium for the thoughts of the soul. Epictetus, in *Diatr.* 2.23, extensively figures the human senses as *diakonoi* of the mind. In this context, Paul's use of *diakonos* and its common denotations and connotations helps him depict his apostolic role as one of mediator and agent, whose validity comes not from himself but from the one he represents.[19]

New Testament interpreters have taken as a focal point of the term's background its usage in the Cynic-Stoic discourses that merged early in the Roman period. For some, the Cynic-Stoic *diakonos* is the closest analogue to Paul's vision of "apostleship," so much so that some have seen Paul (or his opponents in Corinth) as having imported a technical, philosophical term and, through it, many of the philosophical ideas from that context. Central to the discussion is a text among the *Diatribes* of the first- and second-century C.E. Stoic Epictetus, already encountered in this study. *Diatr.* 3.22 describes Epictetus's vision of a true Cynic using vivid metaphors and examples, among which is the notable use of the term *diakonos*. Rather than focus on the intellectual pedigree of the term—a debate that risks incorporating wholesale into Paul's rhetoric entire thought systems—I look at how both Epictetus and Paul adopt and adapt terms and concepts to build rhetorical constructions, attempting to create and define social roles.[20]

Recent work on Epictetus's presentation of Cynicism reads it as part of a general trend in the early Roman period of domesticating the picture of the Cynic sage within Roman sensibilities, purifying it of its provocative and obscene role in order to salvage its strength in resisting social convention and promoting moral rectitude. What seems most unique about Epictetus's presentation is his depiction at the beginning and end of his lecture of the Cynic vocation as a *divine* calling. One cannot choose such a rigorous lifestyle through one's own volition (as seemed to be the case among the Cynic charlatans decried by Epictetus) but only through the behest and compulsion of God: "Anyone who takes up such a great matter without God is under God's wrath; he desires to do nothing else but shame himself publicly" (*Diatr.* 3.22.2). Early on in the discourse, he compares the divine call to serving a role in a universal household:

> A person does not come into a house that is well-managed and say to himself, "I should be the head household slave." Or, if he does, the lord of the household will turn, see the man arrogantly giving orders, then drag him out and beat him to smithereens. So it is in this great city: for here there is a master of the house who orders all. "You there, you are the sun; you have the ability to travel around and make the year and seasons . . . Go, travel about and move all things from the greatest to the smallest. You there, you are a calf; when a lion shows up, do what comes naturally to you. You there, you are a bull; come over here and fight. For this is your lot, it is proper and in your power to do. You there, you have the ability to lead the campaign against Ilium; be

Agamemnon. You there, you have the ability to fight Hector one-on-one; be Achilles." But if Thersites had come and contended for leadership, he either would not have attained it or, if he attained it, would have shamed himself before numerous witnesses. (3–8)

The metaphor of the universal household allows Epictetus to emphasize that the Cynic call is based on divine authorization with reference to personal ability and persona. (See Chapter 2 for my discussion of *persona* and Roman philosophies of social roles.) The notion of the world as a universal household ordered by God extends throughout the discourse and conditions later discussions of the Cynic rejection of household ties. More importantly, the focus on divine calling emphasizes two aspects of the Cynic mission. First, the true Cynic receives his appointment at God's will and because of his personal aptitude. The Cynic is called to be messenger and scout because his persona is suited to it. Second, one can never choose to be a Cynic.

In *Diatr.* 3.22, Epictetus redefines the Cynic by cycling through traditional and innovative motifs, rejecting focus on personal appearance and affect (9–12) and positing other figurative analogues, such as universal "teacher" and "pedagogue" (17). For Epictetus, the Cynic is a hybrid between "a messenger [*angelos*] sent from Zeus, speaking to people about good and evil, and showing them they are wandering in error, seeking the true good and evil elsewhere, where it is not, and not discerning where it is; and, as Diogenes said . . . as a scout [*kataskopos*]. Truly, the Cynic is a scout, finding out for people which things are friends and which things foes" (23–24). The figure of the Cynic as *angelos* and *kataskopos* serves a complex strategy of addressing a key aspect of a Cynic stereotype—namely, homelessness or travel. Although the Cynic is a preacher without a home, Epictetus emphasizes that it is the non-Cynic who is actually "wandering in error." "The good . . . is not where you expect or wish to find it. For if you had wanted to, you would have found it residing within yourselves and would not have wandered abroad" (38). Though the Cynic is technically homeless, he is at home in himself, his own virtue, and his divine vocation.

Epictetus quickly translates his focus on who is truly "wandering" and who is at home into an antithesis between "freedom" and "slavery." The penury and suffering that the Cynic lifestyle entails implies servility, at least through the lens of popular opinion. While the body and all related to it are enslaved to sickness and worldly vicissitudes, only rational assent is free. By means of a diatribe in which he takes on the persona of the Cynic, Epictetus addresses the nature of the good and how the Cynic embodies it:

And how is it possible for someone who has nothing, who is naked, homeless, hearthless, disheveled, without a slave, without a city, to live in tranquility?

Look, God has sent you the man who will show you in deed that it is possible. "Look at me, I am homeless, without city, without belongings, without slave; I sleep on the ground; no wife, no children, no praetor's mansion; but only earth and sky and one paltry cloak. But what do I lack? Am I not without pain, without fear, am I not free? . . . In what way do I encounter those whom you fear and gawk at? Don't I treat them like slaves? Who, when seeing me, doesn't think he's seeing his king and master?" (*Diatr.* 3.22.45–49)

Despite a list of apparent misfortunes (presented in much the same way as the Pauline *peristasis* catalogues), Epictetus performs what seems to be a fairly standard redefinition of the suspiciously servile aspects of the Cynic condition. So, when pressed by audience members about whether a Cynic will accept help from a friend when sick, he responds that he will accept only a fellow Cynic, a "worthy attendant" (*diakonon axion*) both of the Cynic and of God. Or, when asked whether the Cynic can maintain a family, Epictetus asserts that he must conserve single-minded commitment to his divine mission: "The Cynic should be always undistracted, wholly devoted to the services of God [*diakoniai tou theou*], able to travel around visiting among men . . . [lest] he destroy the messenger and scout and herald of the gods" (69). Here, Epictetus's deployment of *diakon-* terminology bears a generative double meaning: the Cynic rejects the *diakonia* of household chores in favor of his divine *diakonia*. The Cynic serves in God's household, at the behest of the Lord of the universal mansion.[21]

As Epictetus reiterates at the end of the discourse proper: "Think it over more carefully, know yourself, ask your little daemon, do not try it without God" (*Diatr.* 3.22.53). The emphasis on Cynicism as a divine vocation is Epictetus's ultimate rhetorical attempt to redefine the lifestyle for Roman sensibilities. In the words of Margarethe Billerbeck, "the rejection of friendship, marriage, begetting of children, and engagement in politics called for positive reinterpretation, if Cynicism, especially among Romans, was not to become suspect as a subversive movement . . . By raising Cynicism to a religious level and to the status of an exceptional existence within the human community, Epictetus . . . relieves the Stoic sage of having to choose whether or not he will play the Dog. It is for Zeus alone to call him to an imitation of Diogenes."[22] Epictetus brackets and suffuses his discourse on the Cynic call with an emphasis on God's volition and authentication behind the vocation. For the Stoic teacher, the Cynic founder Diogenes's lifestyle of proclamation and confrontation is to be imitated only by divine compulsion. Unless Zeus himself assigns the role of divine messenger and scout, any who play the Cynic are charlatans striving after mere ostentation.

For at least a century, scholars of Christian origins have struggled to articulate the affinities between Epictetus's description of the Cynic sage and early

Christian discourses on apostleship. Though both "Dog" and "Apostle" share numerous descriptive affinities—itinerancy, poverty, an ideology of proclamation, confrontation, and ethical rigor—attempts to posit close analogues (or, much less, trajectories of influence) have remained unpersuasive to many in the field. I posit that the similarities perceived between *Diatr.* 3.22 and 2 Cor 3 have less to do with the propositional content of the respective ideologies than with the common rhetorical projects entailed in each discourse; that is, each writer responds to a social situation of heightened suspicion over wandering religious practitioners or moralists and deploys rhetorical tools both traditional and innovative to redefine or newly create social spaces. Scholars such as Billerbeck have helped delineate Epictetus's project from this angle. In the previous two chapters, I have argued that Paul similarly raises ambiguous and suspicious topics, such as failed travel plans and itinerant devotees of Eastern deities, in order to provide a rhetorical platform for constructing the category "apostle," partially through addressing the more shady aspects of his own behavior. Both Epictetus and Paul exploit the relatively broad semantic range of the term *diakonos* in order to define figuratively their missions. For Epictetus, the common meaning of "household attendant" or "waiter" allows him to show how the Cynic rejects traditionally valued household attachments and their concomitant duties in favor of a divine office in the universal household of God, serving a specific role at the behest of the Lord of the mansion, who assigns to each on the basis of his persona.

Paul can also use the *diakon-* word group to refer to divine assignments based on individual aptitude and proclivity. In fact, two of the three occurrences of the term in 1 Corinthians (3:5 and, especially, 12:5) are intimately entwined with one of the letter's major themes: the diversity of gifts of the spirit distributed according to God's will. This aspect of Paul's use of the term, however, does not seem to come into play in 2 Cor 3, in which Paul exploits the broad semantic potential of the term to float from the quotidian figure of letter delivery to the more spectacular figure of the divine messenger. Paul could have chosen more common words to denote letter delivery (*apodounai, komizein,* etc.), but only the *diakon-* word group encompassed all activities involving communicative mediation—especially those involving travel—in a way that suited Paul's rhetorical needs. Paul defines his *diakonia* through the figure of letter delivery in that he is a representative of God to the extent that he bears God's very presence. Like a courier, his activity, his mission, is not his own but is completely at the behest of the one who sent him, for whom he strives to be an authentic replacement. Moreover, anyone who receives Paul also receives the one who sent him. Through the remainder of 2 Cor 3, the figurative implications of epistolary delivery suffuse Paul's discussion of missions at the behest of the God of Israel, both his own and that of Moses.[23]

Recognizing a Divine Diakonia in 2 Cor 3:4–18

Paul expands the notion of *diakonia* in 2 Cor 3 by first citing it as a term for letter delivery and then building upon it a series of allusions to Jewish scriptures. For example, as mentioned above, references to stone tablets recall the Mosaic covenant in Exodus. The reference, in turn, points forward to the comparison of Pauline and Mosaic missions in 3:7–18. Moreover, echoes of LXX Jer 38, with its description of God's law written on the hearts of Israel (v. 33) and God's promised new covenant (v. 31), hint at the explicit mention of the new covenant in 2 Cor 3:6. Another scriptural allusion prepares for Paul's argument defending (what we might call) diaconic authenticity by evoking a prophetic commonplace in the Septuagintal tradition, especially with regard to the prophetic call of Moses: the topic of prophetic "sufficiency," or *hikanotēs*, first mentioned in the rhetorical question of 2 Cor 2:16b ("Who is sufficient [*hikanos*] for these things?"). Scholars have viewed the repetition of the term as alluding to Moses's call in LXX Exod 4:10, in which Moses claims "I am not sufficient [*hikanos*] . . . I am stammering and slow-speaking." As he moves away from explicit epistolary imagery in 2 Cor 3:5–6, Paul reiterates that the type of commendation he implies is not a self-commendation: "Not that we are sufficient [*hikanoi*] ourselves to reckon anything as being of our own resources. Rather, our sufficiency [*hikanotēs*] is from God, who even made us sufficient [*hikanōsen*] to be messengers [*diakonous*] of a new covenant, one not of letter but of spirit. For the letter kills, but the spirit gives life" (3:5–6). Paul prepares for his comparison of covenants with an assertion that God supplements the personal insufficiency of his prophetic messengers, employing language evoking the call of Moses in LXX Exodus.[24]

Moses-as-messenger begins to take center stage in the subsequent section (2 Cor 3:7–18), in which Paul's discussion of covenants continues with a rhetorical *synkrisis*, or comparison, in verses 7–11. Far from rejecting the legitimacy of the Mosaic mission, however, the logic of the comparison (functioning on the principle of *a minori ad maius*—or, in later, rabbinic terms, *qal wā-hômer*) relies on the assumed "glory" of the appearance of the Sinai incident in order to bolster the surpassing glory of God's action in Christ. "If the ministry [*diakonia*] of death, engraved in letters on stone, came in glory, so that the sons of Israel were not able to gaze on the face of Moses because of the glory of his face which was being nullified [*katargoumenēn*], how much more will the ministry [*diakonia*] of the spirit be in glory?" (vv. 7–8).

Three additional statements compare the two missions and assess the Pauline mission as superior, including the assertion that "what was glorified has not been glorified, in this way: because of the exceeding nature of glory" (v. 10).

Paul's exposition continues to expound upon the "glory" (*doxa*) granted Moses and his ministry (*diakonia*):

> So having such hope, we act with great openness, and not like Moses, who set a veil over his face so that the Sons of Israel might not gaze at the goal of that which was being nullified [*to telos tou katargoumenou*]. On the contrary, their thoughts were hardened. For up until this very day, the same veil remains over their reading of the old covenant, and is not unveiled because it is being nullified [*katargeitai*] by Christ. Rather, to this day, whenever Moses is read, a veil lies over their hearts. "But whenever he would turn to the Lord, the veil was removed" [Exod 34:34]. The Lord is spirit; and wherever the spirit of the Lord is, there is freedom. And all of us, with unveiled faces, gazing as if in a mirror at the glory of the Lord, are being transformed into that very image, from glory to glory, as from the spirit of the Lord. (3:12–18)

Modern interpreters have struggled with the passage's anti-Jewish implications, the opaque logic of Paul's exposition, and, at the very least, the seeming liberties Paul takes with the story of Moses. As a starting point, we should note that Paul refers not to the event at Sinai generally, but more specifically to the second giving of the law (Exod 32–34) after the Israelites had abandoned hope of Moses returning and began worshipping the golden calf, followed by Moses's reaction of shattering the original tablets. Attention to the differences between the first Sinai theophany and the second covenant ratified after Moses's intercession affects our understanding of Paul's interpretation. On the one hand, the initial giving of the law occurs with God's presence on the mountain in the sight of the entire people of Israel. Later, as a consequence of the golden calf incident, God refuses to be in their presence and personally guide them to the promised land. The refusal is in part cast as an act of mercy granted at Moses's request, since God claims he would destroy the Israelites in his wrath if he were present among them.[25]

Moreover, the second theophany is granted to Moses alone, after he asks God how he will know how and where to lead Israel. God promises, "I will go before you [singular] and give you [singular] rest" (LXX Exod 33:14). Moses beholds God's glory while concealed in the cleft of a rock. The next day, he receives a new recitation of the law in God's presence. Upon descending the mountain, Moses does not realize that "the surface of the skin of his face had been glorified from talking to him. And Aaron and all the elders of Israel saw Moses, and the surface of the skin of his face had been glorified. And they were afraid to approach him" (34:29–30). Nevertheless, Moses has Aaron and "the leaders of the assembly" gather so he can read them the law. Then, the entire people gather to hear him (vv. 31–32). When he finishes speaking, he puts a veil over his face. From then on, subsequent encounters and counsels between God and Moses continue to occur outside the camp, apart from the people's presence: "Whenever Moses went in before the Lord to speak to him he removed the veil until he went back out. Upon exiting, he told all the Sons of Israel whatever the Lord had commanded him. And the Sons of Israel would see the face of Moses, that it had been glorified. And Moses would set a veil on his face until such time as he would go in to speak with Him" (LXX Exod 34:34). In essence, what was supposed to be a covenant relationship in which God physically resided with his people and led them to Canaan became, because of the sin of the people, an arrangement requiring a human mediator, a buffer between Israel and the divine—Moses.

The context of LXX Exod 34:29–35 helps explain specific vagaries of 2 Cor 3:7–18, including Paul's cryptic use of the verb *katargein* ("to nullify, to render inoperative") in 3:7, 11, 13, and 14. One common, modern interpretation sees the term as expressing the annulment of the Mosaic covenant in light of the new covenant in Christ. Some have read the phrase in 3:7 as "the glory . . . which was fading"—that is, they posit that Paul claims Moses veiled himself to hide the temporary nature of his glory and of the "old" covenant with Israel through the law. The interpretation also leads to a translation of 3:13 as "the end [*telos*] of what was fading away [*katargoumenou*]." Such a reading of Exod 34 would be unique to Paul among Jewish readers, since most ancient interpretations posited that Moses's lustrous complexion endured or even increased over his lifetime. In contrast to those readings seeing Paul as referring to a temporary or fading Mosaic glory, some recent interpretations note that most Pauline instances of *katargein* follow closely the word's basic semiotic meaning, "to render idle" or "to make ineffective," in the sense of "nullifying" the binding effects of a contract. In this rendering, focus shifts from the nullification of the actual glory on Moses's face to the nullification of the outcome of that glory. Namely, Moses's veil prevents the destruction that would befall the Israelites were they to gaze on the glory of God reflected in Moses's face. As God claims in Exod 33:3 and 5, the result of his presence among this sinful people would be their destruction. So, if we assume that such an interpretation of Exod 33–34 is behind Paul's argument, 2 Cor 3:13 should be read as "the goal [*telos*] of what was being nullified [*katargoumenou*]." Far from implying the "end" of the old covenant, this refers to the "goal" or "purpose" of the divine presence—the punishment of Israel—which is rendered ineffective by the veil.[26]

Close attention to the details of Exod 34 has reinforced a growing consensus concerning Paul's treatment of Moses as *diakonos* in this section. In 2 Cor

3:12–13, Paul asserts the "great boldness" characterizing his mission, a boldness not found in Moses: "we act . . . not like Moses, who set a veil on his face so that the Sons of Israel did not gaze upon the goal of what was being nullified. On the contrary, their thoughts were hardened" (3:12–14). While older readings interpreted Paul as disparaging Moses for concealing his glory, scholars increasingly note that, according to Exodus, Moses had to conceal his face for the sake of the very survival of his "stiff-necked," mind-hardened people. The subsequent verses (14b–18) enact this transferring of fault by placing the veil over the hearts and minds of Israel, both of old and of Paul's day. The veil is not due to deception on Moses's part, but to the demonstrated inability of Israel to receive God's message and presence.[27]

In this light, the metaphoric scope of the "courier" metaphor of 3:1–3 becomes clear, even in this late section of the chapter. As I discussed above, Philo implied in his life of Moses that Moses was a *diakonos* of the divine (*Mos.* 1.84). Many other Jewish texts similarly emphasized Moses's role as "messenger," "mediator," or "intercessor," specifically in connection with the golden calf scene. Thus, in *Mos.* 2.166, in response to God's anger over Israel's idolatry, Moses became a "mediator and reconciler" on the people's behalf. Likewise, in the first-century C.E. text known as the *Assumption of Moses* (preserved in Latin), the prophet's role as "great messenger" (*magnus nuntius;* 11.17) seems predicated on his intercessions in the wake of the golden calf incident. Furthermore, the text may imply that Moses's role extended beyond his death, remaining a heavenly and eschatological messenger between Israel and God. Similarly, a text found among the Dead Sea Scrolls (4Q377 2 ii 5–12) recounts Moses's post-calf intercessions from Exod 33; line 11 of the text states that when Moses was in the cloud with God, "he spoke like an angel through his mouth, for who was a messen[ger] [*bsr*] like him?"[28]

In what ways does Moses as messenger in Exod 34 highlight the epistolographic features evoked in Paul's letter of recommendation image? First, Moses bears not just a stone text, but, in the glory of his face, a reflection of the presence of the text's author—God. Recall that the major issue in the wake of the calf was how God could dwell in Israel's midst without destroying Israel. The apparent solution was that only Moses could be in God's presence, first on Sinai to receive the law a second time, and then subsequently in the tent of meeting outside the camp. Being in God's presence transferred God's "glory" onto Moses's face. Far superior to a courier doing a mere impression of a letter's author, Moses himself presents the true presence of the one who sent him. As 2 Cor 3:13–14 already indicates (having shifted the veil from Moses's face to Israel's heart), Paul is less interested in targeting Moses than the Israelites' inability to perceive or withstand the divine "glory" in his face.

In fact, Moses is a superior messenger, *like Paul*, fulfilling the communicative limit case established not just by ancient epistolographic practice and theory, but by a whole trajectory of Greco-Roman philosophical reflections on the nature of human communication. *Like Paul*, who bears the Corinthians as a "letter" of spirit "written" on his heart, Moses bore God's presence in his very complexion.

That Paul focuses on the Israelites' *reception* of Moses and the law brings us to the second feature of epistolographic practice that orients Paul's exposition of Exod 34. In ancient letter-writing conventions—particularly in the case of letters of introduction—the recipient was expected to receive the courier as a substitute for the letter writer's presence. In Paul's case, his recommendation was the very spirit of God borne in his heart, which, when accepted by the Corinthians, similarly dwelled among them and became the most effective recommendation imaginable: communication as a transferal of real presence. In contrast, because of their "stiff-necked" nature, the Israelites were unable to gaze upon Moses's divine glory—for them, experiencing the full effects of Moses's mission would truly have resulted in a "ministry of death." In this way, the Israelites did not (and, according to Paul, did not even in his day) receive the full effect of God's message—his very presence among them.

It is this sort of presence that texts such as Jer 38:31–33 envision—at least, in Paul's usage in 2 Cor 3:3 and 6 and thus in Paul's description of his mission and the Corinthians' reception of it. Already in 2 Cor 3:1–3, Paul depicts the Corinthians as fulfilling a communicative limit case by receiving and being a "letter" as the true presence of God. In light of the evocation of Exod 34, the notion of God's presence is recapitulated and reemphasized as Paul wraps up his scriptural exposition in 3:16–18: " 'But whenever he would turn to the Lord, the veil was removed' [Exod 34:34]. The Lord is spirit; and wherever the spirit of the Lord is, there is freedom. And all of us, with unveiled faces, gazing as if in a mirror at the glory of the Lord, are being transformed into that very image, from glory to glory, as from the spirit of the Lord." The three verses present numerous, well-known problems, all surrounding the enigmatic verse 17. I have little space here in which to build upon previous efforts to decipher it, but I will observe that Paul seems eager to solidify an equation between (on the one hand) the terms "glory" (*doxa*) and "Lord" (*kyrios*) from Exod 34 and (on the other) the "spirit" (*pneuma*) found in 2 Cor 3:1–6, on which his epistolary metaphor (and prophetic evocations) rely. That is, Paul wants to make clear that the *doxa* borne in Moses's complexion is, in effect, identical to the "spirit of the Lord" characterizing Paul's ministry. Paul emphasizes the equivalence again at the end of verse 18, in which he explains the statement "from glory to glory" (*apo doxēs eis doxan*) with the phrase "as from the spirit of the Lord" (*kyriou pneumatos*). Again, Paul claims that he and Moses both bore God's presence.

Paul's final expression of his spiritual ministry, however, surprisingly focuses on the spiritual status characterizing both his *and the Corinthians'* life in Christ. This inclusion is indicated by the emphatic *hēmeis pantes,* "we all," introducing verse 18. Paul includes the Corinthians with himself as a contemporary analogue to Moses's face-to-face relationship with God. In Christ, the Corinthian community experiences the situation originally envisioned at Sinai—they dwell in God's presence, bearing God's spirit within them. For Paul, the Corinthians themselves are a concrete instance of the communicative miracle enacted in the preaching of the gospel. In essence, Paul claims that his community in Corinth, through its spirit-filled existence, achieves the epistemological limit case that haunted Plato and Jeremiah alike.

Paul's use of travel and epistolography in 2 Cor 3 manipulates the Corinthians in other ways as well. Note, first of all, the contrasting pedagogical effect of Paul's two allusions to the exodus generation (and, specifically, the golden calf incident) in our surviving correspondence to the Corinthians: 1 Cor 10:1–12 and 2 Cor 3:7–18. First Corinthians 10 employs the "example" of the exodus generation as a warning lest the Corinthians repeat the mistakes of the exodus (as is made explicit in vv. 7–14). In contrast, Paul's use of Exod 34 in 2 Cor 3 serves both as a personal defense of his apostleship and as praise, even flattery, of the Corinthians' new and miraculous status in Christ. Here Paul employs flattery in the service of apologia, as he does so often in this letter.

In fact, in 2 Cor 3, Paul exploits the subservience connoted in his lifestyle and appearance by momentarily situating himself as socially dependent upon the Corinthians. Paul's letter metaphor in verses 1–3 almost defies neat and orderly interpretation, as the Corinthians are figured as letter, letter recipient, and letter sender. The ambiguity is both the strength and the weakness of the image, as it speaks to the impossible wish for the hypostatization of communication itself. But insofar as the Corinthians are depicted as receivers and sources of Paul's recommendation and introduction, they are likewise depicted as parties in a social transaction with God over the services of Paul the apostle. God offers and commends the services of his *diakonos* to those who will receive him—that is, who will accommodate Paul, though a servant, as an authorized representative of the one who sent him. Though it may be an exaggeration to say that the Corinthians and God are pictured as "social" equals here, to say that the notion of the Corinthians recommending Paul to "all men" envisions a situation in which the Corinthians are in a position of patronage to Paul as apostolic client in no way stretches the force of Paul's metaphor.

Paul's depiction of the Corinthian community as a "letter of recommendation," insofar as they have accepted God's spirit through Paul's preaching, and his favorable comparison of them as superior to their Israelite forebears and contemporaries, serves Paul's overall purpose of defending and defining his apostleship within the frame of his itinerancy. As an entrance into Paul's scriptural argument, his "citation" of conventions of letter delivery grounds the notion of receiving God's spirit in a quotidian practice while simultaneously calling to mind profound and prevalent concerns about communication and authenticity. Paul deploys suspicions over his traveling lifestyle and his physical distance from the Corinthians to exploit anxieties over the epistemological distance between human intention and the wandering nature of human language. Paul's assurance that he and the Corinthians bear the same divine spirit, and that he proclaims this fact wherever he goes (that is, that he carries the Corinthians around like a letter of recommendation), emphasizes that they are present with him on his journeys, filling the crucial role of recommending his mission to all people. Paul intensifies the common epistolary motif of *parousia,* of presence despite absence. By 2 Cor 3:18, Paul has pictured himself and the Corinthians jointly standing in God's presence; though these Gentile sinners (along with the apostle to the Gentiles) are outside the camp of Israel, they have gathered in the tent of meeting to be transformed into an image of God's glory.

Theoretical discussions of performativity as "citationality" emphasize the ability of language to have social force by showing how it can either affirm or challenge existing conventions and subject positions. Paul's juxtaposed citations of quotidian epistolographic practices and scriptural anxiety over God's presence among God's people similarly function to strengthen and define a new community of Gentiles paradoxically possessing the spirit of the God of Israel in their hearts, language that, by describing a situation, seeks to enact that situation as a reality. From Paul's Jewish point of view, the existence of the Corinthian community is an instance of God's presence among those to whom he had been radically absent. The "law written on the heart" predicted by Jeremiah has been inscribed within a people not God's own. Those outside the camp have received spirit without the law, the spirit *as* law.

In other contexts, Paul makes clear the effects of the gift of the law to those previously excluded with extensive (though various) use of the term *katargein,* "to nullify" or "render ineffective," employed four times in the passage just treated. In his recent work on Paul, philosopher Giorgio Agamben has focused on Paul's use of this term, relating it to the Roman notion of the *iustitium,* the "state of emergency," understood as the genealogical forerunner to the various types of emergency laws enacted by modern states. The parallels between Paul's cryptic language concerning Christ and the law, on the one hand, and the behavior prescribed under states of exception, on the other, are mutually illuminating. In a state of exception, the totality of the law (the constitution—that is, that which "constitutes" the state) is nullified so that the state might be preserved in the face of some emergency. To understand this figure, imagine the Roman Senate calling on all citizens to take whatever means necessary to save the state. Such a condition grants upon every citizen, even the lowest of status, ultimate power to defend society, even through acts otherwise in violation of the state's founding precepts, its laws. Thus, constitutive law is revoked in order to be fulfilled.[29]

For Paul, God enacts the revocation of his law by granting his spirit to those outside the law, granting blessing for those who were once a curse and creating a new people, a "remnant" united by faith, both Jew and non-Jew. "The remnant is an exception taken to its extreme," writes Agamben, "pushed to its paradoxical formulation. In his rendering of the messianic condition of the believer, Paul radicalizes the condition of the state of exception, whereby law is applied in disapplying itself, no longer having an inside and an outside. With regard to this law that applies itself in disapplying itself, a corresponding gesture of faith ensues, applying itself in disapplying itself, rendering law inoperative while carrying it to its fulfillment."[30] Agamben's meditations on the state of exception, inspired in part by Paul's writings, constitute an example of the general phenomenon of the logics of exception so prevalent in recent work in social and critical theory. Just as the state of exception fulfills law by revoking its specific precepts, the strategic antagonisms erected by the articulation of floating signifiers (according to Laclau) fulfill popular aspirations excluded by hegemonic regimes, and performativity—in both speech and action—isolates and enacts ideas, wordings, and practices from oppressive discourses in order to call into question, even suspend, dominant regimes of knowledge and social control.

In each case, however, the logics of exclusion function only insofar as they cite, evoke, parody, or otherwise play off of tropes within the dominant discourse. Even the most hardened antagonism or most global critique strategically deploys ideological motifs in order to subvert the ruling ideology. For Paul, the law regulated the life of the chosen people; paradoxically, its suspension through Gentile reception of God's spirit made it all the more pressing and relevant. Similarly, the act of God in Christ nullified all ruling assumptions: "We speak wisdom to the mature, but not the wisdom of this age, nor that of the rulers of this age, who are being nullified" (*katargoumenōn;* 1 Cor 2:6). Paul's (almost hidden) promise of the nullification of Rome promises an alter-empire of God fulfilling the aspirations of its subjects. In such a project, rhetorics of exclusion are contingent and strategic; all make reference to existing paradigms despite assertions and appearances to the contrary. Existing cultural hegemonies are worn paths from which the deviations of the wandering signifier are mapped and understood.

5

Whether Home or Away

At the beginning of 2 Cor 4, Paul recapitulates many of the themes and images strung together since the "led in triumph" passage at the beginning of 2:14–17. He describes his *diakonia* (4:1) as being "veiled" only to "perishing unbelievers" (4:3; for language of veiling, see 3:13–18; for Paul's message as having a distinct message for those perishing, see 2:15–16). He goes on to describe the "light of the knowledge of the glory of God" (4:6) by claiming that "we have this treasure in clay jars," referring, with a processional metaphor recalling the imagery of 2:14–17, to the glory paradoxically contained in his paltry body and lifestyle. In epiphany processions, cult objects and fragrances were contained in such vessels, which were far more cheap and breakable than their precious contents. In general, 2 Cor 4 unites the wandering paths of Paul's imagistic rhetoric into a more orderly and festive march. For example, in the section, travel and death, heretofore merely juxtaposed, are explicitly linked: "In every case, we are afflicted but not crushed; distressed but not despaired; pursued but not left abandoned; attacked but not destroyed; always carrying around [*peripherontes*] the death of Jesus in our body so that even the life of Jesus might be made manifest [*phanerōthēi*] in our mortal flesh. For we who are living are always being handed over to death for Jesus's sake, so that even the life of Jesus might be made manifest [*phanerōthēi*] in our mortal flesh. So death is operative [*energeitai*] in us, but life in you" (4:8–12). I briefly discussed this passage in the introduction, but a second visit can profit from my analysis in the study thus far. For example, we can now appreciate how processional motifs continue to stride in the foreground. Life is "made manifest" like the presence of the deity in an epiphany ritual. The dual use of words for "always" (*pantote* and *aei*) again recalls the eternal triumph of Augustus, as did the *pantote* of 2:14. Most crucial for our purposes is the assertion in 4:10 that Paul always carries around the death of Jesus. Here also, the verb *peripherein* recalls processions, especially funerals; the nominal form, *periphoros*, means "pallbearer," and the burden, here, of the "death of Jesus" only reinforces that impression. Here, Jesus's dead body is both mourned corpse and sacred cult object.[1]

Yet *peripherein* conveys a wide semantic range depending on context. It can mean the circumference of a circle in geometry or any type of enclosure in architecture—to employ the English loan word, the "periphery" of any area. And if the motion to which it refers is geographically broad enough, it can mean travel.[2] Some readers, seeking a more material referent for the image, have wondered whether Paul has in mind his evangelical wanderings. In the context of the present study of the prevalence of travel metaphors in the letter, it seems without doubt that Paul once again reframes his travels for Christ with the image of the journey. Here, he draws a direct connection between the suffering nature of his traveling lifestyle and the death suffered by Jesus.

In making such a link, Paul is in good company among the various traditions of the early Jesus movement. In the earliest extant gospel, Mark, Jesus asserts: "If anyone wants to follow after me, let him deny himself and take up his cross, and let him follow me" (8:34). Matthew and Luke, who used Mark as a direct literary source, copy Mark's statement but also add a separate version from their other common source, a lost collection of Jesus's sayings that scholars call "Q." Matthew includes it in Jesus's lengthy commissioning of the twelve disciples to go out to "the lost sheep of the House of Israel": "And he who does not take up his cross and follow after me is not worthy of me" (10:38). Luke (14:27) frames it as a quick statement to the large crowds following Jesus, perhaps to make sure they knew what they were getting into. Even the noncanonical *Gospel of Thomas* (55) contains a version of the saying. In each case, travel is put forth as a performative interpretation of the meaning of the crucifixion. Or to put it another way: in citing the crucifixion, itinerant proclaimers of the Jesus movement cast their form of life as cruciform in that it filled self-sacrificing and restorative functions. Paul is no exception to the general trend within the international community, but the ways in which he deploys the travel-death connection are unique to his circumstances. For as we have seen, Paul must assert his self-emptying as well as his status. His shameful lifestyle must be given as paradoxical proof of his divine commission. Paul posits a common denominator between travel and death through the rhetorical logic of exclusion that governs the letter.

The logic of exclusion joining wandering and death is nowhere clearer than when Paul again links the two in 2 Cor 4:16–5:10, in which he casts life and death as journeys. The passage draws heavily on the language of philosophical consolation over death (discussed in Chapter 1) in such a condensed and complex way that I treat the passage in three sections, quoting each section in full at the outset. I read Paul as entering into a self-consolatory discourse (of the type discussed in Chapter 2 with reference to ancient self-killing) that simultaneously appropriates ancient motifs concerning travel and death while dissociating himself from other aspects of the discourse. Specifically, Paul raises a dualistic anthropological framework through the Platonic motifs of the "inner and outer" human being and a "body-as-tent" metaphor. For ancient sages, meditation upon the postmortem separation of the soul from the body provided comfort and resolve in the face of all tribulations, including one's final departure. With each traditional trope he raises, however, Paul subsequently effaces the distinction between soul and body, insinuating aspects of the type of eschatological transformation schema we see in other Pauline passages, especially 1 Cor 15. The effacement of dualism leads to a valuing of earthly suffering as the decisive force in activating not only personal, eschatological glory, but also the social spread of Christ's spirit through the growth of Pauline communities. For Paul, eschatological transformation and the importance of earthly suffering result in an ambivalence toward the true "home" of life in Christ, an ambivalence that, in turn, implies Paul's desire to be reunited with the Corinthians. Paul's language performs all this rhetorical work by inhabiting an outsider position of doubly exiled consoler, a traveler outside the realm of society and an as-good-as-dead sufferer. As he does numerous times earlier in the letter, Paul evokes a genre or system of thought in order to exempt himself from its sphere, distancing himself from its tropes in order to fashion a unique self-definition. Having shown that he can master the center of a discursive tradition, he disidentifies with it, preferring the margins with regard to all social regimes. Paul foregoes the solace and status of consolation in order to continue on his lonely exile from humanity and God, though with the sure hope of a blessed homecoming.

Travel and Death in 2 Cor 4:16–5:10

4:16–18—ANTHROPOLOGICAL DIVISION AND MUTUAL TRANSFORMATION

Therefore, we do not lose heart. On the contrary, even if our outer person is decaying, our inner person is being renewed day by day. For the temporary lightness of our affliction activates in us to a surpassingly exceeding degree an eternal weight of glory, since we do not set our sights on things seen but things unseen; for things seen are temporary, but things unseen are eternal.

Paul begins the section with a dichotomy between the "outer" and "inner" person (*exō* and *esō anthrōpos*), establishing, at least on the surface, a dualistic anthropology (with language almost certainly of Platonic origin) at odds with Paul's statements in other letters. On this point, we should take seriously the notion that he is less interested in expounding propositional anthropologies than in forming his audience's understanding of his character. As I will argue, Paul periodically effaces the dualism implied by dualistic language, insinuating instead a transformative eschatology. Moreover, the rhetorical strategy of the passage operates by raising notions of dualism and disdain for earthly vicissitudes only to reject such schemes in favor of the importance of a transforming and transformed suffering.[3]

As mentioned in Chapter 1, the distinction between soul and body was indispensable in philosophical discussions of death and dying, especially within the consolatory tradition. In the *Phaedo,* Plato has Socrates defend his "hope" concerning his fate with a discussion of the nature of the soul in relation to the body (66B–67C). More explicitly, Cicero claims that if one could achieve certainty about the composition of the soul and its relation to its corporal shell, the problem of death would be solved. And even though attainment of certainty is doubtful, meditation upon the soul's nature stands at the center of consolatory rationalizations (*Tusc.* 1.11.23–24). Since the finality of death and decay of the body seem to argue against life after death, imaginative construals of an enduring human existence understandably pictured the existence of the soul separate from its material remains. This was the default language of death and its consolation regardless of specific anthropological schemata. Just because Paul employs the language of anthropological dualism, then, does not on its own convey a definite anthropology. What we can see, however, is that Paul exploits dualistic language in order to negotiate a transition between two passages—one concerning hidden glory despite manifest ignominy, the other an exposition of the proper attitude in the face of death in the ancient tradition of self-consolation. The simple language of "inner and outer" human beings, when considered in the context of ancient discourses, is generic and general—though simultaneously a fitting figure within the Pauline passage. "Outer" and "inner" convey the notions of "ostensible" and "actual" glory that dominated 4:1–15 (a theme that continues in the language of "things seen and unseen" in 4:18) while preparing for the dualistic language generically required by the discussion of death and dying in 5:1–10.[4]

Despite the implied dualism, however, hints of a more familiarly Pauline eschatology and anthropology emerge in 4:16–18. Specifically, the language of transformation found here differs from the language of separation of soul from body found in most consolations. Paul speaks in verse 6 of the "day-by-day renewing" of the inner person despite the outer person's "decaying." Especially significant is verses 17–18a, in which Paul describes how "the temporary lightness of affliction activates in us to a surpassingly exceeding degree an eternal weight of glory, since we do not set our sights on things seen but things unseen." Two major points should be made about this important sentence. First, many of its elements mirror aspects of the *consolatio mortis* tradition, especially the notion of being more mindful of heavenly things (comparable to Paul's "things unseen") than earthly, as well as the process instigated by a heavenly focus, preparing the soul for its heavenly, postmortem destination (see, for example, Plato, *Phaed.* 80D–81D). The main difference between Plato and Paul, however, is that Paul describes the process as a physical *transformation*, not a gradual *separating* of the soul from the body. The notion of eschatological renewal matches the schema of 1 Cor 15 and underlies much of the language throughout our present passage.

Second, Paul's depiction of his travels serves as the basis for the formulation in verses 17–18a. The process of renewal described here is one that occurs during Paul's lifetime (as he says, "day by day"). Moreover, the verbal marker in the phrase "the temporary lightness [*elaphron*] of affliction" recalls the description of Paul's changeable travel plans as a possible instance of acting with *elaphria* ("lightness" or "vacillation") in 1:17, the only other instance of the *elaphr*-root in the Pauline corpus. The combination of the term with the notion of "affliction" is made possible by the close connection between travel and suffering in ancient discourses, a connection Paul evokes as early as 2 Cor 1. At the very least, the "affliction" to which he refers here reflects back on the recent discussion of suffering in 4:1–15 (especially to the recapitulation of the processional motifs in 4:7 and 10–11, which associate his travels with Christlike suffering on behalf of the proclamation of the gospel), if not to similar discussions in preceding sections of the letter. Such sufferings were products of Paul's itinerant, apostolic activity.

We should also take into account Paul's expression of the abundance of glory produced by his suffering travels, especially in light of the importance of the social logic of semantic abundance informing recent theories of social change. The glory produced by Paul's *personal* sufferings is a *communal* glory, that is, a glory exceeding Paul's own person insofar as it results in the increase of the communities he founds. Paul himself emphasizes this abundance with the odd and awkward repetition *kath' hyperbolēn eis hyperbolēn* (that is, the "surpassingly exceeding degree" to which glory outweighs suffering) in verse 17. The complex phrase can be explained if we remember the social function of "glory" in 2 Cor 3 and 4. Paul receives glory from God only to pass it on to the communities he founds, including the Corinthians. One could say that the transferal of glory, roughly synonymous with *pneuma,* or "spirit," constitutes a physical description of the founding of Pauline communities. Throughout the letter, the notion of "excess" characterizes the pneumatic transfer that, for Paul, enables the social spread of his movement. In other words, communal glory surpasses the personal, apostolic suffering that produces it. While the language of anthropological dualism and transformation prepares for Paul's appropriation of the ancient discourse of self-consolation, his specific formulations always keep his travels and the social spread of his movement in the near background.

5:1–5—EARTHLY SOJOURN AND HEAVENLY ABODE

For we know that if our earthly tent of a home is destroyed, we have a building from God, an eternal house in the heavens not made by hands. For even in this we groan, yearning to clothe ourselves over with our dwelling from heaven (for if it is indeed true that, once we have been so clothed,[5] we will not be found naked). For even we who are in a tent groan because we are weighed down, for which reason we do not want to be unclothed but clothed over, so that mortality might be swallowed by life. And the one who activates us for this very purpose is God, who gives to us the down payment of the spirit.

In 2 Cor 5:1–5, Paul continues his strategy of raising and effacing a dualistic view of the human being by adopting further the language of consolatory literature, though his mixed metaphors and strange wordings have weighed down not a few scholars. In attempting to escape the exegetical quagmires of the passage, I argue that Paul dissociates himself from the philosophical, consolatory attitude that the vicissitudes of earthly life are to be despised and abandoned. Paul's exclusions of consolatory logics, however, have wide-ranging effects for both his eschatological beliefs and his social strategy for his communities.

Paul continues to assert his "knowledge" concerning his present life and his postmortem fate through a dualistic figure strongly evoking the consolatory tradition of death as travel. "We know that if our earthly tent of a home is destroyed, we have a building from God, an eternal house in the heavens not made by hands" (5:1). Commentators have long noted relevant parallels among Pythagorean and Platonic texts, especially similar descriptions of the body as a paltry tent in Ps.-Plato, *Ax.* 365E–366A, cited in Chapter 1, in which the *skēnos,* or "tent," of the body is "not the human person." The true person is trapped in such a tent and prison that "nature has fashioned . . . for suffering." In its figurative usage for the human body, a tent connotes temporariness and fragility. Much like the "clay jars" in 4:7—the apostolic body bearing God's pneumatic glory—the "tent of a house" is fragile and cheap, yet for that reason highly portable. The temporary nature of a tent well expresses a common philosophical attitude toward the sufferings attending travel. As a contrast to his earthly tent, Paul presents a heavenly dwelling, a "building" or "edifice" prepared for and assigned to Paul so assuredly that he can speak of it as a present possession.[6]

Once again, the notion of two homes raises the possibility of anthropological dualism. The tent imagery understood in the context of Greco-Roman usage would normally imply the soul's ability to separate from the paltry, tentlike body. A close reading reveals, however, that Paul nowhere explicitly describes such a dualism and only hints at the idea of separation in verses 3–4. So when compared with other ancient authors who describe life in the body as a temporary sojourn, Paul's description of two "homes" here may add a note of ambivalence with regard to which mode of existence is truly "home." Such ambivalence characterizes the discussion of life and death throughout the passage. Moreover, his shift to clothing imagery in the following verses implies a clear ideological preference for an eschatological model of bodily transformation, the type of scheme he describes elsewhere. Paul's ambivalence represents a distancing from the dualism and contempt for earthly life normally found in consolatory literature. Instead, Paul asserts that the sufferings experienced in his paltry tent of a body will result in transformation to a heavenly body.

As mentioned above, 2 Cor 5:2–4 confusingly exchanges the sojourn/home imagery for clothing imagery. Again, we can read Paul as replacing dualism with corporal transformation. Paul reiterates that his focus is on his heavenly destination: "in this [tent] we groan, yearning to clothe ourselves over with our dwelling from heaven." The image of putting on one "dwelling" or body over another expresses transformation, and Paul specifies his meaning in the next verse: "if it is indeed true that, once we have been so clothed, we will not be found naked." Paul's reference to nakedness has been variously interpreted. In light of the confluence of consolatory topoi in the passage, it is highly likely that the figure has to do with the "nakedness" attributed to the soul in postmortem judgment as described in Plato and recurring throughout the consolatory tradition.[7] In the ancient construal, the stripping bare of the soul divests each individual of the earthly status markers obfuscating a person's virtue. Similarly, though Paul asserts his focus on "things unseen" (4:18), he has spent much of 2 Cor 4 claiming that his external sufferings and ostensible lifestyle themselves enact the present process of glorification, affecting not only his own soul, but the social spread of the Jesus movement. To strip away the bodily marks of Paul's apostolic activity would seem to violate his logic of judgment, since physical evidence of his suffering will be a central criterion. Paul's claim that "once we have been so clothed, we will not be found naked" seems far less mundane when read in contradistinction to myths of the otherworldly court appearance of the naked soul, myths rejecting the significance of visible, ostensible aspects of a person's life. Verse 3 represents Paul's quick appropriation and reevaluation of a well-known understanding of divine judgment in order to assert his own formulation.

Paul attempts to clarify his appropriation and alteration of the language of dualism in verse 4. Just as I have read the preceding verses as adopting and adapting the dualism that characterized philosophical consolation, I also tend to take verse 4 in this vein. Moreover, verse 4a recalls the internal afflictions described in 2 Cor 4 (as well as in 1:8–11, which also uses language of being "weighed down") in the face of death and eschatological judgment. As I argued in Chapter 2, Paul depicts himself as contemplating suicide in 1:8–11 in the face of potential failure in Corinth. With the prospect of the dissolution of his relationship with the Corinthian community, Paul rhetorically ponders the option of self-killing, the method of escaping punishment so in vogue among his upper-class contemporaries. Yet Paul rejects the option for three reasons: he decides to place his trust in "the God who raises the dead" (1:9), he asserts his blamelessness with regard to the Corinthians (1:12), and he notes the inescapability of eschatological judgment (1:13b–14). Paul's reflections on death in 2 Cor 4:16–5:10 similarly focus on judgment. His view of the final trial in part guides his correction of consolatory dualism; because Paul's success as an apostle depends upon his travels and suffering on behalf of his community, the physical evidence of his work endures through death until his appearance before Christ as judge. Thus, I read 5:4 as specifying again why Paul as apostle is and must be so "weighed down" by affliction: "For even we who are in a tent groan because we are weighed down, because we do not want to be unclothed but clothed over." That is, Paul again specifies that, rather than despise his earthly sufferings, he endures them and counts them as significant insofar as they will provide the proof of his successes as apostle and result in the eschatological reward of a pneumatic "overcoat"—that is, as he states more literally in verse 4c, "so that mortality might be swallowed by life."[8]

Perhaps Paul suspected (or knew for a fact) that he was up against the same dualistic assumptions that once prompted some Corinthian followers to ask: "How are the dead raised? With what kind of body do they come?" (1 Cor 15:35). In any case, it seems as if Paul's anthropology and eschatology (and his efforts to clarify them) were driven by ethical concerns, such as asserting his understanding of apostolic existence in Christ, especially with respect to eschatological judgment. The point seemed important enough to Paul that he temporarily (in vv. 2–4) exchanged travel imagery for clothing imagery.

Indeed, we again see Paul enter the realm of consolatory literature when he briefly interrupts his strategy by inserting yet another common, consolatory topos in 5:5—that of life construed in economic terms. Writers of consolation would often rationalize their situations with the help of the following metaphor: life is but a loan from God, so do not be surprised when God asks you to pay it back. After all, God does not even charge interest! In 2 Cor 5:5, in contrast, spiritual life in Christ is made possible when God "gives to us the down payment of the spirit" (*ton arrabōna tou pneumatos;* evocations of 2 Cor 1 continue, as *arrabōna* occurs only here and in 1:22 among the undisputed Pauline correspondence). The "down payment" initiates a process by which Paul's spiritual wealth, as it were, abounds with life and glory (with a view toward the social spread of the gospel) finalized when "God activates" (*katergasamenos*) the final somatic transformation.

To summarize: in 2 Cor 5:1–5, Paul emphasizes that his suspicious, suffering, wandering behavior paradoxically enacts a process whereby his inner, spiritual nature overflows into the communities he founds and, moreover, begins a process whereby he will be rewarded with physical transformation at the eschaton. Paul initiates his assertions using travel imagery, but his rejection of dualism causes him to drop "housing" and "travel" imagery for a complex clothing metaphor as well as the economic construal of the spirit as "down payment." Having dispensed with his adaptation of dualist anthropology, he returns to travel imagery in 5:5–10 and his ambivalence about where his "home" truly is.

5:6–10—AT HOME OR AWAY

So, being of good courage at all times and knowing that when we are at home [*endēmountes*] in our body we are away from our home [*ekdēmoumen*] with the Lord (since we walk by faith, not by sight)—in any case, we are of good courage and would much prefer to leave our home in the body and be at home with the Lord. For this reason, we strive, whether at home or away [*eite endēmountes eite ekdēmountes*], to be pleasing to him. For all of us must appear before the judgment seat of Christ, so that each might be repaid for the things he did through his body, whether good or bad.

Paul begins his return to travel imagery in verse 6 with an assertion of "being of good courage at all times" (*pantote*). In earlier parts of the letter, the notion of what Paul does "always" or "continually" usually has some relation to his wandering activity. Within the context of explicit travel imagery, the *pantote* of verse 6 should be no exception. The verse continues with a second participial construction (one that attaches to no main clause): "knowing that when we are at home [*endēmountes*] in our body we are away from our home [*ekdēmoumen*] with the Lord." The notion of life as an exile from a true, heavenly home was common among consolations on both death and literal exile, as I have discussed. To speak, however, of being "in the body" as "being at home" (*endēmein*) seems too positive for a discourse on death. True, writers on exile might assert that a wise man should be content and self-sufficient despite the travails of being abroad (or, more generally, the vicissitudes of life itself). But self-sufficiency would rarely be expressed through the knowledge of being away from heaven. On the contrary, a consoler would recommend that contentment is derived from focusing on one's true, divine home. Here, Paul juxtaposes two consolatory topoi—death as a journey from an earthly home and life as an exile from a heavenly home—in such a tight space that the borders between them begin to blur.[9]

The adoption of consolatory language again threatens to import anthropological dualism, implying that death would be a departure *from* the body. With respect to this verse, Manuel Vogel has put forth that Paul adopts language of dualism to take advantage of its ethicizing component—namely, the sense of the wisdom and bravery of distancing oneself from earthly life. There is much to commend this reading as a basic component not just of verse 6, but of the passage 4:16–5:10 as a whole. The following verse (which, in the context of the anacolouthon of v. 6, should be rendered as parenthetical) reinforces the precept that the wise person hopes in a return to a heavenly home in the face of the fact of death, or that "we walk by faith, not by sight" (v. 7), a verse recalling Paul's focus on "things unseen" in 4:18. Throughout the passage, Paul appropriates the ethicizing rhetoric of distancing oneself from life found not only in the consolatory tradition, but, as Vogel shows, throughout various types and eras of Greco-Roman literature.[10]

One wonders, however, why Paul would reinsert dualistic language after carefully rejecting dualistic schemata in verses 1–5. An answer could be found in the juxtaposition and blurring of "home" language for both earthly and heavenly life. Within the space of eight words in verse 6bc, Paul refers to both his earthly body and postmortem existence with the Lord as "home." The categories are further blurred in the resumption at verse 8, in which Paul *switches* terminology: "we would much prefer to leave our home in the body and be at home with the Lord." As noted above (and as emphasized by Vogel with respect to verses 6–8), many ancient writers explained that while the wise man longs to leave the tribulations of life and constantly sets his eyes on heavenly matters, he devotes his concentration to enacting virtue on earth. Paul appropriates this idea along with the dualistic system it evokes. Since Paul asserts his "faith" that God will glorify him after death, he "would prefer" or even "resolves" to leave his bodily home, a resolution tempered by the claim in verse 9, that "we strive . . . to be pleasing to him [God]." As in 1:8–11, Paul states that, though self-killing might seem a preferable option, he continues his earthly journeys on behalf of the gospel.[11]

The participial constructions modifying the ethical assertion in verse 9, however, further blur the travel motifs appropriated from the *consolatio mortis* tradition. As noted above, Paul plays with the notions of life as exile and death as journey by switching the positions of *endēmein* and *ekdēmein* in verses 6 and 8. In verse 9, Paul collapses any distinction between the two terms with the construction *eite endēmountes eite ekdēmountes*, "whether at home or away," completely dropping prepositional specifications such as "in/ away from the body" or "away from/with the Lord." Though in verse 8 Paul acknowledges the attractiveness of abandoning the body to join the Lord, in verse 9 he seems to dismiss the importance of the categories altogether. The most obvious exegetical recourse is to interpret the strategic blurring of these categories in light of Paul's subtle rejection of anthropological dualism in 5:1–4. For Paul, the contempt for earthly life and the yearning for death are ultimately unproductive.[12]

To see in more detail that Paul, in verse 9, rejects or blurs the dualism normally implied by consolatory travel motifs, we should examine his past experiences with assertions of dualism among the Corinthians. For example, in response to the query in 1 Cor 15:35, "How are the dead raised? With what kind of body do they come?," Paul immediately exclaims, "Fool!" (*aphrōn;* v. 36). A more striking verbal parallel appears in the letter preserved in 2 Cor 10–13 in the context of the so-called fool's speech, in which Paul confronts the evaluative criteria of some in Corinth—namely, those who see strength and authenticity solely in terms of transparent, spiritual power. When Paul turns to an ironic, third-person account of his own mystical experiences of ascending to heaven, he mocks the anthropological speculation that tended to adhere to such narratives: "I know a man in Christ who, fourteen years ago (whether in the body I do not know, or apart from the body, I do not know—God knows [*eite en sōmati ouk oida, eite ektos tou sōmatos ouk oida, ho theos oiden*]), such a man was snatched up into the third heaven. And I know that this same man (whether in the body or apart from the body I do not know—God knows [*eite en sōmati eite chōris tou sōmatos ouk oida, ho theos oiden*]) was snatched up into paradise" (2 Cor 12:2–4). Though Paul does not speak here about death, he treats a related issue, an ascent to heaven, often depicted in ancient literature as a foretaste of postmortem glory. (See such ascents as Enoch's in *1 En.* 1–36 or in the "Scipio's Dream" portion at the conclusion of Cicero's *De Republica*.) When Paul discusses heavenly journeys, many of the elements of his discussion of death in 2 Cor 5:6–9 are foreshadowed: the issue of remaining in the body or leaving it, an anacolouton breaking the syntax (in v. 2, rendered partially in my translation as a parenthetical), unnecessary repetition of relevant terms and concepts, and a "whether-or" (*eite-eite*) construction suggesting indifference. In each passage, Paul rhetorically dismisses dualistic conceptions since, in his experience, he associated dualism with those who would eschew the often grueling work of the gospel for the quick attainment of spiritual glory. Just as he accused the Corinthians of being fools in 1 Cor 15:36, Paul claims that, with his enumeration of sufferings and glories in the gospel in 2 Cor 11:16–12:13, he similarly speaks as a "fool" (*aphrona*). Paul blames the Corinthians' dualistic construction of the body, an anthropology and ethic he deems "foolish," for their desire for immediate glory. The main difference in 2 Cor 5 is that, in the interests of preserving their newly repaired relationship, Paul refrains from explicitly calling them "fools." Instead, in keeping with the tone of the letter thus far, Paul's language more likely flatters the Corinthians than rebukes them. Rather than chastise them for their dualistic conceptions and resulting errant ethic, Paul subtly appropriates and reshapes their expectations of Paul as apostle.

As he does so often throughout the Corinthian correspondence, Paul frames old information with a new rhetorical strategy. My thesis has been that he chooses travel plans as an overarching epistolary situation because, as a motif, travel encompasses all that seemed suspicious and ignominious about his quasi-exilic life yet still bears sufficient polysemy to provide fuel for a reconstruction of his image. In the case of the passage in 2 Cor 4:16–5:10, travel motifs allow Paul to revisit the mistaken assumption that suffering and leadership are incompatible through the consolatory connection between travel and death. Ancient authors who fashioned self-consolation in the face of exile and dying effectively removed themselves from the fear naturally associated with earthly vicissitudes. They took an outsider position of self-mastery with regard to the social shame surrounding tribulation. Through rational arguments and plausible (though often mythic or metaphorical) depictions of fate, they achieved the necessary rhetorical distance to redefine their situations. Death and exile are merely journeys. Life in society is the true evil. Any departure from it is good. Similarly, in 4:16–5:10, Paul asserts that death will be a transformation figured as a migration.

Yet Paul declines to claim either state—earthly or heavenly—as home. In light of the letter's travel frame and the implicit claim that his travels primarily characterize his work for the gospel, Paul *cannot* claim a true home. Or rather, he devises the ironic statement of verse 9—"we strive, whether at home or away, to be pleasing to [God]." The sentence describes not only the state of his soul with regard to death, but also his wandering and suffering lifestyle as apostle. As a near-exile, Paul's only true home *is* his own body, as other exiled authors similarly claimed. The double assertion of his social and ontological homelessness fits his transformational eschatology, insofar as his afflictions gradually begin the process of his glorification during his lifetime. Paul's apostolic wandering is the earthly portion of a journey back to God. In order to reach his heavenly home with the Lord he must temporarily cling to his bodily home, wherever he may be. His only hope of a true homecoming is to remain "pleasing" to God until the day of judgment. As Paul reminds his readers, this is a universal, not just an apostolic, necessity: "For all of us must appear before the judgment seat of Christ, so that each might be repaid for the things he did through his body, whether good or bad."[13]

By appropriating and manipulating the language of consolations over death and exile, Paul defends his apostolic lifestyle by taking over a well-known outsider position while shifting the position to fit his own conception of ethics and authenticity. He does not content himself to occupy the role of sagacious, self-consoling outsider but proceeds to step outside of the well-defined persona to create a new position even *outside* the outsiders. Paul's specific adaptations to the consolatory tradition fashion a new role of leader-as-social-outsider: the apostle. By depicting himself as radically peripheral to normative ideologies, Paul claims a vantage point from which to arrange a new society.

We cannot leave this passage until we note one more rhetorical resonance: in verse 8, Paul asserts that he would prefer to travel "home" to the Lord but accepts that he must "be pleasing to the Lord" through his wanderings and sufferings. The verbal and conceptual parallels between 4:18–5:10 and 1:8–22, however, allow the reader to recall what he has set as the ultimate goal of his current journey—Corinth. Just as Paul yearns throughout life to journey home to God, he similarly expresses regret that he could not travel directly to Corinth and is instead sidetracked in Macedonia (1:15–16, 2:12–13), though only because he wishes to cause the Corinthians joy instead of pain (1:23–2:11) and was eager to learn from Titus the state of his relationship with them before visiting in person (as later revealed in 7:5–8). In effect, the linguistic parallels between 2 Cor 1 and 5 establish parallel goals. Despite his desire to be back in Corinth, Paul must set his travel plans in whatever way best pleases God. Through his clever appropriation of travel motifs in 5:6–10,

Paul once again implies that, despite his seemingly vacillating travels, he keeps a special focus on the Corinthian community. Though he ultimately would prefer his promised dwelling with God, he presently yearns for his "home" in Corinth.

As a subtext to Paul's manipulation of common travel motifs, I have also traced thus far through my reading of 2 Cor 1–9 Paul's flattering of the Corinthian community in the interests of further mending his relationship with them. The theme of judgment with which the preceding passage ends, however, leads Paul to target the Corinthians' behavior and attitude in the following sections, since the mention of the final trial may lead them to consider more closely their standing before God. From 2 Cor 4:16–5:10, Paul continues: "So, knowing the fear of the Lord, we persuade men, but we are always clearly in the sight [*pephanerōmetha*] of God. I hope that we are also always clearly in the sight [*pephanerōsthai*] of your consciences" (5:11). Having dropped the consolatory motifs of 4:16–5:10, Paul begins in 5:11 to address the Corinthians more directly.

So, as in 3:1, he rejects the notion of "commending ourselves to you again" (5:12). Since he is already well-known to them, he should have no need of reintroduction. On the contrary, by this time, the Corinthians should be able to commend and defend him. Immediately after dismissing the need for reintroductions, Paul returns to language that (one could imagine) may mirror his initial and fundamental message. Stripping away the consolatory motifs, he discusses the relationship between apostleship and death in light of the central event of the death of Christ:

> If we appear a little crazy, it is for God; if we appear reasonable, it is for you. For the love of Christ holds us prisoner [*sunechei hēmas*],[14] since we decided that, because one died on behalf of all, all have died; and he died on behalf of all so that those who are living might no longer live for themselves but for the one who died on their behalf and was raised . . . So if someone is in Christ, he is a new creation. The old things have passed away; behold, they have become new! (5:13–15, 17)

Verbal cues recall the earlier consolatory motifs: the *eite-eite* (here, "if-if") construction in verse 13 echoes the dual focus of apostolic life in verse 9; the "those who live" who "no longer live for themselves" in verse 15 mirrors the "we who are in a tent" (5:4) who yearn to be transported and transformed. Yet this passage about "newness" in Christ also reminds the Corinthians of what was so new about the gospel when they first heard it—the message of the Messiah who died for all so that all are now dead. As a community in

Christ, dead to the world, they are the ultimate outsiders. As an alternate society, they are a "new creation."

Another theme of my overall argument is that the variety of images that make up 2 Cor 1–9—indeed, the sheer pace of imagery that uniquely characterizes the letter—serves the rhetorical function of evoking numerous cultural discourses in order to define Paul as apostle (as well as his new, international movement) in relation to them. Paul enacts a series of identifications and exclusions in order to take an outsider position not simply toward society as a whole, as if in one, broad, rhetorical stroke, but with respect to specific subject positions, both respected and reviled, in order to trace the finer details of his position. As Alain Badiou has surmised (with reference to Paul's opposition of his message to "Greek" and "Jewish" expectations in 1 Cor 1:17–29), a truly "new" discourse contrasts itself not merely to one, dominant discourse (say, the totalizing "wisdom" of Greek philosophy), nor to a discourse defined as an exception to the dominant (for Badiou, the Jewish discourse of prophetic "signs"), but to all prevailing discursive regimes. While one can argue with Badiou's characterization of Greek and Jewish discourses (and his analysis, based on Paul's language in 1 Cor 1, can be seen as largely heuristic), Paul's rhetoric in 2 Cor 1–9 seems to parallel Badiou's model, isolating specific expectations and assumptions in order to define more precisely his self-image through strategic exceptions. Hence Badiou's preoccupation with describing the "diagonal" trajectory by which Paul engages every regime of discourse; Paul rejects the option of direct, perpendicular opposition to an ideological barrier in favor of proposing nuanced alternatives to every kind of established cultural value.[15]

The seemingly excessive manner in which Paul redefines himself with respect to prevailing expectations reveals more than just a theory of his rhetorical strategy, however. That he must take such great steps at such a late stage in his relationship with Corinth—indeed, that he must remind the Corinthians of their entrance into the gospel (after twice asserting that he should not have to)—seems to constitute an embarrassing rhetorical development, the apostolic equivalent of a rebuilding project. The subtle shift in tone hits a sudden pinnacle in the next passage, in which Paul adopts yet another travel motif, depicting his letter and his journey as an emergency embassy from Christ to intervene within a troubled community.

6

Ambassadors of God's Empire

"This is the care of a true *princeps,* or even a god," claims Pliny the Younger in his *Panegyric* to the emperor Trajan. "To reconcile competing cities, to pacify angry peoples less by exercise of power than by reason, to intercede against the injustices of magistrates, to undo what should not have been done: in short, like the swiftest star to see everything, to hear everything, and be present at once with aid wherever your help is sought" (80.3). As I discussed in the introduction, the advent of imperial Rome instituted a system of governance and communication (and attending propaganda reinforcing its efficacy) allowing the emperor to claim powers of influence transcending geographic distance. Or, as Clifford Ando explains:

> The extraordinary efficiency of the Roman imperial bureaucracy made all this possible. Someone, somewhere, may, in fact, have determined what the provinces [of the empire] should and should not know of the emperor's deeds. No one ever questioned, however, that a continual stream of information about the emperor's benefactions to his people would prepare them to receive favorably his requests for information, for money, and for obedience. Rome did not rely on the inertia or the awe of her subjects to compel their quietude; her guardians instead defined, distributed, and ultimately decorated the landscape of their *imperium,* while their images stood in every square, their names marked every road, and their coins jingled in every market in the empire.

As we survey the last few chapters of 2 Cor 1–9, we read Paul attempting rhetorically to construct his own global network of envoys spreading the news of God's reconciliation with the Gentiles and his request that they respond in kind with their worship and obedience, expressed in large part through financial donations to the assembly of Christ-believers in Jerusalem. Like Caesar's traveling heralds who brought Rome to the provinces and the provinces to Rome, Paul's co-workers represented his interests as he represented Christ's. Rome's ambassadors evoked the support of its subjects through expressions, in various media, of the empire's magnanimity. Similarly, Paul attempted to win the hearts of non-Jews with a gospel of grace from the king of the universe. Just as the material network through which imperial ideology was spread shifted the global map, reorienting it toward Rome, Paul redraws international boundaries in order to turn the nations toward Jerusalem and place powerful locales at the margins. By portraying himself and his fellow wanderers as ambassadors, Paul legitimates his traveling lifestyle as a mission on behalf of a divine king, albeit with the normal tribulations that attended all embassies. While Paul implicitly acknowledges that his demand for acceptance and hospitality makes him appear to be just another practitioner of foreign cults, he asserts his sincerity by acknowledging standard understandings of benefaction as reflected in philosophical texts. Finally, through his appeal for the collection to the saints in Judea, Paul reorients the world toward Jerusalem with an organic depiction of the international relations among God's new people.[1]

Ambassadors of the Divine Emperor

After contemplating a metaphorical journey to his heavenly home in 2 Cor 4:16–5:10, Paul comes back to earth, as it were, with an explicit repetition of the core of his gospel message, that "since Christ died for all, all have died; and he died on behalf of all so that those who are living might no longer live for themselves but for the one who died on their behalf and was raised" (5:14–15). In what follows, from 5:18 until the end of the letter, Paul subtly continues to persuade and shame his audience into accepting him, his message, and his financial collection through a repetition of ideas, motifs, and key terms. The long section (and its series of travel motifs) is further united by a focus on the connection between travel and money. After all, Paul's overall focus on travel, shame, and death was occasioned by suspicions over his refusal of financial support in conjunction with his plan to collect a donation to the Jesus-believing community in Jerusalem. Paul must both answer suspicions and reorganize preparations for the collection.

Paul broaches the issue of financial support in 5:19–6:1 with a self-depiction as an ambassador for Christ, an image striking for many reasons: by figuring Paul as *repeating* God's message of reconciliation, it implies that the community never fully adhered to its initial call. Furthermore, the image reverses the normal movement of ambassadorial solicitation, picturing the stronger party (Christ) as petitioning the weaker (Corinth)—though, as Pliny the Younger noted, the swiftness of Roman propaganda often seemed to preempt any rifts with the emperor. Finally, among the many travel motifs throughout the letter, ambassadorship presents the most socially honorable and upper-class analogue for apostleship. The beneficence of the ancient ambassador was most clearly expressed (notably on memorial inscriptions) through the assertion that the ambassador, though offered travel funds by his city, refused them and funded the embassy on his own. Likewise, Paul famously requested no financial support from Corinth (see 1 Cor 9:15, 2 Cor 12:13–15), sacrificing his efforts and means on behalf of his community.

A number of key terms mark Paul's shift to ambassadorial language at 5:18. After having described his mission as a "mediatorial service [*diakonia*] for reconciliation [*katallagēs*]," Paul describes his present activity as "acting as an ambassador [*presbeuomen*] on behalf of Christ, as God exhorting [*parakalountes*] through us; we beseech [*deometha*] you on Christ's behalf, be reconciled [*katallagēte*] to God" (5:20). Technical language for embassies in this verse include *presbeuein* ("to act as ambassador"), *parakalein* ("to exhort"—a word used to mean "comfort" earlier in the letter, exhibiting another example of Paul's clever semantic slippage), and *deesthai* ("to beseech").[2]

Scholarship on Paul's ambassadorial language, however, has noted important discrepancies between normal diplomatic practices and Paul's figuring of his own divine embassy. Most embassies in the ancient world were supplicatory—that is, a subjected city would entreat a ruler for favors or forgiveness. Yet in Paul's formulation, it is God who offers reconciliation without first having been supplicated. Cilliers Breytenbach, who posits ambassadorial efforts at the cessation of hostilities (that is, for "reconciliation") in time of war as a background for Paul's language here, notes Paul's strange adaptation of normal practices in this case. Similarly, Anthony Bash notes how Jewish depictions of Moses as envoy cited the prophet's supplications to God on behalf of sinful Israel (as in Exod 34—again, the background of Paul's discussion of Moses in 2 Cor 3). In contrast, Paul claims in his proclamation that God, paradoxically, has initiated diplomatic relations with his wayward subjects.[3]

In building upon the work of Breytenbach, John T. Fitzgerald has further shown how Paul also adapts the more general concept of reconciliation, whether understood as diplomatic or interpersonal. In ancient literary and documentary texts, it is understood that the offending party in a ruptured relationship was expected to supplicate the offended for reconciliation. Fitzgerald finds that some form of the phrase "be reconciled to me" was invariably used. In contrast, Paul depicts God as making the same entreaty ("be reconciled to me") despite being the superior and wronged party in the relationship. Normal paradigms of reconciliation encouraged the offended party to accept readily the supplications of the offender in the spirit of benefaction—that is, to be *eukatallakton*. In Paul's formulation, God outstrips even the broadest ancient expectations of conciliatory magnanimity by initiating reconciliation with the sinful.[4]

Despite the radically innovative picture of God and his beneficence that Paul offers in this passage, Breytenbach has shown convincingly that Paul ultimately strives not just to depict God's generosity and clemency (toward both the individual and the ecclesiological community), but further to depict himself as apostle and to repair his relationship with Corinth. That Paul is speaking about God in order to speak about himself becomes more evident when we examine the broader context of Paul's appeal, especially in light of rhetorical strategies employed earlier in the letter. As argued at the end of the previous chapter, Paul follows his self-depiction in 4:16–5:10 as wise self-consoler with what appears to be more traditional expressions in 5:11–15 of God's act in the death of Jesus. Paul's repetition of older and more literal language of salvation through Christ's death continues as he turns to ambassadorial motifs. Paul depicts his ministry as the ongoing effort to spread God's conciliatory proclamation far and wide and, in effect, reminds the Corinthians of the initial message that brought them to worship the God of Israel through Christ in the first place. Of course, this is not the first time in the letter Paul has reminded the community of its initial calling. As I argued in Chapter 4, Paul's language of "recommending himself" (first introduced with the letter of recommendation metaphor in 3:1) serves as an embarrassing reminder of their long and close relationship. Paul subtly asserts that he should not have to ask for the Corinthians' emotional and material support. Similarly, in 5:19, Paul once again reminds the Corinthians of his initial message to them: the God of Israel has graciously extended the hand of friendship to the Gentiles.[5]

The notion that reconciliation with Paul really entails reconciliation with God fits well with ancient ambassadorial practices. It was widely understood that receiving an ambassador or envoy was, in essence, receiving the one who sent him. Once again, Paul evokes assumptions previously raised with the couriership motif of 2 Cor 3, framing himself as a substitute and agent for Christ. Yet the passage comprises a smooth yet sudden transition in the tone of the letter, as Paul for the first time punctuates his rhetoric with a fearful note of warning, reinforced in ambassadorial terms in 6:1, in which he "exhorts" the Corinthians "not to accept the grace of God in vain." To this reminder of the original gospel message, Paul adds a feature that deepens the embarrassing implications for the Corinthians' previous treatment of Paul. In 5:20, the apostle depicts his present mission as a special embassy subsequent to his initial sending to Corinth by God, this time at the behest of Christ as God's agent: "we beseech you on Christ's behalf, be reconciled to God." In effect, Paul implies that the Corinthians have endangered their newfound friendship with God. Paul repeats his initial call and proclamation to the community, suggesting that the Corinthians are back at square one. Their near rejection of Paul has threatened their standing before God.[6]

As discussed in Chapter 1, the rift between Corinth and Paul (framed by Paul as a rift between Corinth and God) stemmed from accusations that Paul's collection to Judea was an attempt to rob the community. It is not surprising, then, to find that ambassadorial expectations evoked by Paul's language could serve to address suspicions of financial malfeasance. A common element of urban dedicatory inscriptions to envoys was the notation that an ambassador paid for the trip himself or even declined financial help offered by the city. If the favorable response of the emperor was included in the inscription, it often contained a formulaic affirmation from the emperor that the ambassador had earned financial compensation for the journey, to be paid by the city. A successful ambassador was seen as deserving compensation for his dangerous journey, yet many ambassadors enhanced their image as benefactors by footing the bill. Numerous inscriptions from the first century B.C.E. and first century C.E. proclaim that an ambassador performed his duty [*kata*] *dōrean* ("as a gift" or "for free"), *ek tōn idiōn* ("from his own funds") or *par' heautou* ("by his own means"). By comparing himself to a faithful ambassador of God and Christ, Paul implicitly addresses issues of financial support and sincerity, all in preparation for a discussion of the envoys he has sent to Corinth in service of the collection.[7]

Since the social image of an ambassador rested on an understanding of his beneficence as well as his willingness to confront the dangers of travel, Paul likewise, in 2 Cor 6:3–10, builds upon his ambassadorial language with a list of hardships (traditionally known in scholarship as *peristasis* ["affliction"] catalogues). Although undertaken by upper-class members of local communities, who could afford to absorb the costs of such long journeys, embassies on land and sea naturally faced the sorts of dangers that all travelers encountered. The motif of ambassadorship allows Paul to unite the status and suffering attending his vision of apostleship. Within the structure of this list, issues of travel and poverty play such a frequent role that close analysis of terminology benefits the current study. The first grouping of troubles describes sufferings construed in a general sense: "in afflictions, in distresses, in tight situations" (*en thlipsesin, en anankais, en stenochōriais;* 6:4b). The third term might refer to narrow escapes from external pressures. The verbal form of the term recurs just below in 6:12, however, in which Paul refers to the Corinthians' attitude (and perhaps lack of hospitality) toward him: "you are not closed off [*stenochōreisthe*] among us, but rather, you are closed off [*stenochōreisthe*] in your affections." The second group of three afflictions (6:5a) is more concrete: "in floggings, in imprisonments, in riots." Perhaps this group delimits the first as referring to external and physical afflictions.[8]

Fitzgerald labels the third group of afflictions (5b) as "occupational hardships" of an "apostle and artisan": "in labors, in sleepless nights, in periods of starvation" refer primarily to Paul's activity as a tentmaker. A more specific context, however, can be found in his life as a *traveling* artisan and apostle—especially in light of the common "on-the-road" travails that ambassadors experienced. As discussed in the introduction, some of Paul's *peristasis* catalogues evoke specifically itinerant dangers. This is particularly true of 2 Cor 11:22–33, in which Paul mentions his labors, imprisonments, floggings, brushes with death, hunger, thirst, sleeplessness, and nakedness, among other "on-the-road" hardships. The list in 6:3–10 (and especially the triad of v. 5b) mirrors many of these elements.[9]

A traveling context is most clearly emphasized in the second major section of the catalogue, in which afflictions are contrasted with descriptions of Paul's endurance. The first pair, *hōs planoi kai alētheis* (v. 8b), is usually translated "as deceitful and yet true." That *planoi* ultimately implies Paul's suspected mendacity is beyond doubt. We should keep in mind, however, the base meaning of *planos,* "wandering," and its ironic implications in the context of a letter thematically characterized by travel motifs. Subsequently, Paul describes himself "as unknown, but actually recognized" (v. 9a). A traveling context once again helps explain the phrasing, since as a traveler Paul would be a stranger in most contexts, known only to those groups who had welcomed him and accepted his message. That the Corinthians have failed in properly "recognizing" Paul's role and status in relation to the community has been a constant theme in the letter thus far: in 1:13–14, Paul asserts that he "writes nothing other than what you can read and recognize [*epiginōskete*]; I hope that you will recognize until the end [*heōs telous epiginōesthe*] (just as you have also recognized us in part [*epegnōte apo merous*]) that we are your boast, just as you are our boast, on the day of the Lord." In this element of the catalogue, Paul once again asserts that, though his journeys make him a stranger in all places, he should be recognized, received, and remembered by the communities he has founded.

The third element in this construction similarly recalls a prominent theme of the letter first expressed at its outset: "as dying, yet, behold, we live" (v. 9b). As I have argued throughout this book, Paul intimates from the outset that he has felt himself close to death by virtue of the constant dangers presented by his travels and, more significantly, the despair he felt over his ruptured relationship with the Corinthians, leading him to contemplate a dignified departure from life through self-killing. Once again, Paul juxtaposes travel and death in 6:8–9, following descriptions of his ostensible appearance as "wanderer" and "stranger" with a statement that he "lives" despite his nearness to death. The depiction is reinforced by the following pair, "as being disciplined but not dying" (v. 9c). Together, the final two couplets of verse 9 constitute a fairly certain allusion to LXX Ps 117:17–18: "I will not die; rather, I will live and recount the Lord's deeds. The Lord has disciplined me severely, yet he has not handed me over to death." Though most commentators note the allusion, few have wondered why Paul chooses this specific psalm. But when interpreted in light of the processional imagery introduced early in the letter (and to which Paul returns in 6:11–13 and 7:2—see below), we can begin to see in more detail why Ps 117 lies behind this passage. Following the verses paraphrased by Paul, Ps 117 continues with the exhortation: "Open for me the gates of righteousness; when I enter through them, I will praise the Lord. The very gate of the Lord!—the righteous will enter through it. I will praise you because you heard me and became salvation for me" (vv. 19–21). Farther on, the psalmist continues the processional imagery: "Blessed is the one who comes in the name of the Lord . . . The Lord is God and has illuminated us. Prepare the festival with bound garlands up to the horns of the altar" (vv. 27–28). The use of "bound garlands" (*pukazousin*), a Judean festal commonplace, was just the kind of ritual activity that may have led some non-Jews to confuse such processions with Bacchic cultic practices. The processional motifs and the expectations concerning Dionysian cultic practitioners recur just below, in 6:11—a verse, incidentally, invoking Ps 118:32.

The final three pairs in the catalogue of hardships appear in 6:10: "as grieving yet always joyful, as poor yet making many rich, as having nothing yet possessing everything." Each pair reflects an aspect of the preceding part of the letter or a past controversy between Paul and the Corinthians. The notion of Paul's grief (*lupē*) over his troubles with his community found clear expression in 1:1–2:13 and recurs in 7:4–15. In the final two pairs, Paul chooses to end his list with a reference to financial issues. In the face of suspicions of financial misdealing, Paul asserts that, despite his ostensible material poverty, he is spiritually rich and actually enriches others.

It is initially perplexing, however, why Paul would end his catalogue with the issues of his emotional and financial state and not the more natural climax found in 6:9, the contrast between death and life. Once again, Paul's ordering of themes reveals the ultimate function of the passage—namely, to recapitulate topics that came before and to transition to the remaining part of the letter. Thus, while the bulk of the *peristasis* catalogue (6:4–9) summarizes Paul's afflictions as miserable wanderings connoting death, the final three clauses foretell the contents of the rest of the letter (7:4–9:15): the joyful relief Paul feels in light of Titus's report of the Corinthians' willingness to reconcile (7:4–16) and participate in the collection to Jerusalem (2 Cor 8 and 9). By building on ambassadorial language with a carefully constructed list of itinerant woes, Paul defends his sincerity and depth of commitment to his mission and the Corinthians, further preparing for his ultimate request.

Divine Hospitality Revisited in 6:11–13, 7:2–16

In order to resurrect the collection in Corinth, Paul must first discuss the co-workers (most notably Titus, a controversial figure in Corinth) sent in advance of Paul's arrival. In preparing to defend and commend Titus, Paul returns to the motif of Dionysian processions and divine hospitality. Duff has argued that the language of epiphany processions—first mentioned in 2:14–16a and then broached again in 4:7–11 and 5:14—finds its final expression in 6:13 and 7:2. In this section, Duff points to the role of the herald in an epiphanic procession, who was expected to prepare the way for the cult image and its attendants. The herald urged the crowd to make way and encouraged only the pious and reverent to observe the image, chastising the impure to stand aside.[10]

At 6:11, after professing spiritual riches despite material poverty in verse 10, Paul asserts his complete openness toward the Corinthians: "Our mouth is open to you, Corinthians, our heart is opened wide." In the context of the implied suspicions over Paul's honesty, his language connotes not only love, but sincerity, as confirmed by his profession of "great openness" in 7:4. Paul turns the Corinthians' charges of dishonesty and malfeasance into rejections of friendship: "You are not closed off [*stenochōreisthe*] among us; rather, you are closed off [*stenochōreisthe*] in your affections." At this point, Paul once again entreats his community with two imperatives: "As an equal payback (I am speaking as to children), you also, open wide for us, make room for us" (6:13 and 7:2a). The heart continues as the metaphorical ground for the entry of Paul and his co-workers, heralds and envoys of God. Notice, in addition, the recurrence of imperatives, absent from the letter until the entreaty of 5:20, "be reconciled to God." The imperatives here mirror the earlier request of

5:20 for the Corinthians to repair their relationship with God by repairing their relationship with God's apostle. By opening their hearts to Paul and his divinely led triumph, they accept the image of Christ that he "carries around" with him (cf. 4:10).[11]

Following this passage, Paul returns to charges of financial wrongdoing: "We wronged no one, we ruined no one, we defrauded no one. I do not say this as a condemnation against you; for, as I said before, you are in our hearts to die with us and live with us" (7:2–3). Once again, Paul broaches the charge of possible malfeasance in close juxtaposition to the mixed metaphor of the Corinthians allowing him into their hearts like an epiphany procession down Main Street. The juxtaposition is significant if we recall a similar connection in 2:12–16a, in which Paul's discussion of his progress toward Macedonia through Alexandria Troas (in which "a door was opened to him") leads to the first expression of his traveling ministry as a divinely led procession encountering both resistance and welcome. The depiction is followed by the rejection of any accusation that he sells his message for profit like "hucksters [*kapēleuontes*] of the word of God" (2:17a). In 2 Cor 2 and 7, evocations of Bacchic processions are linked directly to accusations of fraud.

After laying out a description of his love and devotion toward the community, Paul sets out to show that his co-workers are apostolic servants in the same mold. As he describes his encounter with Titus in Macedonia, he transfers his own apostolic self-definition to his co-worker, reduplicating the social logic of his ministry. Paul's redeploying of themes central to 2 Cor 1–6 in 2 Cor 7–9 not only helps show the thematic unity of 2 Cor 1–9; identifying such themes helps us discern how he rhetorically establishes the social logics of his fledgling, international community.

Envoys, Money, and Social Reproduction (7:2–9:15)

The logic of social excess that Paul establishes serves as the foundation for the ideological replication he enacts in 2 Cor 7–9. Such a logic is expressed through two new social forms: first, Paul depicts his co-workers (first Titus, then the anonymous "brothers" whom Paul sends with him) as servants in Paul's own image, bearing an emotional excess toward the Corinthians identical to that which Paul claims to bear; second, he establishes a social logic by which any emotional excess on the Corinthians' part is to be expressed monetarily and devoted to the collection. In this way, Paul creates a logic for the exchange of symbolic and financial capital—suffering, emotions, money—as a process that binds together his new international movement. At the same time, he gradates how this logic operates across the international movement, creating a worldwide hierarchy with Christ at the center, Paul and his co-workers in a pivotal, mediating role, and Corinth at the margins.

After his repeated calls in 7:2–3 for the Corinthians to open their hearts to him, Paul rephrases his exhortations in emotive language that in part recalls early passages of the section 2:14–7:4 as well as the very beginning of the canonical work (that is, the repetitive, emotional language in 1:3–7). At 7:4, Paul declares: "Great is my openness toward you, great is my boasting about you. I am filled [*peplērōmai*] with consolation, I am overflowing [*hyperperis-seuomai*] with joy in all our affliction." The movement between the two verbs in these statements—*peplērōmai* and *hyperperisseuomai*—reflects the social necessity of "excess" so central to the letter. Paul enhances his "fullness of consolation" to an "overflowing of joy." The fact that abundance, for Paul, results in social growth becomes ever more clear in the subsequent section, in which the confidence and comfort experienced by one Pauline co-worker overflow into the next, an emotive transfer that results in social replication.

In his account of his encounter with Titus, Paul expresses the social transfer of emotional overflow that he has described as the ministry of the spirit, though the exchange occurs in a surprising direction. Paul's numerous afflictions allow him no "relief" until "the God who consoles the lowly consoled us through the presence [*parousiai*] of Titus—indeed, not only with his presence but also with the consolation through which he was consoled about you, reporting to us your longing, your mourning, your zeal on my behalf, so that I rejoiced all the more" (7:5–7). The wording recalls the outset of the letter (1:3–7) in which Paul blesses God for consoling him in his sufferings. In fact, the general statement in 1:7 that "our hope about you is secure, knowing that, just as you are sharers in our sufferings, so also are you sharers in our consolation" finally finds particular instantiation in Paul's account of his encounter with Titus: Paul shared the internal affliction and regret he felt over the Corinthians with his "painful letter" (preserved in 2 Cor 10–13); Titus, through his visit, learns that the Corinthians also "mourned" over the situation and expressed a willingness to reconcile; overflowing with joy and consolation, Titus then shares the news with Paul. In Paul's reckoning, just as God causes his servants to suffer in replication of Christ's sufferings, "godly grief" yields eagerness, zeal, longing, and joy (7:10–11).

Paul, however, does not merely rejoice in the message of reconciliation. Titus's own emotional state causes him even more relief, and he expresses this relief in such a way and to such an extent that the passage reads like a recommendation—even a defense:

Because of this [emotional change in you], we have been consoled. But over and above our consolation we rejoiced all the more exceedingly [*perissoterōs mallon*] in Titus's joy, because his spirit was refreshed by all of you. Because, if I had been boasting to him about you in any way, I was not made ashamed. On the contrary, just as we say the truth in all things to you, so also did our boast to Titus prove true. And his heart goes out all the more [*perissoterōs*] to you, remembering the obedience of all of you, that you received him with fear and trembling. I rejoice because I have confidence in you in every matter. (7:13–16)

As in other commendatory passages, Paul follows the Greco-Roman convention of portraying envoys as adequate substitutes for their senders and, in turn, as faithful representatives of those to whom they were sent. As discussed above, however, 2 Cor 12:14–18 implies that both Paul and Titus were implicated in Corinthian charges of insincerity and fraud. Thus, having defended himself by expressing his exceeding joy and confidence in the Corinthians, Paul extends his defense to include Titus, describing him as having the same type of abounding emotion toward Corinth.[12]

The depiction is all the more important as Titus arrives to finalize the community's collection for Judea (8:6). That a previous insult to Paul and Titus is in view in 2 Cor 8 is made clear in Paul's subsequent commendation of two anonymous "brothers" to be sent with Titus, the first of whom serves as a clear provision against charges of fraud: "We have sent with him the brother who is praised in the gospel among all the communities—not only that, but he has also been selected by the communities as our fellow traveler [*sunekdēmos*] in our ministering of this gift for the glory of the Lord and for our own desire, since we are making preparations [*stellomenoi*] for this very thing: that no one blame us in our ministering of this generous gift. For we keep in mind what is good not only before the Lord but also before people" (8:18–21). In making provisions for sending envoys on behalf of the collection, Paul sends a "fellow traveler" (*sunekdēmos*) selected by other Christ-believing communities as an ostensible safeguard against suspicions of fraud. Here, he explicitly makes travel plans augmenting his earlier attempt to send Titus and a single "brother" (2 Cor 12:18), a plan that had raised doubts among the Corinthians in that it contradicted earlier plans to send Corinthian representatives with the money (1 Cor 16:1–4). That Paul is making explicit "travel preparations" in sending this "famous brother" is implied by the use of *stellomenoi* in 8:20, which, in its meaning of "preparation," may have been picked up by Paul through its use in Wis 14:1, where *ploun tis . . . stellomenos* refers to "someone preparing to set sail." The sending of the famous brother is a travel preparation designed to supplement the wandering, deceptive connotations of Titus's activity and to provide independent attestation to the authenticity of the collection.[13]

More important, however, is Paul's introduction of the envoys in light of his protestations of sincerity throughout the earlier parts of the letter. Just as he frames the beginning of the letter with a rhetoric of self-revelation and sincerity, Paul asserts that Titus and the two brothers hold the same zeal on the Corinthians' behalf as is felt by Paul himself. The strategy begins in 7:13 (cited above), where Paul claims that "we rejoiced all the more exceedingly in Titus's joy, since his spirit was refreshed by all of you." Soon after, in verse 15, Paul asserts that Titus's "heart goes out all the more toward you, remembering the obedience of all of you, that you received him with fear and trembling." Later, Paul explicitly claims that his co-worker has the very same affection as Paul toward Corinth: "Thanks be to God who has given into Titus's heart the same eagerness on your behalf as I have, since he not only accepted our exhortation, but, being all the more eager, set out for you on his own accord" (8:16). Through repeated references to the zeal or affection felt among Paul, Titus, and Corinth on the behalf of the other parties, Paul articulates a logic of social exchange mirroring the apostolic transferal of spirit first described in 2 Cor 3–4, a transformative, emotive exchange initiating an impulse to respond in kind—that is, an "exceeding" or "overflowing" gift of the spirit and God's grace (cf. 4:15). Paul's proclamation of the gospel, Titus's management of the collection, and the Corinthians' (eventual) warm reception of Titus—in Paul's fashioning, all serve as terms in the social logic of spiritual exchange initiated by God's gift in Christ.

As in earlier parts of the letter, Paul's revelation of his inner disposition and that of his co-workers closes the physical distance of their traveling mission. The revelation of inner devotion and longing, however, fills an even more specific social function within the context of the collection, especially if we understand the endeavor in light of ancient logics of benefaction. The scheme Paul establishes in his commendation of Titus and the two brothers resembles the Stoic theory of benefaction presented in Seneca's *De beneficiis*, as discussed in Chapter 2. Based on earlier works by Chrysippus and Hecaton, *De beneficiis* founds its discussion on Stoic theories of sense perception in order to claim that gratitude is the enduring and most significant social result of benefaction. In fact, for Seneca, a benefit is not truly the object given or deed performed but rather the intention and goodwill behind it. A Stoic paradox famously expresses the notion that gratitude is the heart of benefaction: "he who receives a benefit gladly has already returned it." Seneca explains the paradox thus:

Whenever anyone attains what he aimed at, he receives the reward of his effort. When a man bestows a benefit, what does he aim at? To be of service and to give pleasure to the one to whom he gives. If he accomplishes what he wished, if his intention is conveyed to me and stirs in me a joyful response, he gets what he sought. For he had no wish that I should give him anything in exchange. Otherwise, it would have been, not a benefaction, but a bargaining. A man has had a successful voyage if he reaches the port for which he set out . . . He who gives a benefit wishes it to be gratefully accepted; if it is cheerfully received he gets what he wanted. (2.31.2–3, LCL)

For Seneca, gratitude and indebtedness are no mere abstract virtues, but the very glue that holds society together. The emotive residue of gratitude ensures the continuation of social exchange and the perpetuation of social logics.

In Paul's establishing a fledgling group, it was of the utmost necessity for him to articulate repeatedly the logic of selfless giving, a logic building on the notion of benefaction reflected in writers such as Seneca, but one that takes on new meaning in a new, international movement founded on an understanding of God's benefaction through Christ's crucifixion. Throughout the letter, Paul depicts his own reception of God's grace, taking up Christ's example and applying it to his own apostolic situation. In strategic spots, he goes on to outline the influence of his mission on the Corinthians and mold an emotional response on their part. In describing his plans for the collection and reestablishing his provisions for traveling co-workers, Paul more explicitly describes the emotional excess driving his vision of the worldwide Jesus movement. He outlines the social exchange of emotions, service, and money uniting the movement across physical and cultural distance.

Sandwiched between Paul's description in 7:5–15 of Titus's attitude upon their meeting and the "formal" recommendation in 8:16–24 of Titus and "the brothers" appears Paul's first description in 8:1–15 of the proper attitude toward the collection. This attitude, however, is initially framed as being exemplified by the Macedonian congregation (vv. 1–5) through "the grace of God given among" them (v. 1). "In a great test of affliction, their excess [*perisseia*] of joy and extreme poverty have overflowed [*eperisseusen*] into the wealth of their sincerity" (v. 2). This giving occurred "of their own free will, as they begged us with great exhortation" to contribute, "not merely as we had hoped; on the contrary, they gave their very selves, first to the Lord, and, then, to us, through the will of God" (vv. 3–4). Here, the degree of the Macedonians' willingness to contribute constitutes a self-giving even before the setting aside of any money—a wholeness of devotion not only to Christ, but also to Paul and his leadership structure. Paralleling the Senecan depiction of benefaction that privileged inward response over external return, Paul explicitly cites the Macedonians' aspiration to self-sacrifice as the greater part of their gift, a self-giving that takes on greater meaning against the cruciform template that underlies the movement. The fact that they gave despite affliction and suffering testifies all the more to their inward disposition. Paul's mentioning of the Macedonians' generosity toward the collection undoubtedly serves to spur on the Corinthians in their giving, initiating a bit of competition among the communities (as many interpreters have noted). Additionally, however, Paul's depiction of the Macedonians' role in the collection parallels the "exceeding" emotional disposition already described as characterizing the apostolic existence of Paul and his co-workers. Thus, 8:1–5 serves as yet another articulation of his social logic of excess-in-suffering, this time in the case of a Pauline community responding to God's favor granted through the Pauline apostolic network.[14]

The Macedonians' response directly prompts Paul to continue his solicitation of the Corinthians through Titus. In a quick transition, Paul states that the Macedonians' eagerness to participate wholeheartedly in the collection "led us to exhort Titus, so that, just as he had begun it before, so also he might complete among you even this same benefaction" (8:6). In response to Titus, the Corinthians are to imitate further the apostolic emotive "excess" modeled by Paul, Titus, and the Macedonians: "Indeed, just as you are surpassing [*perisseuete*] in every aspect, in faithfulness and speech and knowledge and all eagerness and love which came from us and is among you, so also you might be surpassing [*perisseuēte*] in this favor" (v. 7). Again, the emotive response to the reception of the gospel takes ideological priority, but the external response—a financial contribution—still remains for the "completion" of their expression of gratitude.

The translation of suffering and emotion into money, however, becomes more explicit when Paul depicts Christ's crucifixion, the basic model for apostolic activity and the new social logic it exemplifies, in economic terms: "For you know the gracious gift of our Lord Jesus Christ, that for your sake he made himself poor, though he was rich, so that you yourselves might become rich through his poverty" (8:9). Paul's figurative language here refers to Christ's crucifixion as resulting in the spiritual wealth of the Corinthian community, but in its context it serves to equate Christ's death with the financial sacrifice asked of the Corinthians. A close reading reveals the tension present in this equation: surely donating a little money pales in comparison to Jesus's suffering and death! Adding to the tension, Paul goes on to assert that he does not wish to place any burden on the Corinthians whatsoever: "If your desire to give remains, it is acceptable according to what one has, not what one does not have. For it should not be that there is relief for others but affliction for you, but rather, you should give out of equality" (*isotētos;* 8:12–13).

Some scholars take seriously the assertion of "equality" as Paul's guiding social principle for his vision of the international Jesus movement—that he sincerely embeds Corinth in a relationship of mutual, fair exchange—but in light of the imbalance of self-sacrifice depicted in the passage, reference to "equality" more likely serves as the type of rhetorical misrecognition so crucial to ideologies of benefaction. Much like Roman patronal appeals to *amicitia,* Paul's references to *isotēs* actually reinforce an international hierarchy based on sacrifice and indebtedness. And while Christ's death (cast in monetary terms) provides the ultimate example of this ideology, the social payoff of Paul's strategy is the legitimation of the traveling ministry of himself and his co-workers. Moreover, by establishing the principle of his own Christlike suffering on Corinth's behalf, Paul offers Corinth the opportunity to respond in kind to his Christ-modeled beneficence.

By establishing a social logic of wandering sacrifice through most of the letter, Paul seeks to establish in 2 Cor 8–9 an international hierarchy based on this logic. The hierarchy of the Jesus movement, however, is necessarily juxtaposed with existing societal values and international status markers. Paul's appeal for the collection in 2 Cor 8 depicts the Macedonian community's zeal for the endeavor as leading Paul to continue his efforts in Corinth, a depiction perhaps intended to shame Corinth into action. When Paul returns to the Macedonian situation in 9:1–5, however, the direction of influence is reversed: Paul intimates that he told the Macedonians that the Corinthians were ready and willing to contribute and that the claim prompted the Macedonians' generosity. In light of his recent troubles in Corinth, one wonders whether Paul has been caught overstating his case in Macedonia. Be that as it may, he must ensure that the Corinthians are indeed prepared to contribute in order to avoid "embarrassment" (9:4) and the very charges he had narrowly escaped in Corinth—namely, *pleonexia,* or "fraud" (9:5; cf. 7:2). In this construal, it seems as if Paul has leveraged the prestige of Corinth to ensure success in Macedonia, accumulating financial and political support, as contingents from the donating communities seem to travel with Paul as he proceeds toward Achaia (9:4).

The rhetorical strategies seem so opposite that some scholars have cited the disjunction as evidence for 2 Cor 8 and 9 being separate letters. Yet the tension more likely results from Paul's situation in making his appeal. Paul believes his service to Judea will accrue prestige proportional to the importance of the communities involved. As Corinth is the home base of his Achaean sphere of involvement (cf. 1:1), the participation of the Corinthians in the collection would bring relief and devotion to the center of the Jesus movement from the heart of Greece and Greekness. Again, Paul's decision to refer to regions and not to cities in 2 Cor 9—as in 2 Cor 1 and 2—draws upon the international reputations of each region. Moreover, his mentioning that his promises of Corinthian involvement led Macedonia to contribute may well have flattered Corinthian self-understandings of their city being a bastion of Greek cultural superiority. Paul even depicts the Corinthians as spiritually superlative, "surpassing in every aspect, in faithfulness and speech and knowledge and all eagerness and love which came from us and is among you" (8:7). Here, we yet again see the discrepancy between Paul's controversy in Corinth and the rhetoric he deploys in its wake. By nodding to Corinth's eminence in the region and flattering the Corinthians concerning their status in Christ, Paul rhetorically manipulates an existing, perceived international hierarchy.

Yet this evocation comes alongside a very different mapping of international relations—a Mediterranean hierarchy as construed within Paul's understanding of the Jesus movement. In light of the connection between suffering and glory emphasized throughout the letter, 2 Cor 1–9 conspicuously fails to attribute suffering to the Corinthians. Most clearly, in 8:1–15, Paul posits suffering as the mark of generosity through the examples of Macedonia and Christ, yet he tells the Corinthians that they need not sacrifice or experience any trouble for their contribution. In fact, as discussed above, he asserts that their generosity should be proportionate to their exceeding spiritual gifts, not their sufferings. The notion that the Corinthians need not sacrifice on behalf of their donation is especially glaring in such close proximity to the description of Christ, who "for your sake made himself poor, though he was rich, so that you yourselves might become rich through his poverty" (8:9). If, for Paul, suffering leads to status, Paul here places Corinth at the bottom of the hierarchy of the Jesus movement.

Thus, the tension between 2 Cor 8 and 9 can be explained in part as the tension between two conceptual maps of Paul's international sphere of activity—both of which the apostle had to take into account. First is the perceived prestige among various regions so often exploited in Paul's rhetoric and imagery. Corinth, as the center of Achaia, represented the antique fame of Greece, whereas Paul's message from Judea bore an air of marginality and foreignness. While evoking this construal to his benefit, Paul simultaneously overlays a new apostolic map with its center in Jerusalem. Following Christ's example of self-inflicted "poverty," the Judean community confers spiritual benefits despite its material lack (8:14). Of course, throughout the letter, Paul often recounts his traveling, international sufferings for his mission. Even the Macedonians displayed abundant generosity despite poverty and affliction.

The Corinthians, in Paul's explicit description, do not fit the pattern. The combination of flattery and omission from the Christ-modeled scheme of suffering and glory is of a kind with other instances of flattery in the letter in which Paul asserts that his suffering is on behalf of the Corinthians. In 2 Cor 8 and 9, however, the cumulative weight of the shaming technique is increased, as Christ, Judea, Paul, his co-workers, Macedonia—indeed, it seems the entire Jesus movement—suffers on behalf of the international community. Corinth is left at the edge of this map, oriented toward Christ, Judea, and Paul as instructive models, despite Paul's "opinion" that they need not overly trouble themselves.

The discrepancy between Paul's model of glory-in-suffering and his assertion that the Corinthians, though rich, should give only of their excess follows in the paths Paul laid earlier in his claims that his sufferings are purely on the Corinthians' behalf. As he includes the models of Christ (as he does in 5:14–15 and 8:9), his traveling co-workers (7:6–7, 13; 8:16–17, 23), and the Macedonians (8:1–6), all examples reinforce earlier depictions of himself as selfless and sincere in his message and travels. In effect, Paul argues that his apostolic form of life mirrors the central, cruciform ethic of the international movement. As always, his self-depiction is the rhetorical heart of the discourse—a fact that becomes especially apparent in his final appeal to the Corinthians—that they complete the collection under the leadership of Titus so that, when Paul arrives with a Macedonian contingent, he may not be "ashamed" and appear "greedy" (9:4–5). As Paul is bearer of Christ's gospel to the Gentiles, success of its expansion rests on his reputation.

The Bountiful Fields of Jerusalem and the Effacement of the Traveling Apostle

Throughout this book, I have argued that Paul is the main focus of his own rhetoric and imagery, a rhetoric in which travel serves as an ideal floating signifier. As-good-as-dead in terms of worldly status yet glorious in his self-sacrificing devotion, the Wandering Apostle defies status quo evaluation yet catalyzes the emergence of God's new social creation. At times, as in 2 Cor 9:1–5, Paul must speak explicitly about the centrality of his role in spreading the gospel, including his own fears of shame and embarrassment. But almost in reaction to this degree of explicitness, Paul will also pull himself out of the picture, describing the glory of God, Christ, or even the Corinthians themselves. The conclusion of the extant part of our letter is a prime example of Paul's effacement of his role. After warning the Corinthians of the potential embarrassment of lack of preparation, he turns in 9:6–15 to an agrarian, almost utopian picture, overflowing with scriptural citations, of the international Jesus movement. In drawing the lines of relationship between Achaia and Judea, Paul fades from view. More significantly, however, he replaces what thus far in the letter has been his main apostolic trait—travel—with a social activity of markedly higher status in ancient estimations—agriculture.

Second Corinthians 1–9 concludes with an appeal to agrarian wisdom, most ostensibly to encourage the Corinthians to donate generously, willingly, and cheerfully (cf. 9:7). Beginning in 9:6, Paul creates his own version of a proverb familiar to most ancient hearers, Jews and Gentiles alike: "He who sows sparingly, sparingly will he also reap; and he who sows bountifully, bountifully will he also reap." The beginning of the statement recalls Prov 11:24, but the end, playing with and emphasizing *eulogia* ("bounty" or "blessing") as a key word for this section, is all Paul's. The appeal to generous sowing and reaping was ubiquitous in the ancient world, at home in Jewish wisdom circles as well as in scholastic and popular philosophy of any stripe. Such an appeal to common sense bolsters Paul's appeal to Corinth's generosity, promising abundant returns. Next, in a rhetorically remarkable sentence that encompasses the key concepts of both 1 Corinthians ("all" or "wholeness") and 2 Cor 1–9 ("excess"), Paul displays how the international community will be united through the free exchange of divinely granted abundance: "God makes it so that every [*pasan*] gift abounds [*perisseusai*] in you, so that being utterly, always, and in all things [*en panti pantote pasan*] self-sufficient, you might abound [*perisseuēte*] in every [*pan*] good work" (9:8). More than any other statement in 2 Cor 1–9, this flourish shows the rhetorical excess required of social construction.[15]

Paul's agricultural language contributes at least two facets to his depiction of the collection. The first is a status implication associated with farming activity. Paul raises the notion of "self-sufficiency" (*autarkeia*) in relation to the agrarian themes of 9:6–15. Many scholars have rightly noted the philosophical (especially Stoic and Cynic) usages of "self-sufficiency" at this time. But the appeal of self-sufficiency in Stoic rhetoric was to individual power and status. For many ancients, the social location that best personified self-sufficiency was farming (as discussed in the introduction), which necessitated land ownership, an automatic status symbol. Moreover, the upper-class ideal of land-owning became spiritualized as a connection to nature and detachment from worldly affairs. Agriculture even became a stock ethnographic topos, contrasted with travel and mercantile activity (too shifty and risky to be noble). We have seen how this notion was employed even by Jewish writers such as Josephus and the author of the *Letter of Aristeas* to extol the virtues of their nation. For *Aristeas,* the fertile environs of Jerusalem speak to its glory as much as the opulent splendor of its Temple. As a status motif, thriving agriculture was a mark of landed prestige.

Second, agricultural language contributes to Paul's depiction of the collection as temple worship. As scholars have noted, Paul is careful to choose agrarian scriptural passages from contexts that speak of temple worship in general and, in some cases, the eschatological pilgrimage of the nations to Jerusalem. So, his quotation (in 9:9) of LXX Ps 111:9 ("He scatters, he gives to the poor, his righteousness remains forever") not only praises generosity in "sowing" terms, but evokes the larger context of Pss 110 and 111 (almost certainly a united pair) that begin as songs of "confession" or "thanksgiving" (*exomologēsomai*, 110:1; cf. the collection as Gentile *homologia* in 2 Cor 9:13). Later, in Ps 110:6, God is praised for giving his people "the inheritance of the Gentiles." After alluding to the psalm, Paul then (9:10) cites Isa 55:10, which, in its context, compares God to the rain that "gives seed to the sower and bread to the hungry." The section of Isaiah uses other images of material abundance to describe Israel's promised future, including the worship of the Gentiles: "Behold, I have made him [David] a witness to the Gentiles, a leader and commander of the Gentiles; Gentiles who did not know you will call upon you, and peoples who did not know you will flee to you for the sake of your God, the Holy One of Israel, because he glorified you" (55:4-5).[16]

Paul does not explain to his Corinthian audience the contextual import of his citations. Yet with the description that follows of the effects of the collection, Paul makes clear that their donation amounts to a financial offering to the God of Israel. Thus, the Corinthians' "sincerity . . . enacts through us thanksgiving [*eucharistian*] to God" (2 Cor 9:11). "Thanksgiving" could be understood as a cultic act among ancient hearers. More specifically, the next verse describes the collection efforts as *hē diakonia tēs leitourgias tautēs*, "the administration of this financial service," a phrase rendered clumsily into English, since both *diakonia* and *leitourgia* (in classical Greek cities, usually a personal, voluntary funding of civic-cultic festivals) can be translated vaguely as "service." Scholars correctly note that *leitourgia* had both political and cultic connotations—though within the context of a discussion of "thanksgiving" and "prayer" (*deēsis* in 9:14), the term most likely conveyed a cultic meaning to its audience. The service "not only provides for the lack among the saints, but also abounds [*perisseuousa*] through thanksgiving of many people to God." Finally, the collection service (again, *diakonia*) is a "proof" that will cause the Judean community to "glorify God for the obedience of your confession of the gospel of Christ and your sincerity expressing fellowship with them and with all, since they also are longing for you with prayer on your behalf because of the exceeding beneficence [*tēn hyperballousan charin*] of God among you" (9:13–14). Through the collection, as Paul understands it, the scriptural prophecies of the Gentiles flocking to worship at Jerusalem are fulfilled.[17]

Paul's notion of Gentile financial offerings as eschatological worship had other close cognates in Jewish practice. Scholars have long wondered whether the Gentile donations could also have been understood in terms of the temple tax. After all, the tax itself was a form of worship among the Jewish Diaspora—a way of making offerings to the Temple despite great distance. The offerings were carried by envoys called *hieropompoi* (according to Philo), who took on these dangerous journeys upon uncertain roads, travels understood to "lead them to piety" (*Legat.* 216, LCL trans.). Since the contributions were understood as the Diaspora form of temple worship, and since temple festivals had such a close connection to harvest season, it is no wonder that the contributions took on an agrarian understanding. Philo repeatedly refers to the money as "first-fruits" (*ton athroisthenta ek tōn aparchōn; Legat.* 156, 216, 312; *Spec.* 1.178). In many ways, the temple contributions served to replace the presence of Diaspora Jews who could infrequently (if ever) make a pilgrimage to the center of their devotion. They interpreted their monetary donations in terms of the produce of the soil long offered by their ancestors in the environs of Jerusalem. Agricultural expressions for the temple tax worked to efface the distance of Diaspora. Paul, as we have seen, similarly translates the Corinthian gift of money into agrarian terms of bountiful harvest. Why should we not view the collection as a more international expression of the Gentile pilgrimage and worship depicted in Jewish traditions?[18]

A Gentile collection understood as an analogue to the Diaspora temple tax also served Paul's purpose in establishing a new, alternative, Jesus-believing and Jerusalem-centered society. For as ancient evidence suggests (and despite Roman provisions for its legality and safety), many non-Jews viewed the Diaspora contributions as subversive and antisocial. So, Cicero praises Flaccus, who, as governor of Asia Minor, prohibited the transport of the donations as "barbaric superstition" (*Flacc.* 28.67, LCL trans.). Moreover, Josephus portrays the emperor Titus as chiding the Judean rebels in 70 C.E., who had used the contributions so graciously allowed by the Romans to revolt—using, as he claims, the Romans' own money against them (*B.J.* 6.335–36). Especially vexing for some Romans was the fact that non-Jewish proselytes occasionally donated to the Temple; according to Tacitus, "the worst rascals among other peoples, renouncing their ancestral religions, always kept sending tribute and contributions . . . and the earliest lesson they receive is to despise all gods, to disown their country, and to regard their parents, children, and brethren as of little account" (*Hist.* 5.5, LCL trans.). The monetary donations to Jerusalem presented a flow of devotion diverted from its ideal orientation (Rome), a practice all the more concerning if it attracted those not allied with this minor people by birth. How much more provocative, then, if Paul's collection represented the turning of the Gentiles of the Mediterranean toward a new international center?[19]

Multiple perspectives of the collection served one complex purpose: Paul's endeavor to establish a new, global movement, one necessarily alternative to the international society ruled from Rome. Through the collection, Paul urges Achaia, with all its historic, cultural prominence, to turn from West to East. Moreover, in borrowing from the rhetoric of the Diaspora Jewish communities, picturing its transported financial donations as local harvest offerings, Paul encourages the Corinthians to view themselves as bringing the produce of their generous sowing and God's providence to the altar of God. It is as if Paul depicts an agrarian utopia in which the fertile fields of Jerusalem encompass the Mediterranean. After all, the language of sowing pervading 2 Cor 9:6–10 implies no distance. No mediator or envoy conveys seed from the farmer's hand to the soil, and the harvester can reap, transport, and offer on his own. Paul's rhetoric shrinks geographic distance in order to create within his Corinthian audience a sense of community with the Jerusalem saints. The effacement of distance, however, also effaces the role of the traveling apostle, who nevertheless interjects himself in 9:11 (the collection occurs "through us") and 12 (with reference to *diakonia*). As the broker of a new, international society, Paul must always construct his pivotal role, requiring alternation between explicit defense and self-emptying. Even when putting forth an agrarian image of a direct relationship between farmer, seed, and God, Paul slips in his own role. No one need transport the seed to the soil, yet Paul performs just this strange function. In 2 Cor 1–9, travel is the social and rhetorical excess that makes the newness of the Jesus movement possible, an excess that escapes full expression, leaving a remainder as the fuel for social growth. We have seen this remainder strain Paul's rhetoric throughout the letter; no wonder we find the letter concluding in thanksgiving for God's "indescribable gift" (9:15).

Conclusion

Readers of 2 Corinthians have long observed that, however the composition of the letter or the events behind it are construed, all was rectified between Paul and Corinth by the time he wrote his letter to the Romans. At the closing epistolary salutations of Romans, Paul begins with a commendation: "I commend to you Phoebe, our sister, who is a servant-leader [*diakonon*] of the community in Cenchreae [Corinth's eastern port], so that you might welcome her in the Lord in a manner deserving of the saints and provide her with whatever she may need from you. For she has been a benefactor of many people and even of myself" (16:1–2). Sending Phoebe displays both adaptation and flexibility on Paul's part. Instead of charging one of his own subordinate co-workers with delivery of the letter, he chooses a prominent member of his community, whom he calls a "benefactor." Yet he sends her as a *diakonos*, a "courier" or "mediating servant" (I here translate "servant-leader" to avoid possible anachronistic understandings of the usual translations, "minister" or "deacon"), presumably expected to fulfill the normal epistolographic functions of delivery, reading, and explanation. Paul entrusts a woman from the Corinthian community to be his first voice in Rome, the first interpreter of what would become a central pillar of Christian theology and Western thought.

Paul may have found it necessary to display his ability to mend fences with his communities and work alongside fellow envoys not of his network as an important part of his message to Rome. He writes to the Christ-believers in the empire's capital in a spirit of cooperation, looking for both material and spiritual support in his travels and collection efforts. "I greatly desire to see you," he writes at the letter's beginning,

> so that I might share some spiritual gift with you, so that you might be strength-ened—that is, that there might be mutual encouragement among you through each other's faith, both yours and mine. I do not want you to be unaware, brothers, that I have often planned to come to you (but have thus far been prevented from coming) so that I might have some harvest even among you, just as I have among the rest of the Gentiles. To both Greeks and barbarians, the wise and the ignorant, I am a debtor; thus my desire to preach the gospel even among those of you in Rome. (Rom 1:11–15)

Just as he now admits of "benefactors" in Corinth, Paul calls himself a "debtor" to Gentiles of all subject positions—and seeks a similar relationship with Rome. His attitude reflects, in part, an underlying tone of his letter, an ambassadorial call to harmony among God's people, both Jews and Gentiles. As a faithful envoy, Paul's message and behavior model that call.[1]

As quoted at the beginning of this book, Paul viewed his planned trip to Rome as a central point in his evangelical career: "from Jerusalem and all around until Illyricum I have fulfilled the gospel of Christ, and so I have the ambition to proclaim the gospel not where Christ has been mentioned by name, lest I build upon another's foundation; but, rather, as it is written: 'Those to whom he has not been reported will see, and those who have not heard will understand'" (Rom 15:19b–21, citing Isa 52:15). He then outlines his plan to continue to Spain with his message after visiting Rome, once he has delivered the collection to Jerusalem that Macedonia and (finally) Achaia have been generous enough to provide (15:23–32). Yet though he expresses pride in his accomplishments (he has "reason to boast," though only in "what Christ has activated through me" [15:17–18]), he acknowledges his need for their "prayers on his behalf" so that he might eventually find "rest" in visiting Rome (15:30–32).

The rhetoric of Romans betrays the effect that writing 2 Cor 1–9 had on Paul's strategies. Alternately bold (with various apostolic personae in the fore-ground) and humble (confessing dependence on those to whom he preaches), his role oscillates between presence and absence much in the way it increas-ingly faded in and out of focus over the course of his final letter to Corinth. Nowhere is this more apparent than in what scholars increasingly see as the central portion of Romans, chapters 9–11, in which Paul outlines his version of God's ultimate plan for the relationship between Jews and Gentiles.

Paul begins the section by lamenting the rejection of Christ among the majority of Israel. As a solution, he offers a unique scheme based on a creative reading of Jewish scriptures: "Through their [Israel's] transgression, salvation has come to the Gentiles in order to make them jealous" (Rom 11:11). Or, later, explained as a "mystery": "a hardening has occurred over part of Israel until the full number of Gentiles enters; and, in this way, all Israel will be saved" (11:25b–26a). In order for Jews and Gentiles to receive the gospel, however, an initial remnant of Israel was necessary to disseminate the message—a remnant in which Paul proudly claims membership: "So, I say, then, has God rejected his people? By no means! For I am an Israelite, from the seed of Abraham, the tribe of Benjamin!" (11:1).

Through the apostolic remnant, the gospel is made available to all people. Yet earlier in Rom 9–11, Paul's picture of the spread of the gospel conveys much more immediacy than the eschatological scheme whereby the Gentiles' salvation mediates that of Israel. In Rom 10, Paul references Deuteronomy to express the imminence of God's word:

> The righteousness of faith says: "Do not say in your heart, 'Who will go up to heaven?'" (that is, to lead Christ down) "or, 'Who will go down into the abyss?'" (that is, to lead Christ up from the dead). But what does it say? "The word is near you, in your mouth and in your heart"—that is, the word of faith that we proclaim [*kēryssomen*]; for if you confess with your mouth, "Lord Jesus!" and you believe in your heart that God raised him from the dead, you will be saved. (10:6–9, paraphrasing Deut 30:12–14)

The message about Christ—indeed, Paul implies, Christ himself—is as near to the believer as words in the mouth and thoughts of the heart, though it is proclaimed by Paul. The paradox of an unmediated word of faith that is, nevertheless, mediated by the apostle, finds more striking expression as the passage progresses:

> There is no difference between Jew and Greek, for he is Lord of all, making all who call upon his name rich. For everyone who calls upon his name will be saved. So how will they call upon one in whom they have not believed? And how will they believe one from whom they have not heard? And how will they hear without someone to proclaim? And how are they to proclaim unless they are sent? As it is written, "How timely are the feet of those proclaiming the gospel." (10:12–15, citing Isa 52:7)

Ostensibly, apostolic proclamation involves simple communication between hearts and mouths. Yet as Paul strings questions together, a pair of feet step in. It is tempting to read Paul's expression here as a near Freudian slip, as a series of questions that has outrun its natural course. What have feet to do with proclamation, belief, and confession? But has Paul's language really wandered here? Or has Paul intentionally slipped in his apostolic feet? After all, the letter is, as I noted above, intended not just to prepare the way for his visit to Rome, but to secure Roman support for his broader travel plans. In Romans, Paul's itineraries do not merely communicate future missions; they convey the necessary, performative, and cruciform aspect of the word of proclamation. Though wandering appears shameful and suspicious, the gospel is fully proclaimed only through the act of apostolic travel. And while, for Paul, Christ provides unmediated spirit and presence to believers (like a letter written on the human heart; see 2 Cor 3:1–3), Paul is the vanishing go-between in this arrangement of immediacy. The word of proclamation is inseparable from the wandering apostolic body—an idea that, while appearing in Rom 10, Paul first forcefully conveyed through the travel motifs of 2 Cor 1–9.[2]

Paul the Wandering Signifier makes and breaks a series of transient attachments to existing expectations and values over the course of his letters. Perhaps most illuminating, as the conclusion of this book has shown, are the instances in which he briefly omits his role from a global vision of God's people in Christ. The instances are particularly surprising in light of the central role Paul elsewhere asserts for himself, casting his apostleship as fatherhood, foundation-laying, a cause for boasting, a paradigm for cruciform imitation. An exegetical answer emerges in our readings of 2 Corinthians (and Romans): Paul would both assert his central, mediatory role in a diverse movement of many international leaders *and* claim that, in Christ, God's spirit appears present and unmediated among peoples once excluded from his favor.

Analysis of the logic of Paul's rhetoric, however, has offered other clues. Although Paul, in the images comprising 2 Cor 1–9, defends and defines his role as leader in Corinth, the matrix of tropes indicating his apostleship cannot merely point to him but to what he, in turn, represents: the presence of God through Christ and the truth that presence conveys, a truth itself communicated through a series of signifiers, central to which is the cross. The series of identifications and disidentifications, seemingly endless, only points to its ultimate referent through their mutual self-referentiality, an observation now common among theorists of the rhetorical constitution of social movements. The floating signifiers of new social rhetorics can only refer to the future community, the social reality they are deployed to build, by referring to each other. And since the cycle of signifiers contributes not just to communal creation, but to communal maintenance and adaptability, they march in an endless and erratic procession.[3]

Paul as signifier, however, at times follows far more direct itineraries. Although his persona as apostle makes frequent, transient attachments at various discursive stops, oftentimes his apostolic image travels from the very center of a discursive regime to beyond its outer limits, disappearing entirely. So, he momentarily inhabits subject positions as sagacious self-consoler, Bacchic proclaimer, trustworthy courier, only to depart just as quickly lest he take on unwanted connotations of the figure. Because the apostle is also mediator, a signifier central to the network of signifiers he constructs, he must periodically vanish to preserve the illusion of direct reference to larger social and spiritual realities. In order to create a community in which Christ is present, he must efface his own role, traversing heaven, earth, and the many prevailing discourses of empire, to bring about the performative miracle of social newness. There must be no envoy guiding seed to the earth, no herald bringing the word of faith to hearts and mouths—and yet such a wanderer must exist in order for the connection between spirit and society, meaning and human action, to occur. Because a main signifier of Paul's emerging hegemonic discourse was a hegemonic actor, that is, an individual—himself—that signifier needed to alternately occupy the center and fade from view, to make perpetually the transient journey from home to away and back again.

In the end, Paul's juxtaposition of travel and death was in part provided by his point of departure and return for his incursions into the many centers of imperial discourse—the cross, radically marginal but established as a new center, allowing Paul to empty himself of personal status but, more importantly, to temporarily depict a global community without his mediating presence. Yet surrounding those moments where cross replaces apostle, Paul's feet step in, since referentiality always leaves an excess that cannot be totally effaced. When the cross is established in the heart of a city or a subject position, when a people receive a vision of its unity despite diversity, it is always borne by wandering apostles.

The role of travel in 2 Cor 1–9 can help illuminate the role of hegemonic agents, of leaders, in the rhetorics of new social movements, often construed as organic formulations. For theorists, the contingency of Paul's situation as a fringe proclaimer of a marginal ethnicity under imperial subjection may contribute to more general meditations on the discursive oscillations of leaders as signifiers. Furthermore, I hope ancient historians find in Paul another perspective, that of the subjected, on imperial ideologies, at the very least revealing the workings of dominant ideologies through parodic performance. Through the approach outlined here, perhaps biblical scholars will seek as the goal of exegesis not so much propositional and systematic statements relying on a notion of representation-as-correspondence, but the rhetorical mechanics of social imagination, the ways in which language and human action created new realities among the audiences of the gospel. Such an approach goes beyond social history construed as the translation of theological precepts into local assumptions; it takes seriously the notion that what Pauline language attempts to communicate and enact cannot be expressed otherwise than through the cycle of images initiated by the first followers of Jesus and continued in numerous trajectories throughout Christian history, accreting upon biblical interpretations and practices for two millennia.

Finally, inspired by recent, broad-based interest in theopolitical approaches, Paul's wandering form of life can continue to provide resources for theological and otherwise interventionist thought by modeling the creativity of strategy required to visit existing discursive locales, transforming them for alternate and excluded subject positions. Such an approach heeds the contingent paths of the traveling God of Israel, always in some sense an outsider, not so much descending from heaven but, rather, arriving at the outskirts of society to redraw its boundaries and stratifications, to redefine the center and reinscribe the margins, to create a new people.

Notes

Introduction

1. See Paul Zanker, *The Power of Images in the Age of Augustus,* trans. Alan Shapiro (Ann Arbor: University of Michigan Press, 1988), 168. For an attempt to compare Augustus's *ludi saeculare* to Jewish and Christian eschatological worldviews, see Dieter Georgi, "Who Is the True Prophet?" *HTR* 79.1–3 (1986): 100–26. For a good summary of the games and how they fit into Augustus's larger program, see Karl Galinsky, *Augustan Culture: An Interpretive Introduction* (Princeton, NJ: Princeton University Press, 1996), 100–6.

2. "4 Ezra" is the title given to a section of a text found in Vulgate manuscripts, 4 Esdras (2 Esdras in most English translations), a sixteen-chapter composite work, of which chapters 1–2 (5 Ezra) and 15–16 (6 Ezra) are Christian interpolations. 4 Ezra (2 Esdras 3–14) is a late-first-century text reflecting on the Roman destruction of the Jerusalem Temple in 70 C.E. The Latin version is a translation of a lost Greek translation of the Hebrew original, also lost. My citations of this text follow the New Revised Standard Version, though I occasionally alter translations to emphasize language of travel in the Latin version.

3. For the role of Isaiah's heralds in Paul's presentation in Romans, see J. Ross Wagner, *Heralds of the Good News: Isaiah and Paul in Concert in the Letter to the Romans* (Leiden: Brill, 2002).

4. With the term "subject positions," now common in postcritically informed research, I mean to denote different, socially defined ways of being—defined by matrices of social and cultural practices, expectations, patterns of discourse, socioeconomic factors,

etc. I see reference to "subject positions" as an attempt to evade treating the Subject as an a priori, noncontextual reality. For an early attempt to define the concept, see Michel Foucault, *The Archaeology of Knowledge,* trans. A. M. Sheridan Smith (New York: Pantheon, 1972), esp. 53–55.

5. Translations of the *Carmen saeculare* are taken from Michael C. J. Putnam, *Horace's Carmen Saeculare: Ritual Magic and the Poet's Art* (New Haven, CT: Yale University Press, 2000), with punctuation altered for clarity in places. I am indebted to many of Putnam's thematic interpretations.

6. For an interpretation of the absence of a "Golden Age" in the *Carmen* as a critique of luxury, I follow Duncan Baker, "The Golden Age Is Proclaimed? The Carmen Saeculare and the Renascence of the Golden Race," *Classical Quarterly* 46.2 (1997): 434–46.

7. Emma Dench, *Romulus' Asylum: Roman Identities from the Age of Alexander to the Age of Hadrian* (Oxford: Oxford University Press, 2005), esp. 96–117, highlights the discursive role played by geographic and social mobility during the late Republic and early Empire; see 114–15 for accusations against the background of Octavian and the Julii, a family with roots in Alba who became a leading family in the city of Rome. On freer travel and trade as a sign of the emperor's powers, see Clifford Ando, *Imperial Ideology and Provincial Loyalty in the Roman Empire* (Berkeley: University of California Press, 2000), 54, 389 (where the citation from Philo appears; I follow his translation, which is guided by the LCL). Mary Beard, *The Roman Triumph* (Cambridge, MA: Belknap Press of Harvard University Press, 2009), 119–24 and 133–42, contains a recent and perceptive discussion of the triumph as a ritual location for meditations on the dangerous permeability afforded by Roman conquest.

With reference to "Augustan" or even "imperial ideology/propaganda" throughout this study, I evoke in a shorthanded way a complex set of phenomena, involving various communications and actions of leaders as well as responses by imperial subjects. At times, I use "self-fashioning" or "self-definition" as a clearer synonym. For an important critique of a facile notion of Augustan "propaganda," see Galinsky, *Augustan Culture,* 39–41. In general, I am influenced by the focus on Roman imperial strivings for *consensus,* a central emphasis in Ando, *Imperial Ideology,* passim.

8. On 2 Cor 11:25–28 as a list of common ancient travel hardships, see Jerome Murphy-O'Connor, "Traveling Conditions in the First Century: On the Road and Sea with St. Paul," *Biblical Review* 1.2 (1985): 38–47.

9. Lionel Casson, *Travel in the Ancient World* (London: George Allen and Unwin, 1974), 67–73, 122, 163–76; Wayne A. Meeks, *The First Urban Christians: The Social World of the Apostle Paul* (New Haven, CT: Yale University Press, 1983), 17–18; Raymond Chevallier, *Voyages et déplacements dans l'Empire Romain* (Paris: Armand Colin, 1988), 53–55, 115–19. See now (in a volume that thankfully appeared during the course of my final revisions) Ryan S. Schellenberg, " 'Danger in the Wilderness, Danger at Sea': Paul and the Perils of Travel," in *Travel and Religion in Antiquity,* ed. Philip A. Harland (Waterloo, Ontario: Wilfrid Laurier Press, 2011), 141–61, who rightly argues that far too little attention has been paid to the material hardships of travel as a fundamental aspect of Paul's apostolic lifestyle—though my study attempts to

take into account both physical exigencies and Paul's rhetorical and performative representation of such exigencies.

10. Statius, *Silvae* 3.2.76–80, 86–88 (trans. from *The Silvae of Statius,* trans. Betty Rose Nagle [Bloomington: Indiana University Press, 2004]). For a discussion of the *propemptikon* genre and its focus on the danger of travel, see Francis Cairns, *Generic Composition in Greek and Roman Poetry* (Edinburgh: Edinburgh University Press, 1972), 10–11, 120–21, 130.

11. M. I. Finley's chapter on farming (*The Ancient Economy,* 2nd ed. [Berkeley: University of California Press, 1985], 95–122) makes this central argument. His observations are built upon by Lionel Casson, "Energy and Technology in the Ancient World," in *Ancient Trade and Society* (Detroit: Wayne State University Press, 1984), 140–48. Finley cites and discusses Cicero, *Off.* 1.151 at 41–44; see also Casson, "Energy and Technology," 143, who touches upon the figure of Trimalchio from Petronius's *Satyricon,* a freed slave who becomes wealthy off of trade but then immediately becomes landed. The novel lampoons him as a particularly offensive and ridiculous example of the nouveau riche.

12. Translations of *Aristeas* are from R. J. H. Shutt, "*Letter of Aristeas,*" in *OTP* 1.7–34.

13. There is currently no consensus among New Testament scholars about the literary integrity of 2 Cor, and all proposed reconstructions must be considered hypothetical. For detailed defenses of the viewpoint I adopt, see James Houghton Kennedy, *The Second and Third Epistles of St. Paul to the Corinthians* (London: Methuen, 1900), and Francis Watson, "2 Cor. X–XIII and Paul's Painful Letter to the Corinthians," *JTS* 35.2 (1984): 324–46. The main theories are as follows:

1. The entire canonical book consists of one Pauline letter.

2. 2 Cor 1–9 and 10–13 represent fragments of two separate letters; some (including me) reverse the chronological order of the letters, identifying 2 Cor 10–13 as the tearful letter mentioned in 2 Cor 2:4.

3. Some see 2 Cor 8 and/or 9 as separate, short letters.

4. Some see 2 Cor 2:14–7:4 as a letter fragment inserted into another letter fragment consisting of 2 Cor 1:1–2:13 and 7:5–16. (To me, 2:13 and 7:5 do not fit together neatly; 7:5 reads as *resumptive of,* not *consecutive to,* 2:13.) Observations 3 and 4 lead many scholars to see the canonical book as consisting of as many as five original Pauline letters which scholars set in various chronological orders.

5. Finally, many (including me) see 2 Cor 6:14–7:1 as a later, non-Pauline interpolation, since it contains numerous terms not used elsewhere by Paul, it seems to interrupt the flow of the narrative, and it seems to contradict ideas Paul expresses earlier in the Corinthian correspondence.

My reading implicitly (and in places explicitly) argues for the unity of 2 Cor 1–9 (minus the interpolation at 6:14–7:1) as a letter subsequent to that found in 2 Cor 10–13, largely on thematic, rhetorical, and chronological grounds.

Travel as a coherent theme throughout 2 Cor, and especially spanning chapters 1–7, has been posited by a few interpreters: the observation appears as an addition to later, German editions of Bengel's *Gnomon,* a suggestion mentioned by Alfred Plummer, *A Critical and Exegetical Commentary on the Second Epistle of St. Paul to the Corinthians,* 5th ed. (Edinburgh: T & T Clark, 1956), xiv. See also John T. Fitzgerald, *Cracks in an Earthen Vessel: An Examination of the Catalogues of Hardships in the Corinthian Correspondence* (Atlanta, GA: Scholars Press, 1988), 160. The most extensive examination is the conference paper by Benjamin Fiore, "Root Metaphors in Paul—Pauline Comings and Goings: The Travel Image," *Proceedings, Eastern Great Lakes and Midwest Biblical Societies* 11 (1991): 174–84.

14. The phrase is the subtitle of one of the best-known post-Marxist works to draw attention to Paul: Alain Badiou, *St. Paul: The Foundation of Universalism,* trans. Ray Brassier (Stanford, CA: Stanford University Press, 2003). Postcolonialism has brought renewed interest in European travel writing interpreted as discursive support for colonial knowledge and domination. For an early attempt, see Mary Louise Pratt, *Imperial Eyes: Travel Writing and Transculturation* (London: Routledge, 1992). For an overview, see Peter Hulme and Tim Youngs, eds., *The Cambridge Companion to Travel Writing* (Cambridge: Cambridge University Press, 2002), esp. Mary Baine Campbell, "Travel Writing and Its Theory," 261–78. In general, European travel writing tended to serve, in a number of rhetorical modes, to bolster colonial expansion and the self-image of the colonizer both at home and abroad. In my reading (and that of many classicists), Roman discourse about travel often betrayed significant ambivalence about global expansion and its effect on traditional culture.

15. An important, early attempt to pair social-historical approaches with a feminist hermeneutic is Elizabeth Schüssler Fiorenza, *In Memory of Her: A Feminist Theological Reconstruction of Christian Origins* (New York: Crossroad, 1983). For a recent, compelling argument in favor of combining materialist or "nonidealist" approaches with postcolonialist and gender studies concerns, see Davina Lopez, *Apostle to the Conquered: Reimagining Paul's Mission* (Minneapolis: Augsburg Fortress, 2008), 6–17.

16. Schüssler Fiorenza, *In Memory of Her,* 218–36, suggests a decentering of Paul's role within modern reconstructions of the international spread of the Jesus movement. In particular, his accommodations for women's roles in leadership within the Jesus movement were more likely reactions to women attaining those roles in Corinth and the central role of women in the non-Pauline communities than the product of his own theological innovation.

17. For a concise statement of this insight, see Wayne A. Meeks, "The Christian Proteus," in *The Writings of St. Paul,* ed. Wayne A. Meeks and John T. Fitzgerald, 2nd ed. (New York: Norton, 2007), 690.

18. A fuller discussion of this passage occurs at the beginning of Chapter 5.

19. On discourses of "excess" and "exception" as being socially constitutive, see Giorgio Agamben, *The State of Exception,* trans. Kevin Attell (Chicago: University of Chicago Press, 2005), 60, 73; Badiou, *Saint Paul,* 13–15 and 65–74 (though his *Being and Event,* trans. Oliver Feltham [London: Continuum, 2005], makes similar points through the much more complicated route of set theory); and Ernesto Laclau, *On Populist Reason* (London: Verso, 2005), 149–56, 223–24. Laclau, discussed in more detail below, speaks of new social movements establishing "strategic antagonisms" with existing hegemonic discourses in order to create the illusion of exclusion, though such movements creatively redeploy existing signifiers in the interests of specific social demands.

20. On avoiding language of "middle class" when referring to ancient cities and focus-
    ing on language of "subsistence," see Steven J. Friesen, "Poverty in Pauline Studies:
    Beyond the So-called New Consensus," *JSNT* 26.3 (2004): 323–61.

21. Recent book-length arguments about the corporate "body of Christ" metaphor
    within the context of ancient political rhetoric, yet with a Pauline adaptation to
    include concern for the marginalized, include Margaret Mitchell, *The Rhetoric of
    Reconciliation: An Exegetical Investigation of the Language and Composition of 1
    Corinthians* (Tübingen: J. C. B. Mohr, 1991), and Dale B. Martin, *The Corinthian
    Body* (New Haven, CT: Yale University Press, 1995).

22. Excerpt from Chrysippus, *On Passions,* cited in Galen, *Plac.* 4.2.15–17 (*SVF* 3.462);
    see I. G. Kidd, "Posidonius on Emotions," in *Problems in Stoicism,* ed. A. A. Long
    (London: Athlone, 1996), 202; A. A. Long and D. N. Sedley, eds., *The Hellenistic
    Philosophers,* 2 vols. (Cambridge: Cambridge University Press, 1987), 1.413–14,
    420. For an earlier attempt linking the literary theme of travel with what Walter
    Burke called "fictional death," see Eric J. Leed, *The Mind of the Traveler: From
    Gilgamesh to Global Tourism* (New York: Basic Books, 1991), 8–9 and 224–27,
    providing a penetrating interpretation of dismembered mythic travelers in terms of
    masculine subject formation. My analysis takes the travel-death connection in more
    poststructuralist and social-constructivist directions.

23. When Laclau speaks of floating signifiers, he tends to speak of vague, generic values
    such as "justice." Certainly, as seen above, Paul takes recourse to cognate concepts
    such as "righteousness" and "peace." But in practice, effective floating signifiers tend
    to take on figures of an ostensibly more specific content. So, Laclau also points to
    Althusser's analysis of the Russian revolution circulating around demands for "bread,
    peace, and land" (*On Populist Reason,* 97). And insofar as hegemonic regimes also
    produce floating signifiers to retain cultural dominance, one could turn to the Ameri-
    can scene and identify icons such as "the Marlboro Man" and "Coke" as attempts
    both to express and to forge a unified, cultural identity. (Ernesto Laclau [*On Populist
    Reason,* 104–5] borrows the examples from Slavoj Žižek, *The Sublime Object of
    Ideology* [London: Verso, 1989], 96.) The term "floating signifier" was originally
    coined by Claude Lévi-Strauss; see *Introduction to the Work of Marcel Mauss,* trans.
    Felicity Baker (London: Routledge, 1987). On floating signifiers as creating tempo-
    rary or "transient" attachments to social realities, see Laclau, "Subject of Politics,
    Politics of the Subject," in *Emancipation(s),* 2nd ed. (London: Verso, 2007), 56–65;
    "Identity and Hegemony: The Role of Universality in the Constitution of Political
    Logics," in Judith Butler, Ernesto Laclau, and Slavoj Žižek, *Contingency, Hegemony,
    Universality: Contemporary Dialogues on the Left* (London: Verso, 2000), 49–53;
    and *On Populist Reason,* 88–89.

24. Giorgio Agamben, *The Time That Remains: A Commentary on the Letter to
    the Romans,* trans. Patricia Dailey (Stanford, CA: Stanford University Press,
    2005), 56.

25. Jacob Taubes, *The Political Theology of Paul,* ed. Aleida Assmann and Jan Assmann,
    trans. Dana Hollander (Stanford, CA: Stanford University Press, 2004), 24–25; see
    Agamben, *Time That Remains,* 55. Forms of *perisseia* ("excess") occur twenty times
    over the course of the letter; forms of *hyperballein* ("to exceed") occur five times;

pleonassein (also "to exceed") roots occur three times. Throughout this study, I also point out the central rhetorical role of this concept.

Chapter 1. Traveling Leaders of the Ancient Mediterranean

1. On Hermes and Apollo as travelers, especially as compared in the *Homeric Hymn to Hermes,* see Silvia Montiglio, *Wandering in Ancient Greek Culture* (Chicago: University of Chicago Press, 2005), 86–90. On Acts 14:8–18, see Luther H. Martin, "Gods or Ambassadors of God? Barnabas and Paul in Lystra," *NTS* 41 (1995): 152–56. See also Gen 18:1–15 and Heb 13:2.

2. For *theoxenia,* see Michael H. Jameson, "Theoxenia," in *Ancient Cult Practice from Epigraphical Evidence,* ed. R. Hägg (Stockholm: P. Åströms Förlag, 1994), 37–41. For arrivals of the gods, see Walter Burkert, "*Katagógia-Anagógia* and the Goddess of Knossos," in *Early Greek Cult Practice: Proceedings of the Fifth International Symposium at the Swedish Institute at Athens, 26–29 June, 1986,* ed. Robin Hägg, Nanno Marinatos, and Gullög C. Nordquist (Stockholm: Paul Åströms Förlag, 1988), 84–87. The mythic travels of gods and goddesses often corresponded with the cycle of seasons, especially in the case of Demeter and Persephone. The myth behind the City Dionysia is recounted in the scholion to Aristophanes's *Ach.* 1.23; see the discussion in Robert Garland, *Introducing New Gods: The Politics of Athenian Religion* (Ithaca, NY: Cornell University Press, 1992), 158–59 (Garland, at 42, asserts that the festival probably originated with Athens's annexation of Eleutherai during the sixth-century reign of Athenian tyrant Pisistratus and that its political function was the celebration of Athens's Attic hegemony); Christina Sourvinou-Inwood, *Tragedy and Athenian Religion* (Lanham, MD: Lexington Books, 2003), 72–73.

3. In this case, the translation from Apuleius is Jack Lindsay's (*The Golden Ass* [Bloomington: Indiana University Press, 1960]). Cybele/Magna Mater was famously brought to reside in Rome in response to a reading of the Sibylline Oracles; see Livy 29.10.4–11.8, 14.5–14, and Ovid, *Fast.* 4.247–372, and the discussion in Elizabeth R. Gebhard, "The Gods in Transit: Narratives of Cult Transfer," in *Antiquity and Humanity: Essays on Ancient Religion and Philosophy; Presented to Hans Dieter Betz on His 70th Birthday,* ed. Adela Yarbro Collins, and Margaret Mitchell (Tübingen: Mohr Siebeck, 2001), 453–56. Propertius's frustrations with Isis are highlighted by John F. Miller, "Propertius' Tirade against Isis (2.33a)," *CJ* 77 (1981–1982): 104–11.

4. See the discussion in John J. Collins, *Between Athens and Jerusalem: Jewish Identity in the Hellenistic Diaspora,* 2nd ed. (Grand Rapids, MI: Eerdmans, 2000), 38, 67–68, 122–23. For Ptolemy IV Philopator, see 3 Macc 2:29 and a fragment from Artapanus preserved in Eusebius, *Praep. Ev.* 9.27. For Antiochus IV Epiphanes, see 2 Macc 6:7–8. Plutarch discusses Dionysiac rites and Sukhoth in *Quaest. Conviv.* 4.6. For a speculative but compelling rereading of the actions of Antiochus IV Epiphanes as Judean-Dionysiac religious "reform," see JoAnn Scurlock, "One Hundred Sixty-Seven BCE: Hellenism or Reform?" *JSJ* 31.2 (2000): 125–61.

5. For the admission of Magna Mater to Rome, see Livy 29.14.5–14 and Ovid, *Fast.* 4.247–348. Dionysius of Halicarnassus 2.19.3–5 gives regulations for the cult. Livy 39.8–14 describes the controversy in 186 B.C.E.; the corresponding inscription is *ILS*

18. On wandering cultic practitioners, see now Ian W. Scott, "The Divine Wanderer: Travel and Divinization in Late Antiquity," in *Travel and Religion in Antiquity,* ed. Philip A. Harland (Waterloo, Ontario: Wilfrid Laurier Press, 2011), 101–22.

6. For archaic artistic depictions as reflecting colonial travels, see Brunilde S. Ridgway, "Architectural Sculpture and Travel Myths," *DHA* 17.2 (1991): 95–112. For François Hartog on Odysseus's journey as an exercise in epic anthropology, see *Memories of Odysseus: Frontier Tales from Ancient Greece,* trans. Janet Lloyd (Chicago: University of Chicago Press, 2001), 16–17. Irad Malkin, in *The Returns of Odysseus: Colonization and Ethnicity* (Berkeley: University of California Press, 1998), also explores the apparent contradiction between those returning home standing in for colonists: "With some ambivalence, and perhaps because of it, the *returns* of the heroes came to articulate the consequences of Greeks' *setting out* for the coasts of the west. The Nostos Odysseus never stops returning, and the *Odyssey* echoes return stories of all kinds" (9, italics original). More specifically, "colonization may sometimes have been responsible for the consolidation of the political community of the city of origin; because of their *ex novo* character colonies provided models of more sophisticated political and social organization to be emulated in the older world" (13). In this way, colonies could be viewed as expressions of the ideals of the home culture.

7. All quotations from the *Odyssey* are from *Homer: The Odyssey,* trans. Robert Fagles (New York: Viking, 1996). See the discussion in Hartog, *Memories of Odysseus,* 32–33: "In contrast to a heroic death . . . at the head of one's warriors, death at sea is totally horrifying, for the dying man loses everything, in return for nothing at all: his life, his homecoming, and also his renown and even his name. Worse still, although he loses his life, he is not truly dead. For until such time as he is given the last rites his shade is left 'wandering in vain along the broad-gated house of Hades' [*Il.* 23.74]." For other texts addressing the fear of not being buried in one's homeland, see Teles, *Peri Phygēs* 29.2; Seneca, *Helv.* 19.1–7, depicts Seneca's aunt, who braved a stormy and dangerous sea voyage in order to bear her husband's dead body home for burial.

8. Montiglio, *Wandering in Ancient Greek Culture,* 9; Hartog, *Memories of Odysseus,* 22 and 24.

9. See Hartog, *Memories of Odysseus,* 80–87 and 157, for a discussion of the legendary "threshold deaths" at the Hellespont and Herodotus's explanation of the Greek-Persian divide. The death of the Achaean soldier Proetsiaus is found in *Il.* 2.698–702, while the Persian Artÿctes is found in Herodotus 9.116. Alexander the Great's sacrifice upon crossing the Hellespont is preserved in Arrian, *Anab.* 7.43. Thucydides 1.3.3 is quoted and translated in Hartog, *Memories of Odysseus,* 79–80. See also Andrew Erskine, *Troy between Greece and Rome: Local Tradition and Imperial Power* (Oxford: Oxford University Press, 2001), 61–92. Regarding the Hellespont, I do not mean to imply that it was a boundary permanently fixed in Greek literary imagination, only that the Europe-Asia divide was a rhetorical option frequently deployed by ancient writers. The tale of Paul's dream in Acts 16:9–12 coercing him to journey from Asia to Macedonia probably expresses the notion that the apostle here crosses the continental divide and thus initiates an important new phase in his worldwide mission.

10. Here, I draw on the classic discussion in W. B. Stanford, *The Ulysses Theme: A Study in the Adaptability of a Traditional Hero* (Ann Arbor: University of Michigan Press, 1968), 100–17. He cites *Tro.* 431–44 at 114.

11. Hartog, *Memories of Odysseus,* 109–10. See the complete collection and assessment of Anacharsis traditions in Jan Fredrik Kindstrand, *Anacharsis, the Legend and the Apothegmata* (Uppsala: Almqvist and Wiksell, 1981). Kindstrand sees "Scythian shamans," often figured as the Hyperborean envoys who brought offerings to Apollo at Delphi, as the historical precursor to the legend (18–23).

12. On laughter and boundary crossing in the Anacharsis legends, see Hartog, *Memories of Odysseus,* 111–13.

13. See the assessment of the antiseafaring apophthegmata in Kindstrand, *Anacharsis,* 116–17 and 145–46; in many cases, other sources attributed similar sayings to other famous figures. See also R. P. Martin, "The Scythian Accent: Anacharsis and the Cynics," in *The Cynics: The Cynic Movement in Antiquity and Its Legacy,* ed. R. Bracht Branham and Marie-Odile Goulet-Cazé (Berkeley: University of California Press, 1996), 151: "Here is an echo of the paradoxical folktale character who has been much traveled yet wants nothing to do with the sea, and wanders about, enduring insults over wine in others' houses . . . Of course, much of the *Odyssey* is built along similar lines. Cynics, from Antisthenes on, admired and imitated Odysseus. This Anacharsis *could* be the last in that long line of copies" (emphasis in the original). See also the evaluation of this tradition in James Romm, "Dog Heads and Noble Savages: Cynicism before the Cynics?" in *The Cynics,* 130–31.

14. Ps.-Anacharsis, *Epistle* 1.13–14. All translations of Ps.-Anacharsis are by Anne McGuire, in Abraham J. Malherbe, *The Cynic Epistles: A Study Edition* (Missoula, MT: Scholars Press, 1977), 35–51.

15. See the depiction of Crates as "Door-opener" in DL 6.86, or the tales of Anacharsis knocking on Solon's door (see above); see also Ps.-Anacharsis, *Epistle* 2. For "temporary" uses of the Cynic persona, such as Dio's, see the discussion in Margarethe Billerbeck, "The Ideal Cynic from Epictetus to Julian," in *The Cynics,* 212–13; Montiglio, *Wandering in Ancient Greek Culture,* 193–203.

16. See the discussion in Derek Krueger, "The Bawdy and Society: The Shamelessness of Diogenes in Roman Imperial Culture," in *The Cynics,* 222–39; for writers attacking Cynic obscenity, see Cicero, *Off.* 1.128, and Theodoret, *Affect.* 12.48. *Chreiai* used for grammatical and rhetorical education are collected in Ronald F. Hock and Edward N. O'Neil, *The Chreia in Ancient Rhetoric. Vol. 1: The Progymnasmata* (Atlanta, GA: Scholars Press, 1986): "In Diogenes Laertius' day, probably the early third century A.D., the chreiai attributed to Diogenes were beyond cataloguing, and even today the extant chreiai may number, according to one estimate, perhaps a thousand. Indeed, what people today most typically know about Diogenes is preserved in chreiai" (3).

17. On the Stoic notion of *adiaphora,* see A. A. Long and D. N. Sedley, eds., *The Hellenistic Philosophers,* 2 vols. (Cambridge: Cambridge University Press, 1987), 1.354–59. On travel as an external, see Horace, *Ep.* 1.11; Seneca, *Helv.* 8.2–6, 10.2–6.

18. On Greek exile, see Simon Hornblower, "Exile (Greek)" and Barry Nicholas, "Exile (Roman)," *OCD,* 580; for cognate Roman punitive practices, see Jo-Marie Claassen, *Displaced Persons: The Literature of Exile from Cicero to Boethius* (Madison: University

of Wisconsin Press, 1999), 11, 20. Giorgio Agamben's study (*Homo Sacer: Sovereign Power and Bare Life*, trans. Daniel Heller-Roazen [Stanford, CA: Stanford University Press, 1998], 71–103) focuses on ancient discussions in Festus Pompeius and Macrobius (*Saturnalia* 3.7.3–8) and refers to Giuliano Crifò, "Exilica causa, quae adversus exulem agitur," in *Du châtiment dans la cité: Supplices corporels et peine de mort dans le monde antique* (Rome: L'École française de Rome, 1984), 460–65, as drawing a connection between exile and the concept of *sacratio*.

19. Euripides's *Phoenissae* (especially Polyneices's speech in 357–406) was confronted in consolations on exile since the genre's earliest incarnations: see Heinz-Günther Nesselrath, "Later Greek Voices on the Predicament of Exile: From Teles to Plutarch and Favorinus," in *Writing Exile: The Discourse of Displacement in Greco-Roman Antiquity and Beyond*, ed. Jan Felix Gaertner (Leiden: Brill, 2007), 87–108, for a discussion of Teles, *Peri phygēs;* Musonius Rufus, *Peri phygēs;* Plutarch, *De exilo* (who addresses and refutes the speech directly beginning in 16 [605F]); and Favorinus, *Peri phygēs*. Additionally, it was a common topos that great intellectuals such as Thucydides, Xenophon, and Marius completed their greatest literary works by means of the otium afforded by exile (cf. Plutarch, *Exil.* 13–14 [604D–605D]; Seneca, *Helv.* 9.4–5). Roman writers note that, when compared to the daily peregrinations which characterized the patron-client system, exile was a relatively sedentary and peaceful state (for example, Seneca, *Polyb.* 9). For the notion, in response to the travails of exile, that heaven is the true home of humanity as a consolation in the face of exile, see Plutarch, *Exil.* 5 [600F].

20. Among other places, I find the phrase "civic death" in Claassen, *Displaced Persons,* 239, with respect to Cicero's writings on his exile. See also 83–85 for discussions of exile and death in Ovid and Cicero. For Cicero's responses to exile, see *Att.* 3.15, *Red. Pop.* 14, and the discussion in Sarah T. Cohen, "Cicero's Roman Exile," in *Writing Exile,* 111–12.

21. See the argument in Silvia Montiglio, "Wandering Philosophers in Classical Greece," *JHS* 120 (2000): 90–91, whose translation of Empedocles I follow.

22. Scholars have puzzled that Aristotle, elsewhere an opponent of the substantial, immortal soul (see *Eth. nic.* 1111b2), seems to imply that very possibility. See the argument in Anton-Hermann Chroust, "Eudemus or On the Soul: A Lost Dialogue of Aristotle on the Immortality of the Soul," *Mnemosyne* 19 (1966): 117–30, that the nature of the soul in the *Eudemus* reflects a generic feature of consolations. Rather than present a coherent, systematic psychology, Aristotle offers therapeutic arguments assuaging grief. For a helpful introduction to philosophical consolations (and an application to Paul's letter to the Philippians), see Paul A. Holloway, *Consolation in Philippians: Philosophical Sources and Rhetorical Strategy* (Cambridge: Cambridge University Press, 2001).

23. For the *Axiochus,* I follow the translation and commentary of Jackson P. Hershbell, *Pseudo-Plato, Axiochus* (Chico, CA: Scholars Press, 1981); Hershbell outlines the philosophical influences on the *Axiochus* in 1–5 and 14–18 and notes the *sēma-sōma* ("prison-body") connection in Orphism and its influence on Platonic literature (1, 23–24).

24. For other references to death as a journey in *Tusc.,* see 1.27 (death is "like a migration or change of place" [*quasi migrationem commutationemque*]); 1.32 ("Hercules went

away to the gods" [*Abiit ad deos Hercules*]) because "when he was among men, he built for himself a roadway" [*cum inter homines esset, eam sibi viam munivisset*]); 1.44–45 (the soul becomes free to examine "the very boundaries of those places"—the very knowledge longed for when the souls "dwelt on earth" [*has terras incolentes*], and a far better accomplishment than Jason's trip all the way to Pontus); 1.82 (to die is to "migrate heavenward" [*in caelum migrare*]); 1.96 (death is "a delightful journey" [*iter iucundum*]); 1.97–98 (an extensive quotation of the end of Plato's *Apol.* [40C]); and 1.118–19 (near the end of *Tusc.* 1: the idea of death should cause joy in that "we journey back to a home eternal and completely ours" [*in aeternam et plane nostram domum remigremus*], 118). For other Ciceronian references, see *Sen.* 83 and 84.

25. In addition to the Senecan passages discussed in detail throughout this chapter, see also Seneca, *Ep.* 63.8, 16; 70.2–5 (discussed in Chapter 3); 99.7, 12; *Brev. Vit.* 2.3, 7.10, 15.4, 18.1, 19.1, to list just some examples among his works. Seneca also refers to life as a journey, even toward death, in *Polyb.* (9.6–7, 11.3).

26. All translations from *Ad Marciam* are from the LCL edition. For other combinations of consolation, cosmology, and "celestial travel" in Seneca, see *Polyb.* 9 and *Ep.* 93.9. Later Greek consolations also feature expressions of death as travel. See in particular Plutarch, *Cons. Ux.* 10 [612A], and, in particular, *Cons. Apoll.* (falsely attributed to Plutarch—Ps.-Plutarch), a hodge-podge of earlier material from consolations on death; see esp. 31 [117F] (where life is a "sojourn" [*epidēmia*]) and 34 [119F–120B], where Apollonius's son's death is called a return journey home. See also 23 [113C–D]: "For just as when it has been decided to migrate to a new fatherland, and the journey is compulsory for all, and none by entreaty can escape it, some go on ahead and others follow after, but all come to the same place; in the same manner, of all those who are journeying toward Destiny, those who come more tardily have no advantage over those who arrive earlier" (LCL trans.).

27. In general, on Paul's itinerary, see the work of Gerd Theissen, in particular "Legitimation and Subsistence: An Essay on the Sociology of Early Christian Missionaries," in Theissen, *The Social Setting of Pauline Christianity: Essays on Corinth,* ed. and trans. John H. Schütz (Philadelphia: Fortress, 1982), 27–67, an essay that explains the conflict between Paul and his rival apostles in Corinth as a dissonance between Palestinian and Pauline models of material support for itinerant preaching.

28. Ronald F. Hock, *The Social Context of Paul's Ministry: Tentmaking and Apostleship* (Philadelphia: Fortress, 1980), 29–31, analyzes Paul's possible tendencies for finding accommodations, distinguishing between his needs for short-term and long-term stays. Peter Marshall, *Enmity in Corinth: Social Conventions in Paul's Relations with the Corinthians* (Tübingen: J. C. B. Mohr [Paul Siebeck], 1987), 137, focuses on Gaius; see his general discussion on Paul and hospitality at 137–43. See also his discussion of Greek and Roman "ambivalence" toward the foreign friend (4). Margaret E. Thrall, *A Critical and Exegetical Commentary on the Second Epistle to the Corinthians,* 2 vols. (ICC; London: T & T Clark, 2000–2004), 1.184, entertains that this may have been the original meaning of the "open-door" figure among earlier missionaries; there is no need to assume, however, that this literal meaning is absent from Pauline usage. As she mentions, Hans Windisch, *Der zweite Korintherbrief* (KEK; Göttingen:

Vandenhoeck and Ruprecht, 1924), 94, notes a parallel in DL 6.86 concerning Crates the Cynic: "He was called the 'Door Opener' (*Thurepanoiktēs*) because he would enter every house and start chastising."

29. For the argument, see Helmut Koester, "Imperial Ideology and Paul's Eschatology in 1 Thessalonians," in *Paul and Empire: Religion and Power in Roman Imperial Society*, ed. Richard A. Horsley (Harrisburg, PA: Trinity Press, 1997), 158–60 (quotation on 160). For another Pauline reference to Christ's *parousia*, see 1 Cor 15:23.

30. For an early version of this argument, see Edwin A. Judge, "The Social Identity of the First Christians: A Question of Method in Religious History," *JRH* 11: 211–14.

31. In Chapter 6 I discuss in more detail the ideological work performed by the collection.

32. For discussions of past scholarship on reconstructing the dispute in Corinth, see Thrall, *Second Corinthians*, 1.49–74.

Chapter 2. Travel, Suicide, and Self-Construction

1. Adolf Deissmann, *Paul: A Study in Social and Religious History*, trans. William E. Wilson, 2nd ed. (New York: Harper and Brothers, 1927), 23. For other descriptions of 2 Cor as especially emotional or personal, see C. K. Barrett, *A Commentary on the Second Epistle to the Corinthians* (BNTC; New York: Harper and Row, 1973), 32; Victor Paul Furnish, *II Corinthians* (AB; Garden City, NY: Doubleday, 1984), 3.

2. Since Chrysostom views 2 Cor as a compositional unity, he sees Paul's promise to visit as occurring in 1 Cor 4:19 and 16:5–6. According to the "identification hypothesis" I support here, Paul promises this visit in 2 Cor 13:1–4.

3. Demetrius is cited and translated in Abraham J. Malherbe, *Ancient Epistolary Theorists* (Atlanta, GA: Scholars Press, 1988), 18–19, as is Cicero 24–25; see similar sentiments in Cicero, *Att.* 9.10.1 and *Fam.* 16.16.2, 12.30.1. *P.Mich.* 8.482 is cited in Klaus Thraede, *Grundzüge griechisch-römischer Brieftopik* (Munich: Beck, 1970), 79. For the importance of the letter writer's *parousia*, see Heiki Koskenniemi, *Studien zur Idee und Phraseologie des grichischen Briefes bis 400 n. Chr.* (Helsinki: Finnish Academy, 1956). For travel plans as enforcing the letter as a substitute for the author's presence, see the discussion in John Lee White, *Light from Ancient Letters* (Philadelphia: Fortress, 1986), 202.

My observations on the importance of travel plans and the epistolary question of the letter writer's "presence," or *parousia*, recall the work of Robert Funk on the epistolary form he denotes as the "apostolic *parousia*," a concept derived in large part from the work of Koskenniemi. He views such forms as taking place in the epistolary frames (that is, at the beginning and end) of Paul's letters. For this reason, he rejects 2 Cor 1:1–2:13 (and 7:5–16) as examples of the phenomenon, since he accepts the five-letter partition hypothesis with regard to canonical 2 Cor. (See Robert W. Funk, *Language, Hermeneutic, and the Word of God: The Problem of Language in the New Testament and Contemporary Theology* [New York: Harper and Row, 1966], 264–66 and 273–74; and "The Apostolic *Parousia*: Form and Significance," in *Christian History and Interpretation: Studies Presented to John Knox*, ed. C. F. D. Moule, W. R. Farmer, and R. R. Niebuhr [Cambridge: Cambridge University

Press, 1967], 251 and 267). Notably, Funk sees Rom as being framed by travel plans, a macrostructure that would resemble what I propose here for the letter preserved in 2 Cor 1–9. See now the helpful discussion in Lee A. Johnson, "Paul's Epistolary Presence in Corinth: A New Look at Robert W. Funk's Apostolic *Parousia*," *CBQ* 68.3 (2006): 481–501, though Johnson's adherence to Funk's typology prevents her from considering passages in 2 Cor 1–7.

4. The first letter is from 80–30 B.C.E., and the second is from the second or third century C.E. Other letters with *eboulomēn* ("I would want") indicating intended travel plans include *P.Mich.* 751, late second century C.E.; *P.Flor.* 156, third century C.E.; and *P.Lond.* 479, third century C.E.. The role of the courier (and not just the letter) as a replacement for the sender will be discussed in Chapter 4.

5. Actually, what appears on the papyrus at this point is *thelō se ginōskein se thelō hoti* ("I want you to know you I want that"). Apparently, Saturnilus could not decide how to phrase the disclosure formula at this point, and his emotions have affected his grammatical construction.

6. The letter is from 114–116 C.E.; ed. and trans. J. G. Winter. For examples of travel apologies in business letters, see White, *Light from Ancient Letters*, 25, 79. White also gives examples from personal letters (his translations): "And I shall make an effort . . . to come to you immediately" (Julius Apollinarios to his father, Julius Sabinus, *P.Mich.* 8.446 [105], 107 C.E.); "I myself hope to come to you soon" (Terentianus to his sister, Tasoucharion, *P.Mich.* 8.481 [112]). For other examples of letters using disclosure formulae to express travel plans, see *P.Oxy.* 14.1773 (third century C.E.), *P.Oxy.* 41.2982 (second–third century C.E.). See the discussion of disclosure formulae below.

7. On *recusationes* and *Ep.* 1.7 as an example of this genre, see Phebe Lowell Bowditch, *Horace and the Gift Economy of Patronage* (Berkeley: University of California Press, 2001), 16, 162–63.

8. Line 34 is the translation of Bowditch, *Horace*, 186. Line 39 is my translation. Scholars disagree over the meaning of this line. Ellen Oliensis, *Horace and the Rhetoric of Authority* (Cambridge: Cambridge University Press, 1998), 161, translates, "Look and see if I can return your gifts with a light heart," meaning something like, "I doubt I will be able to return these gifts; if I do, I'll take no pleasure in it." Bowditch, *Horace*, 187, on the other hand, reads the line as reinforcing the refusal in line 34, translating more freely, "Try me: I'm quite capable of cheerfully returning everything that's been given to me." In light of the following interpretation of the Telemachus-Menelaus episode, I tend to agree with Bowditch's interpretation of this line as a threat of refusal.

9. Trans. Bowditch, *Horace*, 187.

10. The quotation is from Bowditch, *Horace*, 163. See also Oliensis, *Horace and the Rhetoric of Authority*, who reads the *Epistles* as "not only detached or 'philosophical' meditations on society but also strings of attachment that maintain and in some cases modify social connections" (154). For a particularly straightforward explanation of "misrecognition," see Pierre Bourdieu, *Outline of a Theory of Practice*, trans. Richard Nice (Cambridge: Cambridge University Press, 1977), 171.

11. On Roman language of friendship as obscuring social inequality, see esp. Richard P. Saller, "Patronage and Friendship in Early Imperial Rome: Drawing the Distinction,"

in *Patronage in Ancient Society*, ed. A. Wallace-Hadrill (London: Routledge, 1989), 49–62. David Konstan, *Friendship in the Classical World* (Cambridge: Cambridge University Press, 1997), 137, nuances Saller's observations by reemphasizing amicable attachment: "loyalty and intimacy can coexist with the recognition that degree must receive its due . . . There is no prima-facie reason to doubt that Roman writers who speak of friendship intend a relationship of mutual fondness and commitment, whatever the rank of the partners." Seneca, *Ben.* 1.2.3, is cited and translated in Bowditch, *Horace*, 43–44. As she further explains: "A person unable to repay his benefactor in full instead disseminates similar benefactions to those of lower status. In place of a pure reciprocity, a passage of goods and services down a hierarchical network of similar relations pays off the debt to society at large and provides for social cohesion" (51–52).

12. Bowditch, *Horace*, 163.

13. See Bowditch, *Horace*, 178 (citing Stanley K. Stowers, *Letter Writing in Greco-Roman Antiquity* [Philadelphia: Westminster Press, 1989], 29) and 182.

14. For these interpretations, see Oliensis, *Horace and the Rhetoric of Authority*, 161–62, 165, and Bowditch, *Horace*, 188–90; at 221–33, Bowditch reads *Ep.* 1.7 within the broader context of *Ep.* 1.

15. Bourdieu, *Outline*, 22.

16. John Lee White, *The Form and Function of the Body of the Greek Letter: A Study of the Letter-Body in the Non-Literary Papyri and in Paul the Apostle* (Missoula, MT: Society of Biblical Literature for the Seminar on Paul, 1972), 11–15.

17. See David E. Fredrickson, "Paul's Sentence of Death (2 Corinthians 1:9)," *Word & World Supplement Series* 4 (2000): 9–107, for the argument and ancient testimonials.

18. For *taedium vitae* as a general, stock motive for suicide, see Cicero, *Att.* 2.24.4; a second-century C.E. epitaph preserved as *CIL* 9.1164; and the Roman legal collection the *Digesta* 38.21.3.4 and 5. For discussions of these texts and the phrase in general, see Anton J. L. van Hooff, *From Autothanasia to Suicide: Self-Killing in Classical Antiquity* (London: Routledge, 1990), 69, 82–84, 122–23, 154, and 170, and more recently Catharine Edwards, *Death in Ancient Rome* (New Haven, CT: Yale University Press, 2007), 119–21. According to Miriam Griffin, "Philosophy, Cato, and Roman Suicide: II," *GR* 33.2 (1986): 202 n. 21, late antique legal minds "were often content to lump respectable reasons [for self-killing] under the heading *taedium vitae*. This usage is akin to that of Latin writers generally (e.g. Pliny, *Nat.* 2.63.156) and is distinct from the philosopher's use of the phrase to condemn an irrational distaste of life (Seneca, *Ep.* 24.22; 78.25)."

The Vulgate and most Old Latin versions of 2 Cor 1:8 render some version of *taederet nos etiam vivere*. I have found only three instances of early Latin versions diverging from this tradition: Tertullian, *Res.* 48, col. 865A (with *de vita haesitaremus*, "we were at a loss about living"); the Latin commentary on Paul's letters attributed to "Ambrosiaster" (col. 0277C, reading *desperaremus* for the verb); and Jerome, *Comm. Eph.* 2.598 (also using *desperaremus*), though he prefers *taederet nos vivere* later in the commentary (3.636) and, of course, in the Vulgate.

19. The final two observations have been made in numerous works over the past three decades: in addition to van Hooff and Edwards, see Miriam Griffin, "Philosophy,

Cato, and Roman Suicide: I," *GR* 33.1 (1986): 64–77, and "Philosophy, Cato, and Roman Suicide: II," 192–202; Paul Plass, *The Game of Death in Ancient Rome: Arena Sport and Political Suicide* (Madison: University of Wisconsin Press, 1995); and Timothy Hill, *Ambitiosa Mors: Suicide and Self in Roman Thought and Literature* (New York: Routledge, 2004). In relation to Paul, Manual Vogel, *Commentatio Mortis: 2 Kor 5,1–10 auf dem Hintergrund antiker ars moriendi* (Göttingen: Vandenhoeck and Ruprecht, 2006), analyzes 2 Cor 5:1–10 in light of general discussions of death and character; his argument has much to contribute to my discussion in Chapter 5. The standard discussion of suicide in ancient Christianity is Arthur J. Droge and James D. Tabor, *A Noble Death: Suicide and Martyrdom among Christians and Jews in Antiquity* (San Francisco: HarperSanFrancisco, 1991). On *suicidum* as "pig-killing," see Miriam Griffin, "Philosophy, Cato, and Roman Suicide: I," 68, and van Hooff, *From Autothanasia to Suicide*, 137–38. For Paul and suicide, see Arthur J. Droge, "*Mori Lucrum:* Paul and Ancient Theories of Suicide," *Novum Testamentum* 30.3 (1988): 263–86. "The Stoic cult of suicide" is coined in Arthur Darby Nock, *Conversion: The Old and the New in Religion from Alexander the Great to Augustine of Hippo* (London: Oxford University Press, 1933), 197.

20. van Hooff, *From Autothanasia to Suicide*, 108.

21. The phrase "preparation for death" originates in Plato, *Phaed.* 67D, and is echoed in Cicero, *Tusc.* 1.74 (*commentatio mortis*). For a contemporary approach to the age-old notion, see now Simon Critchley, *The Book of Dead Philosophers* (London: Granta, 2008).

22. The quotation is from Hill, *Ambitiosa Mors*, 71. On suicide as a last option for social self-preservation, see Griffin, "Philosophy, Cato, and Roman Suicide: II," 197–98. For more on suicide and the revelation of one's character, see Edwards, *Death in Ancient Rome*, 144–60, drawing on the theatrical metaphor of "playing a character" common to such ancient discussions. Edwards helpfully indicates how we can see in discussions of suicide a rhetoric of both self-revelation and self-construction; while the notion of playing oneself as a role in a play seems necessarily deterministic, the coupled notion of being the playwright of one's own life frames one's attitude toward death as an act of self-fashioning.

23. For the significance of Seneca's praise of Bassus for understanding Roman death, see Griffin, "Philosophy, Cato, and Roman Suicide: II," 198, who also cites a remark of Pliny (*Ep.* 1.22.10) concerning Titius Aristo: "Many people share his impulse and urge to forestall death, but the ability to examine and weigh the reasons for dying, and to accept or reject the idea of living or not, as reason urges, is the mark of a truly great mind" (198–99). With reference to Paul and suicide in Phil 1, N. Clayton Croy, " 'To Die Is Gain' (Philippians 1:19–26): Does Paul Contemplate Suicide?" *JBL* 122/23 (2003): 517–31, parallels much work on reasoned deliberation in the face of death with his suggestion that Paul imitates the rhetorical figure of *dubitatio* in Philippians. I see a similar rhetoric at work in 2 Cor 1:8–11 and 5:1–10.

24. See Ragner Höistad, *Cynic Hero and Cynic King: Studies in the Cynic Conceptions of Man* (Lund: Carl Bloms Boktryckeri A.-B., 1948), 87–102; W. B. Stanford, *The Ulysses Theme: A Study in the Adaptability of a Traditional Hero* (Ann Arbor: University of Michigan Press, 1968), 90–101; Abraham J. Malherbe, "Antisthenes

and Odysseus, and Paul at War," in *Paul and the Popular Philosophers* (Minneapolis: Fortress, 1989), 98–100; and Dale B. Martin, *Slavery as Salvation: The Metaphor of Slavery in Pauline Christianity* (New Haven, CT: Yale University Press, 1990), 86–88, 100–7.

Chapter 3. The Wandering, Foreign God of Israel

1. For the Babylonian text known as the "Cyrus Cylinder," see *ANET* 315–16.
2. For "the many hucksters" as Paul's apostolic rivals in Corinth, see the discussions in Margaret E. Thrall, *A Critical and Exegetical Commentary on the Second Epistle to the Corinthians*, 2 vols. (ICC; London: T & T Clark, 2000–2004), 1.210–15. For the translation of *kapēleuontes* ("those engaging in trade") as "those huckstering," see Victor Paul Furnish, *II Corinthians* (AB; Garden City, NY: Doubleday, 1984), 173.
3. My exposition of recent work on the metaphor largely relies on the work of four scholars: Paul Brooks Duff, whose many articles on the topic will be cited in what follows; Peter Marshall, "A Metaphor of Social Shame: Thirambeuein in 2 Cor 2:14," *NovT* 25.4 (1983), 302–17 (who discusses the preceding passage from Seneca); Cilliers Breytenbach, "Paul's Proclamation and God's Thriambos (Notes on 2 Corinthians 2:14–16a)," *Neot* 24.2 (1990): 257–71; and Roger David Aus, *Imagery of Triumph and Rebellion in 2 Corinthians 2:14–17 and Elsewhere in the Epistle: An Example of the Combination of Greco-Roman and Judaic Traditions in the Apostle Paul* (Lanham, MD: University Press of America, 2005), 1–46. Identification of epiphanic cult processions as an antecedent behind 2 Cor 2:14–17 was first made by Duff in "Honor or Shame: The Language of Processions and Perception in 2 Cor 2:14–6:13; 7:2–4," Ph.D. diss., University of Chicago Divinity School, 1988, and his subsequent articles on the topic. See also by Duff, "The Transformation of the Spectator: Power, Perception, and the Day of Salvation," *SBL 1987 Seminar Papers* (1988): 233–43; "The Mind of the Redactor: 2 Cor 6:14–7:1 in Its Secondary Context," *NovT* 35 (1993): 160–80; "Metaphor, Motif, and Meaning: The Rhetorical Strategy behind the Image 'Led in Triumph' in 2 Corinthians 2:14," *CBQ* 53.1 (1991): 79–92; and "2 Corinthians 1–7: Sidestepping the Division Hypothesis Dilemma," *BTB* 24 (1994): 16–26. On the Roman triumph generally, see now the detailed and insightful study by Mary Beard, *The Roman Triumph* (Cambridge, MA: Belknap Press of Harvard University Press, 2009).
4. See Aus, *Imagery of Triumph and Rebellion*, 8–9, who cites Appian 2.106, as well as Valerius Maximus 2.8.5 and 2.8.7.
5. Beard, *The Roman Triumph*, 119–24, 133–42; on the triumph and Roman engagement with conquered peoples, see also Emma Dench, *Romulus' Asylum: Roman Identities from the Age of Alexander to the Age of Hadrian* (Oxford: Oxford University Press, 2005), 76–80 and 142.
6. For these points and further details and arguments, see the articles by Paul Brooks Duff listed in note 3.
7. Duff, "Metaphor," 83; see also Harold W. Attridge, "Making Scents of Paul: The Background and Sense of 2 Cor 2:14–17," in *Early Christianity and Classical*

Culture: Comparative Studies in Honor of Abraham J. Malherbe, ed. Thomas H. Olbricht, John T. Fitzgerald, and L. Michael White (Leiden: Brill, 2003), 80, 83.

8. Arrian, *Anab.* 5.1ff., gives traditions likening Alexander's birth to that of Dionysus, as does Plutarch, *Alex.* 2–3. See still the discussion in Arthur Darby Nock, "Notes on Ruler-Cult, I–IV," *JHS* 48.1 (1928): 23–26; Nock, 29, also notes that the association between Alexander and Dionysus emerges in the fragments of Greek historians in Egypt (including Leon of Pella, Hermippus, Dionysius Scytobrachion, and Clitarchus) and thus surmises that the connection was first made among the Ptolemies. He also notes (n. 44) the absence of Dionysian propaganda among the Seleucids. For Antigonid use of Dionysian processions, see the discussion of Demetrius Poliorcetes, below. See also Franz Bömer, "Pompa," *RE* 21.2, col. 1936; Duff, "Honor or Shame," 54.

9. The earliest evidence for the Bacchic/Orphic cults and itinerants is now produced and discussed in Fritz Graf and Sarah Iles Johnston, *Ritual Texts for the Afterlife: Orpheus and the Bacchic Gold Tablets* (New York: Routledge, 2007). For Hellenistic patronage of the cults, see the discussion in Walter Burkert, *Ancient Mystery Cults* (Cambridge, MA: Harvard University Press, 1987), 33–34.

10. For Ptolemy IV and Bacchic regulations, see Walter Burkert, "Bacchic *Teletai* in the Hellenistic Age" in *Masks of Dionysus,* ed. Thomas H. Carpenter and Christopher A. Faraone (Ithaca, NY: Cornell University Press, 1993), 263. Plutarch describes the *theoxenia* offered to Demetrius at Athens in Plutarch, *Demetr.* 12.1 ("to treat Demetrius, whenever he visited, with the rites of hospitality shown to Demeter and Dionysus"). Like Plutarch, Aristophanes uniformly castigates Cleon as an archetypical example of a ruler motivated by deception and demagoguery; see *Ach.* 659.

11. See the discussion in Christina Sourvinou-Inwood, *Tragedy and Athenian Religion* (Lanham, MD: Lexington Books, 2003), 76.

12. Cicero's description, *Flacc.* 61, is in defense of L. Flaccum, the Roman opponent to Mithridates in the field. "Euhuius" or "Evius" (Greek: *Euios*) is a Dionysian epithet thought to derive from *eu huie* ("Well done, Son!"), referring to his sonship to Zeus. "Nysius" refers to Dionysus's mythic birthplace at Nysa. "Liber" is the god's Roman name, or more specifically, an Italic god of wine and fertility who was early identified with his Greek counterpart. I. G. Kidd, "Posidonius as Philosopher-Historian," in *Philosophia Togata,* ed. Miriam Griffin and Jonathan Barnes (Oxford: Clarendon, 1989), 42–43, notes the vitriol in Posidonius's prose here, as well as the context in Athenaeus, who strings together stories of unjustifiably arrogant philosophers.

13. Pliny explicitly compares Pompey's achievements to those of Alexander, Hercules, and Dionysus in *Nat.* 7.27. In addition to Pliny's remarks about Pompey and Marius, Nock, "Notes on Ruler-Cult, I–IV," 30 n.48, notes that a later source, Servius's fourth-century *Scholion on Vergil's Eclogues,* implies that Julius Caesar had a Dionysian affinity (5.29).

14. The inscriptional and numismatic evidence for Antony as Dionysus is cited in Joseph D. Reed, "The Death of Osiris in 'Aeneid' 12.458," *AJP* 119.3 (1998): 404–5; the inscription is found in *IG* II2 1043.22–23.

15. See Brian Bosworth, "Augustus, the Res Gestae and Hellenistic Theories of Apotheosis," *JRS* 89 (1999): 2–3.

16. For more on Antony-as-Dionysus in the *Aeneid*, see Clifford Weber, "The Dionysus in Aeneas," *CP* 97.4 (2002): 322–43. Antony as "Osiris" appears in *Aen.* 12.458–461; see the discussion in Reed, "The Death of Osiris," 403–4.

17. Reed, "The Death of Osiris," 405–6.

18. For disidentification, see Žižek in Judith Butler, Ernesto Laclau, and Slavoj Žižek, *Contingency, Hegemony, Universality: Contemporary Dialogues on the Left* (London: Verso, 2000), 103 and 218. To my knowledge, the only phenomenon that came close to resembling Dionysiac reception of a Roman leader between the reigns of Augustus and Nero was the reaction to Germanicus, popular heir to Tiberius, whose premature death under suspicious circumstance is said to have occasioned extravagant, empire-wide mourning resulting in a *iustitium,* or closure of public business, in Rome. See Tacitus 2.73, who claims that a comparison between Germanicus and Alexander the Great was made at Germanicus's funeral, though Tacitus goes on to distinguish the two leaders. *P.Oxy* 2435, a fragment of Germanicus's speech upon arriving in Alexandria, seems to reflect his discomfort with honors offered him in the city of Alexander.

19. On ancient prejudices against mercantile activity (*kapēleia*), see the discussion in the introduction and below in Chapter 6. See ancient parallels with regard to this verse in Furnish, *II Corinthians,* 178.

20. See Calvin Roetzel, "Sex and the Single God: Celibacy as Deviancy in the Roman Period," in *Text and Artifact in the Religions of Mediterranean Antiquity: Essays in Honor of Peter Richardson,* ed. Stephen G. Wilson and Michel Desjardins (Waterloo, Ontario: Wilfrid Laurier Press, 2000), 231–48.

Chapter 4. Delivering the Spirit

1. On the letter, see Hannah M. Cotton, "*Mirificum Genus Commendationis:* Cicero and the Latin Letter of Recommendation," *AJP* 106.3 (1985): 332–34.

2. See J. L. Austin, *How to Do Things with Words,* 2nd ed. (Cambridge, MA: Harvard University Press, 1975).

3. On the performative aspect of language, see Jacques Derrida, "Signature Event Context," in *Limited, Inc.,* trans. Samuel Weber (Evanston, IL: Northwestern University Press, 1988), 1–24 (I quote from 18); and Judith Butler, *Bodies That Matter: On the Discursive Limits of "Sex"* (London: Routledge, 1993), 12–16 and 224–33 (I quote from 232, italics in the original).

4. It is a failing of most prior approaches to 2 Cor 3 to attempt to divorce Paul's reading of Jewish scripture from other ancient conventions that would have guided his interpretations. Paul, a Greek-speaking Jew, himself probably read scripture through the lens of his own, Greek culture. "New Testament scholars should abandon the fantasy that Paul had some biblical doorway into the culture of ancient Israel and a super culture-blocker that prevented him from inhabiting even his own language. Paul reads scripture in terms of his own experiences and of the cultural codes of the Jewish-Greco-Roman society of which he was a member" (Stanley K. Stowers, *A Rereading of Romans: Justice, Jews, and Gentiles* [New Haven, CT: Yale University Press, 1994], 316).

5. For a reading of Paul as rejecting the practice of recommendation letters, see Dieter Georgi, *The Opponents of Paul in Second Corinthians* (Philadelphia: Fortress, 1986), 242–46. For appeals within the general conversation concerning 2 Cor 3:1 to Philemon as a letter of recommendation, see Hans Windisch, *Der zweite Korintherbrief* (KEK; Göttingen: Vandenhoeck and Ruprecht, 1924), 104; Rudolf Bultmann, *The Second Letter to the Corinthians,* trans. Roy A. Harrisville (Minneapolis: Augsburg, 1985), 71; and William Baird, "Letters of Recommendation: A Study of II Cor 3 1–3," *JBL* 80 (1961): 168–69. Among other leaders of the international Jesus movement, Apollos is depicted as employing epistolary references from followers in Ephesus when he wants to cross to Achaia in Acts 18:27; see Margaret E. Thrall, *A Critical and Exegetical Commentary on the Second Epistle to the Corinthians,* 2 vols. (ICC; London: T & T Clark, 2000–2004, 1.218–19. So prevalent were letters of recommendation in the ancient world that it would be surprising if early itinerant proclaimers of Jesus's gospel did *not* employ them. Scholars who see 2 Cor 3:1 as a barb against his opponents' use of such letters point to the prevalence of the theme of self-recommendation throughout canonical 2 Cor (however its compositional unity and chronological order are construed); besides 3:1a and 5, see 4:2, 5:12, and 10:12 and 18.

6. Victor Paul Furnish, *II Corinthians* (AB; Garden City, NY: Doubleday, 1984), 193, and Thrall, *Second Corinthians,* 1.224, also provide this reading.

7. For the milk/solid food metaphor in philosophical pedagogy, see Heinrich Schlier, "*Gala,*" in *TDNT* 1.645–46; see Epictetus 2.16.39 as an example: "Are you not willing already to be weaned like children and share in more solid food?" At 1 Cor 2:4 I read the Greek as *ouk en peithoi sophias,* though this reading is not present in any extant Greek witness and is reflected only in the Latin version of the interlinear Claramontanus. A scribe reduplicated the initial sigma in *sophias;* this sigma was tacked on to the end of *peithoi,* yielding the nonexistent adjective *peithois,* to which later scribes tried to attach a noun.

8. Baird, "Letters of Recommendation," 169, cites Josephus, *A.J.* 6.298. Three other Josephan passages, however, seem to use the phrase to mean "to obey a letter"; see *A.J.* 18.262, 18.268, and 19.10. John N. Collins, *Diakonia: Re-interpreting the Ancient Sources* (New York: Oxford University Press, 1990), 126–27, cites Chariton, *Chaer.* 8.8.5. Furthermore, the noun *diakonos* means "deliverer" or "courier" in Philostratus, *Vit. Apoll.* 6.29. See also the cognate term *komizōn* for "courier" in *P.Oxy.* 1661, *PSI* 642, *P.Eleph.* 9, *SB* 15278, *P.Zen.Pestm.* 42, *P.Cair.Zen.* 59603, *P.Köln* 6.258, and *P.Oslo* 2.51. The recommended usually conveyed his letter of recommendation; see specific examples in Chan-Hie Kim, *Form and Structure of the Familiar Greek Letter of Recommendation* (Missoula, MT: Society of Biblical Literature, 1972), 38–41; see also Hannah Cotton, "Documentary Letters of Recommendation in Latin from the Roman Empire," *Beiträge zur klassischen Philologie* 132 (1981): 5.

9. M. Luther Stirewalt, Jr., *Paul, the Letter Writer* (Grand Rapids, MI: Eerdmans, 2003), 3; see his more general discussion of epistolary practices and the anxieties that attended them at 1–3. See also Furnish, *II Corinthians,* 195, and Hans-Josef Klauck, *Ancient Letters and the New Testament: A Guide to Context and Exegesis* (Waco, TX: Baylor University Press, 2006), 63–65.

10. Klauck, *Ancient Letters,* 65, notes the general practice of couriers as stand-ins, citing *P.Col.* 3.6.14–16 in this regard. See also John Lee White, *Light from Ancient Letters* (Philadelphia: Fortress, 1986), 216. Moreover, Margaret M. Mitchell, "New Testament Envoys in the Context of Greco-Roman Diplomatic and Epistolary Conventions: The Example of Timothy and Titus," *JBL* 111 (1992): 650, cites relevant epistolary parallels, including *P.Oxy.* 3865; *SB* 6799.10; Plato, *Ep.* 9.357D–E; and Cicero, *Fam.* 3.1 (cf. 12.30, discussed below) and 3.5. For some examples from the papyrus letters, see *P.Mich.* 8.498 (second century C.E.) and *P.Lips.* 1.108 (second to third century C.E.).

11. The translation of 12.30.1 is from Abraham J. Malherbe, *Ancient Epistolary Theorists* (Atlanta, GA: Scholars Press, 1988), 27. Cicero does not explicitly state that Chaerippus delivered and read a letter from Cornificius, but it is a reasonable inference, especially in light of references to Chaerippus in earlier letters. So, in *Fam.* 12.22, Cicero ends the letter with an apology: "I should have written more, had not your messengers been in a hurry. So pray make my excuses to our friend Chaerippus" (LCL trans.). That is, Cicero's desire to write a letter that Chaerippus could deliver delayed Chaerippus's departure, a delay for which Cicero apologizes. See also *Fam.* 3.1.2 (cited by Mitchell, above), in which Cicero praises the freedman and courier of Appius Claudius Pulcher, Cilix, who "by his own words followed up in a wonderful way the courtesy with which you wrote. It was a delight to me to hear him holding forth as he told me all about your kindly feeling, and the remarks you made about me day after day" (LCL trans.).

12. Mitchell, "New Testament Envoys," 648–49, relates the practice of asking for hospitality in letters of recommendation to the political practice of receiving official envoys. On "reception" of couriers, see, for example, *P.Mich.* 3216 (third century B.C.E.), *P.Col.* 4.112 (third century B.C.E.), and *P.Oslo* 2.55 (second to third century C.E.) See also *P.Col.* 8.225 (second century C.E.), in which the son, away on military service, writes his father that the recommended will be renting his house until his return; and *P.Oxy.* 8.1162, a fourth-century Christian letter asking that the recipients "receive in peace" the courier. On the assumption of lodging, see the treatment of *P.Oslo* 2.55 by its editor, below. The travels of the recommended are explicitly mentioned in *P.Mich.* 1.93, 1.6, 1.33, and 3216. As Mitchell, "New Testament Envoys," 648, notes, Pseudo-Demetrius's template for recommendation letters states: "You would do well if you deem him worthy of hospitality" (*apodochēs;* this follows Malherbe's translation. The word means "reception" in general, but again, one would assume "hospitality"). On hospitality as a favor to the writer, see *P.Mich.* 1.6 and 1.33 (both third century B.C.E.).

13. On Plato and the logocentric Western tradition, see for just a few examples Paul Ricoeur, *Interpretation Theory: Discourse and the Surplus of Meaning* (Fort Worth, TX: Texas Christian University Press, 1976), 38–40; and Jacques Derrida, *Of Grammatology,* trans. Gayatri Chakravorty Spivak (Baltimore, MD: Johns Hopkins University Press, 1976). To my mind, the most penetrating analysis of Paul along these lines is Mark D. Given, *Paul's True Rhetoric: Ambiguity, Cunning, and Deception in Greece and Rome* (Harrisburg, PA: Trinity Press International, 2001). See also Bultmann, *Second Letter to the Corinthians,* 73; Furnish, *II Corinthians,* 195; and Thrall, *Second Corinthians,* 226–27.

14. On the elevated status of the Corinthians-as-letter, see again Benjamin Fiore, "Root Metaphors in Paul—Pauline Comings and Goings: The Travel Image," *Proceedings, Eastern Great Lakes and Midwest Biblical Societies* 11 (1991): 183. At 3:2, I follow the ancient manuscripts that say the letter is written on "our" (*hēmōn*), not "your" (*hymōn*) hearts, a reading attested only in Sinaiticus among major witnesses, and which would lend support to denying a continuation of the letter metaphor past verse 1. See the discussion in Baird, "Letters of Recommendation," 168–71.

15. The quotation (italics in the original) is from Scott J. Hafemann, *Suffering and the Spirit: An Exegetical Study of II Cor 2:14–3:3 within the Context of the Corinthian Correspondence* (Tübingen: J. C. B. Mohr [Paul Siebeck], 1986), 204. For "incarnation," see Richard B. Hays, *Echoes of Scripture in the Letters of Paul* (New Haven, CT: Yale University Press, 1989), 129–30.

16. For the effect of the letter metaphor as persisting throughout 2 Cor 3, see Baird, "Letters of Recommendation," 171. He counters that Paul's defense of his apostolic legitimacy is still in view in this metaphor (172). See also the observation of Bernd Kuschnerus, "'You Yourselves Are Our Letter': 2Cor 3 as an Example for the Usage of Metaphor in Paul," in *Metaphor, Canon and Community: Jewish, Christian and Islamic Approaches*, ed. Ralph Bisschops and James Francis (Bern: Peter Lang, 1999), 97–100; Gerhard Dautzenberg, "Alter und neuer Bund nach 2Kor 3," in *"Nun steht diese aber Sache im Evangelium." Zur Frage nach den Anfängen des Christlichen Antijudaismus*, ed. Rainer Kampling (Paderborn: Ferdinand Schöningh, 1999), 240–41; and Klaus Scholtissek, "'Ihr seid ein Brief Christi' (2 Kor 3,3). Zu einer ekklesiologischen Metapher bei Paulus," *BZ* 44.2 (2000): 191 n. 23.

17. Collins, *Diakonia*, 77–95. The translation of Plato here is Collins's, who discusses and explains *Pol.* 290C on 85.

18. For Hermes, see Collins, *Diakonia*, 90–92, 100–4. For ancient explanations of *diaktoros*, Collins cites Aristophanes, *Plut.* 1146–70; Lucian, *Char.* 1; and (especially relevant for the discussion below) Epictetus, *Diatr.* 3.1.37–38. Epictetus, citing the appearance of the epithet in Homer, *Od.* 1.37–39, calls Hermes *kalistos angelos*, "finest messenger." For other references to Hermes as *diakonos*, Collins cites Aeschylus, *Prom.* 942; a third-century B.C.E. curse inscription from Athens (published by G. W. Elderkin, *Hesperia* 3 [1937]: 382–95); and *Dial. d.* 7.3. Other Jewish figures referred to as *diakonoi* of God include the archangel Michael in *T. Ab.* (recension A) 9.24; Josephus uses the word group to describe the divine-human mediations of Jeremiah (*A.J.* 10.177) and, remarkably, his own, divinely inspired (though failed) negotiations between Rome and Jerusalem (*B.J.* 3.354 and 4.626; Collins, *Diakonia*, 111–15). Philo, *Mos.* 1.83–84 is discussed at 110.

19. Collins, *Diakonia*, 131–32 and 137–38. Collins interprets Paul's usage in 2 Cor 3 on 207:

> He saw himself of course not as daemon nor as a divine man embodying heavenly knowledge and power but as a man passing on heaven's word, and he chose the term *diakonos* to depict his role of go-between in the same way as the philosopher chose the cognate verb in attempting to speak of the voice carrying thoughts from one soul to another [again, citing Ammonius] . . . In

applying these words to the situation of the Christian preacher Paul expresses a profound and possibly original Christian thought but he cannot be said to have given the words a specifically Christian meaning for he makes use of meanings already current in non-Christian literature.

20. For the close connection between the Cynic "divine messenger" and the Christian apostle, see Karl H. Rengstorf, "*Apostellō,*" in *TDNT* 1.399–400, 409–13. My reference to discussions of *diakonos* as a Cynic-Stoic technical term reflects a small debate between John N. Collins and Dieter Georgi, whose book *Die Gegner des Paulus im 2. Korintherbrief: Studien zur Religiösen Propaganda in der Spätantike* (Neukirchen-Vluyn: Neukirchener, 1964; translated as *The Opponents of Paul in Second Corinthians,* cited above) viewed much of 2 Cor 3 as Paul's response to terms and motifs first raised by his opponents or rival apostles in Corinth. See John N. Collins, "Georgi's 'Envoys' in 2 Cor 11:23," *JBL* 93.1 (1974): 88–96. In the 1986 English translation, Georgi adds a new appendix responding to Collins's critique (Georgi, *Opponents,* 352). In turn, Collins responded in his 1990 book (*Diakonia*) and in John N. Collins, "The Mediatorial Aspect of Paul's Role as *Diakonos,*" *ABR* 40 (1992): 34–44.

21. For comparison with Paul's *peristasis* catalogues, see the discussion in John T. Fitzgerald, *Cracks in an Earthen Vessel: An Examination of the Catalogues of Hardships in the Corinthian Correspondence* (Atlanta, GA: Scholars Press, 1988), 81–82, who highlights Epictetus's assertion that the Cynic sage can endure his sufferings only because he is strengthened by the God who sent him.

22. Margarethe Billerbeck, "The Ideal Cynic from Epictetus to Julian," in *The Cynics: The Cynic Movement in Antiquity and Its Legacy,* ed. R. Bracht Branham and Marie-Odile Goulet-Cazé (Berkeley: University of California Press, 1996), 208.

23. Kim, *Form and Structure,* 39–40, gives examples of common terminology for letter delivery.

24. For a discussion of the prophetic background of Paul's allusion to prophetic insufficiency, see Scott Hafemann, *Paul, Moses, and the History of Israel: The Letter/ Spirit Contrast and the Argument from Scripture in 2 Corinthians 3* (Tübingen: Mohr Siebeck, 1995), 39–91 and 118–19.

25. So in the first giving of the Law, see Exod 19:9–13, where God says he will "come down on Mount Sinai before the entire people" (v. 11), though the people themselves are restricted from the mountain. After the speaking of the Ten Words of the covenant, the people plead for Moses, not God, to speak to them, though Moses explains that God is merely trying to scare them into following his commands (20:18–20). Later, the elders of Israel join Moses on Sinai for a meal with God (24:9–11); the MT twice states simply that the elders "saw the God of Israel" (vv. 10 and 11), while the LXX equivocates in stating that they "saw the place where God stood." When Moses again joins God on the mountain, "the image of the Lord's glory was like a flame of fire on the top of the mountain before the Sons of Israel" (LXX Exod 24:17). The initial arrangement was that God would lead the people through an angel upon whom his name rested (Exod 23:20–23). Though God again promises that his angel will lead them after punishing them for their sin (in 33:2), he refuses to be in their presence

personally: " 'I will not travel with you—since you are a stiff-necked people—lest I completely destroy you along the way.' And when the people heard this terrible statement, they mourned it with laments" (LXX Exod 33:3–4). Yet Moses appeals this decision numerous times, evoking various divine responses: in 33:14, God seems to promise to be with Moses, but the LXX text here may imply that he promises to be with Moses *alone*. Moses, at least, seems to read the statement this way, since he once again asks that, specifically, "I and your people find favor with God" (33:16). God agrees (v.17), but the resolution of this agreement entails Moses's private theophany while concealed in the rock cleft (vv. 18–23). The next day, on Sinai, Moses supplicates once more, and God says he will make a "covenant" with Israel, the effect of which is that he will perform "miracles" among the nations of Canaan, so that these peoples "will see the work of the Lord" (34:10).

26. For example, Furnish, *II Corinthians,* 232, reads Paul as asserting the "fading" of Moses's glory and thus the covenant with the Jewish people. For other Jewish interpretations of Exod 34, see Linda L. Belleville, *Reflections of Glory: Paul's Polemical Use of the Moses-Doxa Tradition in 2 Corinthians 3:1–18* (Sheffield: Sheffield Academic Press, 1991), 40–43, who cites Ps.-Philo, *L.A.B.* 19.16 (Moses's face began to shine [again] at his death), and reads it as implying temporary glory that was periodically renewed; but this involves too much interpretive contortion. Likewise, Daniel Boyarin, *A Radical Jew: Paul and the Politics of Identity* (Berkeley: University of California Press, 1994), 102–3, notes that fourteenth-century Jewish commentator Abraham Ibn Ezra mentioned and rejected such a reading, perhaps in reaction to Christian interpretations of his day. For a thorough exposition of the interpretation I offer here, see Hafemann, *Paul, Moses, and the History of Israel,* 310–13 and 354. For Giorgio Agamben's important meditations on the role of the term *katargein* in Paul's theo-political rhetoric, see the conclusion to this chapter.

27. The reading does not rescue Paul from accusations of anti-Judaism in the way many contemporary readers would hope, except to note the following: Paul's polemic is not identical to the anti-Judaism of later Christian centuries, since, in its historical context, Paul's argument is not one of "Christianity" against "Judaism," but rather that of a very peculiar Jewish teacher who has taken on the extraordinary mission of bringing the message of the Jewish Messiah to non-Jews, incorporating standard, Jewish critiques of Israel's past and present.

28. Jan Willem van Henten, "Moses as Heavenly Messenger: *Assumptio Mosis* 10:2 and Qumran Passages," *JJS* 54.2 (2003): 219–21 and 225–26, citing Wayne A. Meeks, *The Prophet-King: Moses Traditions and the Johannine Christology* (Leiden: Brill, 1967), 125, 160–61. Van Henten also points to 4Q504 1 ii 8–11 as indicating Moses's mediation after the golden calf incident (223). Thus, he concludes: "Moses' role as mediator has its roots in the Hebrew Bible in connection with the golden calf episode" (227).

29. For Agamben's general argument about the *iustitium* and the state of exception, see *The State of Exception,* trans. Kevin Attell (Chicago: University of Chicago Press, 2005). For application to Paul's use of *katargein,* see *The Time That Remains: A Commentary on the Letter to the Romans,* trans. Patricia Dailey (Stanford, CA: Stanford University Press, 2005), 88–112.

30. Agamben, *The Time That Remains,* 105.

Chapter 5. Whether Home or Away

1. Paul Brooks Duff, "Metaphor, Motif, and Meaning: The Rhetorical Strategy behind the Image 'Led in Triumph' in 2 Corinthians 2:14," *CBQ* 53.1 (1991): 89, notes that *peripherein* commonly denoted processions, citing Plutarch, *Is. Os.* 17 [357F] and 36 [365B]; Clement of Alexandria, *Protr.* 4.59.2; and Pausanias 9.22.1–2. See also John T. Fitzgerald, *Cracks in an Earthen Vessel: An Examination of the Catalogues of Hardships in the Corinthian Correspondence* (Atlanta, GA: Scholars Press, 1988), 178–79, noting that the term referred to funeral processions and that funerals and triumphal processions were closely related in the ancient world.

2. For *peripherein* as "travel," see, as examples, Eph 4:14; Herodotus 4.36 (describing Hyperborean devotee Abaris); Philo, *Prob.* 117 (in connection with Hercules and the Cynics); and Ignatius, *Eph.* 7.1 and 11.2.

3. Theo K. Heckel, *Der innere Mensch: die paulinische Verarbeitung eines platonischen Motivs* (Tübingen: J. C. B. Mohr, 1993), believes that Paul, in his controversy with his opponents, received this motif from some supportive Corinthian community members as a handy tool in battle (cf. 145). See the assessment in Hans Dieter Betz, "The Concept of the 'Inner Human Being' (*ho esō anthrōpos*) in the Anthropology of Paul," *NTS* 46 (2000): 315–41. More recently, Fredrik Lindgård, *Paul's Line of Thought in 2 Corinthians 4:16–5:10* (Tübingen: Mohr Siebeck, 2005), argues that Paul is more interested in the rhetorical effect of his language here than in constructing a consistent, systematic anthropology, an insight mirrored in my own reading.

   The Platonic pedigree of the general concept of "inner" and "outer" human beings still presents the most compelling origin for Paul's expression in 2 Cor 4:16. Typically, the idea is traced back to the psychological/anthropological language of Plato's *Resp.* 589A–B, in a discussion of the tripartite psychology characterizing Platonic thought. Here, justice requires that the "inner person" (*ho entos anthrōpos*) should rule over the whole person figured as a "many-headed animal" (*tou polykephalou thremmatos*), probably a reference to the animalistic imagery for the lower parts of the soul. For Plato, the "inner man" represents not the entire soul distinguished from the body, but specifically the soul's rational third. Cognate formulations in Philo similarly refer to the rational and ruling aspect of the human soul, usually the "mind" (*nous; Congr.* 97). Other authors and traditions, however, employ similar terminology to refer to the entirety of the soul in relation to the body. Moreover, the Platonically influenced Hermetic literature at times terms the eternal half of a person the "inner person" (cf. 13.7). So, while reference to the "inner man" always denotes a dualistic distinction within the human being, it was in fact employed in the contexts of disparate anthropologies. The relevant passages from Philo, as well as those from Epictetus and *Corp. Herm.*, were already identified by Hans Windisch, *Der zweite Korintherbrief* (KEK; Göttingen: Vandenhoeck and Ruprecht, 1924), 152–53. As opposed to the dualistic anthropology found in Plato, most readers see Paul as usually expositing a monistic anthropology tied closely to his eschatological schema of transformation, in which material bodies are transformed into spiritual bodies, with "spirit" being understood in the Stoic sense as a finer and more superior type of matter.

On reading this transformation against its ancient background, see Dale B. Martin, *The Corinthian Body* (New Haven, CT: Yale University Press, 1995) 3–15, 125–35.

4. For this exegetical option, taken by some scholars, see Margaret E. Thrall, *A Critical and Exegetical Commentary on the Second Epistle to the Corinthians,* 2 vols. (ICC; London: T & T Clark, 2000–2004), 1.349–50.

5. Here, with many other commentators, I read the *endusamenoi* attested by most witnesses (including P⁴⁶, Sinaiticus, Vatincanus, Ephraemi, and a corrector of Claromontanus) as opposed to the *ekdusamenoi* (in the original of Claromontanus and others) selected by Nestle-Aland. Bruce M. Metzger, *A Textual Commentary on the Greek New Testament* (London: United Bible Societies, 1971), gives the committee decision that the better-attested reading was rejected as "banal and even tautologous" but adds his personal dissent that *ekdusamenoi* is "an early alteration to avoid tautology" (579–80). As I argue, Paul's tautology is not "banal" since it contradicts common beliefs concerning postmortem judgment.

6. Again, I follow the Hershbell translation of Ps.-Plato, *Ax.* For further references to the body as a tent, see Plato, *Phaed.* 81C; Philo, *QG* 1.28; Wis 9:15; and *Corp. Herm.* 13.15, all cited in Windisch, *Der zweite Korintherbrief,* 158. Paul leaves the connection between tent imagery and itinerancy unstated. So, Victor Paul Furnish, *II Corinthians* (AB; Garden City, NY: Doubleday, 1984), 264: "Apart from this passage (see also v. 4) Paul does not use the word 'tent,' even though the author of Acts describes him as a *skēnopoios* ('tent maker') by trade (18:3)."

7. For the nudity of souls during postmortem judgment, see the final portion of Plato's *Gorgias* (523E), directly quoted in Ps.-Plutarch, *Cons. Apoll.* (36 [120E–121E]).

8. My reading here mirrors that of Manual Vogel, *Commentatio Mortis: 2 Kor 5,1–10 auf dem Hintergrund antiker ars moriendi* (Göttingen: Vandenhoeck and Ruprecht, 2006), 302–6.

9. "Always" language occurs in 2 Cor 2:14; 4:8, 10, 11; 5:6; 6:10; and 9:8. On the consoling knowledge that death is a return home, see Plato, *Phaed.* 67B; Cicero, *Tusc.* 1.44–45; and Seneca, *Marc.* 25.1–3. In fact, some early manuscripts of 2 Cor seem to have tried to redomesticate Paul to the consolatory tradition: the original hand of Claromontanus, with the reading *epidēmountes* ("being in exile"), perhaps attempts to depict clearly that earthly life is a sort of "exile" (see the description of life as an "exile," or *parepidēmia* in Ps.-Plato, *Ax.* 365B). Claromontanus also replaces *ekdēmoumen* with *apodēmoumen,* perhaps to reflect the Socratic-Platonic tradition (see *Apol.* 40E–41A). The variant reading negates Paul's blurring of the traditional consolatory conception.

10. Vogel, *Commentatio Mortis,* 323–26.

11. For the wise man's attention to earthly matters despite his heavenly destination, see Vogel, *Commentatio Mortis,* 353–59. Great and detailed interpretive efforts have focused on the precise meaning of *eudokoumen mallon* in verse 8 and whether Paul would "prefer" or "choose" to die and return to God. Of late, the issue has revolved around whether or not Paul puts forth the possibility of suicide, as mentioned in Chapter 2. Those who adopt a translation of "we would much prefer" see Paul as eagerly awaiting the eventual arrival of death, whereas those who render "we choose" or "we are resolved to" are more likely to see also the possibility of Paul considering

a hasty exit, as it were. I do not believe either translation decides the issue; in either case, self-killing is in view. In the context of discussions of death and suicide, the move from a preference for death to the serious contemplation of self-killing was a far easier conceptual step to make in the ancient world than in the modern (again, see the discussion of self-killing in Chapter 2). The common, consolatory process in regard to self-killing was (1) the realization that life is evil and that thus death is good, (2) the desire to kill oneself to escape the evils of life, and (3) the further realization that one must not kill oneself without sufficient reason or divine compulsion. This is the pattern first set forth in Plato, *Phaed.;* in relation to 2 Cor 5:6–8, Vogel, *Commentatio Mortis,* 357–59, cites Epictetus, *Diatr.* 1.9.10–17, 29.28–29, and 3.24.95–96, texts that clearly follow the Socratic mode. See again the discussion in Arthur J. Droge, "*Mori Lucrum:* Paul and Ancient Theories of Suicide," *Novum Testamentum* 30.3 (1988): 263–86, esp. 278–85; Droge focuses, as do most discussions on Paul and suicide, on the similar wording in Phil 1:21–26, but treats our passage at 282.

12. German scholarship on 2 Cor has focused on the seeming rejection of dualistic categories in 5:6–9, at least since Windisch, *Der zweite Korintherbrief,* 165–70. See the discussion in Vogel, *Commentatio Mortis,* 348–52. Vogel disagrees with this line of criticism (among its recent exponents, he includes Heckel, Wünsch, and Kuschnerus), believing that the connection within *ars moriendi* between a desire to leave the body for heaven and the perceived duty to live out a virtuous and divinely ordained lifespan explains the logic (*dio kai*) of verses 8–9. Paul certainly draws on this aspect of the tradition, but this does not explain the almost parodically rapid shift and exchange of travel terminology for life and death.

13. Here, the "all of us" (*tous pantas hēmas*) at the beginning of verse 10 expands the discussion from the apostolic situation that has dominated 4:1–5:9. A similar expansion occurred in 3:18 (*hēmeis pantes*). For the observation, see Furnish, *II Corinthians,* 275; Thrall, *Second Corinthians,* 1.394.

14. For the translation of *sunechei hēmas* as "holds us prisoner," reflecting the practice of leading prisoners in triumphal procession (and thus recalling the central motif of 2:14–16), see Duff, "Metaphor," 86–87.

15. Badiou's attention to "theories of discourses" with respect to 1 Cor 1 can be found in Alain Badiou, *St. Paul: The Foundation of Universalism,* trans. Ray Brassier (Stanford, CA: Stanford University Press, 2003), 40–47. Language of the "diagonal" trajectory of universality occurs on 14 ("Truth is diagonal relative to every communitarian subset"), 28, and 43 ("The opposing of a diagonalization of discourses to their synthesis is a constant preoccupation of Paul's"). In seeing Paul's gospel as a diagonal address to all people and identities, Badiou is in peculiarly conservative, orthodox company: "Upon whatever rung of the ladder of human life men may happen to be standing—whether they be Jews or Greeks, old or young, educated or uneducated, complex or simple—in tribulation or in repose they are capable of faith. The demand of faith passes *diagonally* across every type of religious or moral temperament, across every experience of life, through every department of intellectual activity, and through every social class" (Karl Barth, *The Epistle to the Romans,* 6th ed., trans. Edwyn C. Hoskyns [Oxford: Oxford University Press, 1968], 99, emphasis mine).

Chapter 6. Ambassadors of God's Empire

1. For imperial networks, see Clifford Ando, *Imperial Ideology and Provincial Loyalty in the Roman Empire* (Berkeley: University of California Press, 2000), 410–11; the quotation from Pliny (Ando's translation modifying that of Radice) is on 410, and Ando's analysis that I quote is on 411.

2. See Anthony Bash, *Ambassadors for Christ: An Exploration of Ambassadorial Language in the New Testament* (Tübingen: Mohr Siebeck, 1997), 88–89, for technical terminology for embassies. Bash notes that, as in 2 Cor 5:20, inscriptions commemorating various embassies tended to use *presbeuein* and the preposition *hyper* to denote on whose behalf the embassy was sent.

3. Cilliers Breytenbach, *Versöhnung: eine Studie zur paulinischen Soteriologie* (WMANT; Neukirchen-Vluyn: Neukirchener, 1989), 132–37, 179, 221; Bash, *Ambassadors*, 100–3.

4. John T. Fitzgerald, "Paul and Paradigm Shifts: Reconciliation and Its Linkage Group," in *Paul beyond the Judaism/Hellenism Divide*, ed. Troels Engberg-Pedersen (Louisville, KY: Westminster John Knox, 2001), 248–52. He cites Plutarch, *Pel.* 26.2; *P.Mich.* 8.502; *BGU* 3.846; and *P.Giss.* 17.2.13–14 as examples of the plea to "be reconciled." As he further shows (253), *eukatallakton* and synonyms were frequently attributed to the gods by non-Jewish authors and to God by Jewish authors; see 3 Macc 5:13 and Josephus, *B.J.* 5.415.

5. For Paul's language of ambassadorship as self-defense or construction, see Breytenbach, *Versöhnung*, 222–24; Bash, *Ambassadors*, 105, follows Breytenbach on this point, whereas Fitzgerald, "Paul and Paradigm Shifts," 257, calls reconciliation between Paul and Corinth "the real point" of the apostle's language here. Scholars who see ambassadorial language as being "traditional" or pre-Pauline see the *hōs hoti* of 5:19 as introducing a quotation of sorts. So, Victor Paul Furnish renders the verse: "As it is said: God, in Christ, was reconciling the world to himself, not charging their trespasses to them. And he has established among us the word of reconciliation" (*II Corinthians* [Garden City, NY: Doubleday, 1984]), 306, 317–18). For friendship as a concept closely associated with reconciliation (that is, the repair of a broken friendship or the dissipation of enmity), see Fitzgerald, "Paul and Paradigm Shifts," 257–60.

6. For envoys being received as those who sent them, see Margaret M. Mitchell, "New Testament Envoys in the Context of Greco-Roman Diplomatic and Epistolary Conventions: The Example of Timothy and Titus," *JBL* 111 (1992): 645–49. In observing the close connection between couriership, ambassadorship, and envoys of all kinds, critiques aimed at scholars who conflate various traveling agents in their analysis of 2 Cor (such as Collins's against Georgi [see Chapter 4] or Bash's [*Ambassadors*, 33 n. 62] against Mitchell) are mitigated somewhat. Although it is helpful to distinguish among the specific social roles Paul evokes in 2 Cor 3 and 5–6, Paul himself is exploiting the overlapping functions of couriers and ambassadors in order to portray the "apostle" as authentic agent and stand-in for Christ. Thus, it is not surprising that Paul reinserts the language of *diakonia* at 5:18, 6:3, and 6:4 in order to further exploit the term's semantic slippage. For the distinction between the original embassy

described in verse 19 and the present, Christ-initiated embassy in verse 20, see Bash, *Ambassadors*, 89–93. That Paul's language of reconciliation with God ultimately entails reconciling the Corinthians to himself was early proposed by J.-F. Collange, *Énigmes de la deuxième épître de Paul aux Corinthiens: Étude exégétique de 2 Cor. 2:14–7:4* (Cambridge: Cambridge University Press, 1972), 268–69.

7. Bash, *Ambassadors*, 62–63. Bash paraphrases the standard formula of imperial approval: "I regard the ambassadors as having by a reputable embassy deserved the travel allowance, in case they have not offered to go at their own expense."

8. On the catalogue of hardships, see Bash, *Ambassadors*, 105–7. He cites Plutarch, *Praec. ger. rei publ.* 19 [815D]; Strabo, 13.1.55; Diodorus Siculus 14.93.4; Josephus, *Vita* 13–16; and Epictetus, *Diatr.* 4.1.91 for examples of the risks faced during ambassadorial journeys. John T. Fitzgerald, "Paul and Paradigm Shifts," 324 n. 81, interprets this catalogue as the sufferings of an "abused ambassador"; see the discussion below. In my analysis of the *peristasis* catalogue in 2 Cor 6:3–10, I adopt the structural analysis and many of the interpretations in John T. Fitzgerald, *Cracks in an Earthen Vessel: An Examination of the Catalogues of Hardships in the Corinthian Correspondence* (Atlanta, GA: Scholars Press, 1988), 192–201. For 6:13 and 7:2 as references to the accepting and welcome of Paul in Corinth, see Paul Brooks Duff, "The Mind of the Redactor: 2 Cor 6:14–7:1 in Its Secondary Context," *NovT* 35 (1993): 171–75, as well as the discussion below.

9. Fitzgerald, *Cracks in an Earthen Vessel*, 193, cites Ronald F. Hock, *The Social Context of Paul's Ministry: Tentmaking and Apostleship* (Philadelphia: Fortress, 1980), 34–35, 60, 64, 84–85, 101, for references to the travails of a wandering artisan.

10. I, along with many others, consider the passage contained in 6:14–7:1 to be a later, non-Pauline interpolation into the letter designed to smooth the connection between the letters preserved in 2 Cor 1–9 and in 2 Cor 10–13 by making direct reference to the "unfaithful." On this theory, see Gunther Bornkamm, "The History of the Origin of the So-Called Second Letter to the Corinthians," *NTS* 8 (1962): 258–64, and, more recently and specifically, Paul Brooks Duff, "Mind of the Redactor," 160–80. On the recurrence of processional motifs, see again Duff, "Metaphor," 88.

11. Among his various articles on the subject, see especially Duff, "Mind of the Redactor," 160–80, which focuses on the use of the motif in 6:13 and 7:4 in order to explain the redactional principle that led to the interpolation of 6:14–7:1: a later editor noticed the language of the herald in the present 6:11 and 7:2 and inserted a fragment which asserted that the "unfaithful" should keep away. For a clear example of Bacchic devotees calling the pious to draw near and the impious to make way, see Euripides, *Bacch.* 64–70.

12. Paul's language with regard to Titus and the two anonymous brothers in this section exceeds the normal Pauline expressions of commendation for an envoy. This is the case in both 2 Cor 7:13–16 and 8:13–15. Though 7:6–13 bears much similarity to his expression of the reception of Timothy in 1 Thess 3:6–10 (as noted by Hans Windisch, *Der zweite Korintherbrief* [KEK; Göttingen: Vandenhoeck and Ruprecht, 1924], 227; Furnish, *II Corinthians*, 394; and Mitchell, "New Testament Envoys," 653), the contexts of each case are patently different; Paul's account of Titus comes in the wake of controversy (as noted by Mitchell, "New Testament Envoys," 660)—hence

his expanded commendation in 7:13–15 and 8:13–15, implying that the preceding controversy in some sense included Titus specifically and that the dispute behind 2 Cor 12:14–18 precedes the resolution in 2 Cor 7–8 (contra those who would order 2 Cor 10–13 after 1–9, seeing 12:14–18 as referring to the visit planned in 2 Cor 7–8; for this opinion, see C. K. Barrett, *A Commentary on the Second Epistle to the Corinthians* (BNTC; New York: Harper and Row, 1973), 18–21, and more recently Margaret Mitchell, "Paul's Letters to Corinth: The Interpretive Intertwining of Literary and Historical Reconstruction," in *Urban Religion in Roman Corinth: Interdisciplinary Approaches*, ed. Daniel N. Schowalter and Steven J. Friesen (Cambridge, MA: Harvard University Press, 2005), 321–35.

13. For *stellomenos* as evoking the Wisdom of Solomon, see Margaret E. Thrall, *A Critical and Exegetical Commentary on the Second Epistle to the Corinthians*, 2 vols. (ICC; London: T & T Clark, 2000–2004), 2.551, citing Karl H. Rengstorf, "*Stellō*," in *TDNT* 7.589. The fuller context of the passage from the Wisdom of Solomon could well be behind Paul's choice of expression here. The author uses the sailing example as part of an argument against the idolatrous who might pray to an idol to ensure a safe voyage; such people rely on safety from wooden images just like sailors rely on wooden ships to brave the fickle seas. In each case, God alone provides safety. "For it was desire for profits which devised it [the ship], and technical wisdom which equipped it, but your providence, Father, steers it, so that you have given it a way even in the sea and a safe pathway among the waves" (Wis 14:2–3).

14. On the "proverbial" poverty of the Macedonians in the first century, as well as the differences and rivalry between Achaia and Macedonia, see Hans Dieter Betz, *2 Corinthians 8 and 9* (Hermeneia; Philadelphia: Fortress, 1985), 48–53.

15. On the proverb, see Windisch, *Der zweite Korintherbrief*, 275–76; Dieter Georgi, *Remembering the Poor: The History of Paul's Collection for Jerusalem,* English ed. (Nashville: Abingdon, 1991), 94–95; see especially Betz, *2 Corinthians 8 and 9*, 98–100, in an excursus on "Paul's Agrarian Theology." Among numerous other exemplars scholars have found, see Hesiod, *Op.* 354–60, 381–617; Aristotle, *Rhet.* 3.3.4; and Philo, *Conf.* 152 and *Legat.* 293. Betz, *2 Corinthians 8 and 9*, 103, argues for the latter part of the "sowing" proverb as a Pauline creation.

16. Although, as I argue, Paul effaces his traveling apostolic role from 2 Cor 9:6–15, he may have understood his own role in the immediate context of this Isaian verse (55:11)—just like the rain that provides sustenance, "so it is with my word, should it depart from my mouth, it will not return until it has completed whatever I wanted it to. I will make successful your ways and my commandments. For you will depart with gladness and teach with joy, for the mountains and hills will jump up when they welcome you with joy." Two points emerge from this context. First, it is entirely probable that Paul saw himself and his travels in this prophecy. Second, the idea that God's promise of glory for Israel—"if it should depart from my mouth, it will not return until it has completed whatever I wanted it to"—strikingly resembles Greco-Roman notions of benefaction as expressed by Seneca and cited above: "If a benefactor accomplishes what he wished, if his intention is conveyed to me and stirs in me a joyful response, he gets what he sought . . . A man has had a successful voyage if he reaches the port for which he set out; a dart hurled by a sure hand performs its duty

if it strikes its mark; he who gives a benefit wishes it to be gratefully accepted; if it is cheerfully received he gets what he wanted" (*Ben.* 2.31.2–3, adapted from LCL trans.). Perhaps Paul read Deutero-Isaiah through the cultural lens of benefaction in his desire to convey his notion of "cheerful giving."

17. See Betz, *2 Corinthians 8 and 9*, 116–17, especially noting (n. 220) the prevalence of thanksgiving as "a religious duty" throughout the Hebrew Bible and Jewish literature. Windisch, *Der zweite Korintherbrief*, 281–82, notes that *leitourgia* primarily denoted "eine Dienstleistung für das Staatswesen, die Kommune" (a service for the municipality, the community); it also would have borne for the Corinthian audience "die Bedeutung einer sakralen, den Kultus fördernden Handlung" (the meaning of a sacred deed in promotion of the cult). See also Furnish, *II Corinthians*, 450–51. For defense of the cultic meaning of *homologia* as "confession" here, see Furnish, *II Corinthians*, 444–45 and 451–52; and Thrall, *Second Corinthians*, 2.589–90 (contra Betz, *2 Corinthians 8 and 9*, 122–23, who renders a legal meaning of a "contractual agreement" through "submission").

18. Many studies emphasize the multiple meanings of the Pauline collection; see Stephan Joubert, *Paul as Benefactor: Reciprocity, Strategy and Theological Reflection in Paul's Collection* (Tübingen: Mohr Siebeck, 2000), 5, 8–14, for a defense of a more "holistic" approach to the subject. Even earlier, Keith F. Nickle, *The Collection: A Study in Paul's Strategy* (Naperville, IL: Alec R. Allenson, 1965), 100, identified three meanings of the collection that "were so welded together that each was presented as essentially involved in the other. Correspondingly, the expressions employed to express each of these concerns often possessed overtones which also reflected the other interests." Moreover, Verlyn D. Verbrugge, *Paul's Style of Leadership as Illustrated by His Instructions to the Corinthians on the Collection* (San Francisco: Mellen Research University Press, 1992), notes aspects of Paul's entreaties that resemble ancient "fund-raising" letters. Comparing the collection to the temple tax was extensively defended first by Karl Holl, "Der Kirchenbegriff des Paulus in seinem Verhältnis zu dem der Urgemeinde," in *Gesammelte Aufsätze zur Kirchengeschichte II* (Tübingen: Mohr, 1928), 44–67; see also Nickle, *The Collection*, 74–93. For ancient sources, see especially Philo, *Spec.* 1.78, *Legat.* 156, 216, and 312; and Josephus *A.J.* 14.110–13. See other sources cited by Nickle, *The Collection*, 82–84. See also the interpretation of Stanley K. Stowers, "Does Pauline Christianity Resemble a Hellenistic Philosophy?" in *Paul beyond the Judaism/Hellenism Divide*, ed. Troels Engberg-Pedersen (Louisville, KY: Westminster John Knox Press, 2001), 84: "These celebrations [of temple festivals in Diaspora synagogues] suggest that Jews in the Diaspora were attempting to participate from a distance in festivals of the temple that had a strong agricultural and local orientation . . . The temple tax that supported the daily sacrifices in the temple and the first fruit offerings that signified the ancient pattern of reciprocity and divine giving of productivity were among the major yearly efforts of Diaspora communities."

19. For the discussion and citations, I depend on Sze-kar Wan, "Collection for the Saints as Anticolonial Act: Implications of Paul's Ethnic Reconstruction," in *Paul and Politics: Ekklesia, Israel, Imperium, Interpretation*, ed. Richard A. Horsley (Harrisburg, PA: Trinity Press International, 2000), 201–3. Roman provisions for the safety of the collection are mentioned in Philo, *Legat.* 156; and Josephus, *A.J.* 16.160–70.

Conclusion

1. Robert Jewett, "Romans as an Ambassadorial Letter," *Int* 36.1 (1982): 5–20, was the first to suggest that Romans should be understood within the genre of ambassadorial correspondence, communicating an appeal for cooperation with God and among each other within the community. See now his commentary on *Romans* (Hermeneia; Philadelphia: Fortress, 2006). Rom 13:1–15:13 explicitly turns to the topic of communal relations, especially among Jews and Gentiles.

2. See Werner H. Kelber, *The Oral and the Written Gospel: The Hermeneutics of Speaking and Writing in the Synoptic Tradition, Mark, Paul, and Q,* 2nd ed. (Philadelphia: Fortress, 1997), 149: "Far from being chained to papyrus and scroll, the oral gospel partakes in the itinerant mode of apostolic action." Again, as with so much of Romans, scholars disagree on the interpretation of this passage—specifically, whether Paul targets Jews or Gentiles as the audience of the proclamation of the heralds "on the mountain." I believe both groups are in view. First, although Rom 9–11 is framed by concern over the fate of Israel, 10:12 introduces the fate of all, both Jews and Gentiles, who "call upon the Lord's name." Second, while the "mountain" mentioned in Isa 52 is certainly Zion (52:7 in the LXX continues: "who makes your salvation heard, saying, 'Zion, your God rules' "), the report of the heralds on Zion results not just in comfort and restoration for Israel, but the revelation of salvation to the Gentiles. So Isa 52:10 ("The Lord has revealed his holy arm in the sight of all the Gentiles, and all the ends of the earth will see salvation from God") and 52:15, quoted by Paul in Rom 15:21 ("Thus many Gentiles will be amazed at him, and kings will shut their mouth, because what was not reported to them about him they will see, and those who did not hear will understand"). For another argument to this effect, see J. Ross Wagner, *Heralds of the Good News: Isaiah and Paul in Concert in the Letter to the Romans* (Leiden: Brill, 2002), 170–74.

As an aside, note the correspondence between Isa 52:11 ("Depart! Depart! Go out from there, and do not touch any unclean thing. Go out from its midst, you who carry the vessels of the Lord [*hoi pherontes ta skeuē kyriou*]") with the processional language of 2 Cor 1–9, esp. 4:7 ("But we have this treasure in clay vessels [*skeuesin*]") and 4:10 ("[We are] always carrying around [*peripherontes*] the death of Jesus in the body so that the life of Jesus might be made manifest in our body").

3. For self-referentiality, see one of Judith Butler's early engagements with the writings of Ernesto Laclau and Slavoj Žižek—in particular, Žižek's *The Sublime Object of Ideology* (London: Verso, 1989), 99—in *Bodies That Matter: On the Discursive Limits of "Sex"* (London: Routledge, 1993), 208–9. See also, Ernesto Laclau in Judith Butler, Ernesto Laclau, and Slavoj Žižek, *Contingency, Hegemony, Universality: Contemporary Dialogues on the Left* (London: Verso, 2000), 68: "We have a situation in which: (1) a systemic totality cannot be constituted without appealing to something radically heterogeneous *vis-à-vis* what is representable within it; (2) this something has, anyway, to be somehow represented if there is to be a system at all; (3) as this will, however, be the representation of something which is *not* representable within the system—even more: the representation of the radical impossibility of representing the latter—that representation can take place only through tropological substitution."

Index

I. Subjects

II. Modern Authors

III. Ancient Sources

Hebrew Bible

IV. Papyri and Inscriptions